TO THE BRINK

Stockton, Malone,

and the Utah Jazz's Climb

to the Edge

of Glory

MICHAEL C. LEWIS

Simon & Schuster

SIMON & SCHUSTER
Rockefeller Center
1230 Avenue of the Americas
New York, NY 10020

SIMON & SCHUSTER and colophon are registered trademarks
of Simon & Schuster Inc.

Designed by Leslie Phillips
Manufactured in the United States of America

1   3   5   7   9   10   8   6   4   2

Library of Congress Cataloging-in-Publication Data is available. ·
ISBN 0-684-85686-7
All photos by Trent Nelson of *The Salt Lake Tribune*

ACKNOWLEDGMENTS

S omehow, I know less about how to properly thank all the people who deserve it for their help and support of my capricious attempt at writing a book than I did about writing it in the first place. Yet without them, my work would never have been finished, let alone published.

I'd like to thank, foremost, the entire Jazz organization—from the front office to the coaches and players to the media relations department—for providing its gracious assistance, as well as the actual subject material. I owe a great debt of thanks also to my friends in the newspaper business, notably Steve Luhm, Phil Miller, Dick Rosetta, Lex Hemphill, Joe Baird, Linda Fantin, and Brad Rock, who were willing to endure question after question and provide unending discussion and suggestion without once resorting to physical violence.

For becoming basketball fans solely on my account, I thank my mother, Judy Birch, and her husband, Jerry Birch. For understanding enough to put a brief moratorium on phone calls, I thank my father, Jack Lewis, and his wife, Carole Lewis. For unwavering support in spite of knowing the truth about everything, I thank my friend Candy Dawn Wintrode. For keeping me from repeatedly slamming my head in the door, I thank my friend Andrea Smith. And because he'll throw a fit if the acknowledgments pass without mention of him, I thank my friend Gary Logosz. (Not that he did anything worth a damn.) There are others, too, who deserve my gratitude, and they know who they are, in spite of my inability to list them all here.

Thank you, as well, to my publishers at Simon & Schuster, to my patient and far-too-complimentary editor, Jeff Neuman, and of course, to my agent, John A. Ware, who believed in my idea from the moment it landed on his desk.

Go figure.

TO THE BRINK

CHAPTER

1

Michael Jordan stood, beaming, on the scorer's table at the United Center in Chicago, flakes of multicolored confetti fluttering down around him as he danced amid popping flashbulbs and the roar of the crowd.

Only moments before, Jordan had found teammate Steve Kerr with a perfect pass out of a double-team, and Kerr had drilled a long jump shot to give the Chicago Bulls a two-point lead over the Utah Jazz with five seconds remaining in Game 6 of the 1997 NBA Finals. Then, as the Jazz tried to inbound the ball for a chance at a game-winning shot, the Bulls' Scottie Pippen lunged to intercept the pass. He somehow reached it and shoved the ball forward to teammate Toni Kukoc, who streaked downcourt and threw down a punctuative dunk at the last moment for a 90–86 victory that sealed the Bulls' fifth championship in seven years, and prevented the Jazz from keeping hope alive for their first.

Now the greatest basketball player in the world danced on the scorer's table, his outstretched hand showing five fingers. Later, he would hold up a suggestive sixth.

Lost in the pandemonium were the Jazz, suddenly forgotten and left to brush the enemy confetti from their shoulders as they trudged back to the refuge of their locker room.

A superb collection of role players packed around one of the best basketball tandems of all time in John Stockton and Karl Malone, the Jazz had surprised even themselves by advancing to the Finals for the first time in their twenty-three-year history, but that did not make their 4–2 loss to the Bulls any less disheartening.

Stockton and Malone had been playing side by side for more than a decade in search of an NBA championship, and many fans believed they had just missed the best chance they would ever have at winning one. The two were growing older, after all, and qualifying for the championship round was difficult enough without nature and time conspiring against them, too. Both Stockton and Malone will wind up in the Basketball Hall of Fame one day —Stockton was the NBA's all-time leader in assists and steals, and had built an entire career upon feeding Malone off the pick-and-roll so often that Malone ranked as the tenth-leading scorer in league history—but neither had claimed the ultimate validation of his prosperous career.

Both, unquestionably, deserved it.

"They're the best," said Jack Ramsay, who coached twenty-one years in the NBA and led the Portland Trail Blazers to the 1977 championship. "They are so skilled at what they do. Stockton is the best passer in the half-court that the game has ever seen, and those two guys play together better than any combination of players ever. Malone has a great knack for getting open, and he's a great finisher. Stockton has the unique talent of getting the ball to the receiver at precisely the time he's open and when he can shoot it. Each of them has lifted his game, and the success of the team has grown with it."

Such compliments mattered little now.

Sitting in the locker room, peeling the uniforms from their exhausted bodies, the Jazz could not hear the revelry being conducted out on the arena floor, but they knew what was happening. The commissioner of the NBA, David Stern, was sidling up to a makeshift podium from which to present the championship trophy, and the Bulls were right there to accept it, waving hands and fingers aloft next to the prize.

What the Jazz would have given to switch places.

There was no one cheering the Jazz in their locker room, no one handing them freshly minted championship T-shirts or lighting their victory cigars. No, there in the locker room sat only a dozen lonely players, Coach Jerry Sloan, and a handful of other coaches and staff members, all painfully aware of what opportunity they had just missed.

"No one said one thing," Malone recalled later. "The only thing Coach Sloan said to us was, 'I don't think you guys realize how good you are, or how good you can be.' That's all he said."

What else could he say?

The season already was lost, and the Jazz had long since grown to know Sloan so well that words would have been redundant. No other coach working the sidelines in the NBA had been with the same team longer than the nine years Sloan had been in Utah. His philosophy was simple—work hard, shut up, and play defense—and had been embraced by his two superstars and imposed on their teammates so long ago that it was undeniably the very core from which the team's success sprouted.

Sloan himself was a defensive star in the NBA, the first player whose number was retired by the Bulls. To this day, Sloan's No. 4 hangs in the rafters of the United Center as a testament to the hustle and grit that made him the city's biggest basketball hero until Jordan arrived and began doing what Sloan's teams never could—winning championships.

It was Sloan's belief in defense that guided the Jazz, along with his insistence that the game be played with all five players on the floor, not in the one-on-one fashion that had become increasingly popular in the NBA during the 1990s. Every player had a role on Sloan's teams, and freelancing the offense was not acceptable. He demanded uncompromising devotion to his principles, and had thrown more than one player off his bench during the middle of a game to make a point about it. For the players who could stand the pressure (and not all of them could), Sloan was the best kind of coach. He was a man who understood the game because he played it, and who didn't prance and pose for the benefit of his image, but rather told the truth in plain and sometimes harsh terms.

"I would call him a judge," said Jazz guard Shandon Anderson. "He's honest with you. If you're not getting the job done, he'll tell you. . . . Sometimes he comes in the locker room after the game— we probably won by 10, 15 points—he comes in beating at the chalkboard, cursing. And you're like, 'Did we win or lose?' And then he's like, 'bring it in,' and his whole demeanor changes. You look around again and he's shaking your hand. He's just a guy who's real honest. That's what I respect about him."

Anderson was among the most pained members of the Jazz team that sat in the United Center locker room that night. Not only did he miss two layups in the fourth quarter and have a dunk blocked by Pippen, but he was playing only days after his father had died of throat cancer. Anderson missed Games 3 and 4 of the series at the Delta Center in Salt Lake City to attend his father's funeral in Georgia, and thereby missed the only two games the Jazz won in the final round. He wanted another chance, desperately.

And tragedy did not confine itself to Anderson's locker stall.

That very night back in Utah, Bobbye Sloan was in bed, preparing to turn off the TV after watching her husband's team lose the final game of its season. As she rolled over, comforted some by the knowledge that her husband would be home soon, she felt a sharp pain drive itself through her left breast. She knew right away she was in trouble, and the next morning made plans to have herself examined. What she learned—though she would wait some time before sharing the news—would change her life and the life of the coach of the Utah Jazz forever.

At the time, of course, Sloan was consumed by thoughts of the game, and neither he nor any of his bosses or assistants who made the solemn walk from the locker room to the team bus that night could have felt terribly comfortable with the Jazz's chances of ever securing such a good shot at a championship again.

Although none of them was Stockton or Malone, six players on the Jazz were about to become free agents, able to accept contract offers from any team in the NBA, and the narrow margin by which the Jazz had advanced to the Finals suggested there'd be no easy route to a repeat. They had needed Stockton to swish a miracle three-pointer at the buzzer of Game 6 in the Western Conference finals against the Houston Rockets just to get to face the Bulls, and who knows what might have happened had the shot bounced harmlessly away and forced a deciding Game 7 back in Salt Lake City?

The Jazz had arrived in Chicago as virtual tourists, dazzled and a bit intimidated by the whole Finals experience. They were thrilled at their long-awaited and unexpected arrival, but the media horde was suffocating, and the attention distracting. Cameras were everywhere. All the world was watching.

In their hotel rooms, the Jazz received prank phone calls from radio stations trying to rattle them. Losing Game 1 when Malone missed two late free throws before Jordan nailed a game-winning jumper did nothing to boost their confidence. The Jazz wondered privately whether they truly belonged on basketball's grandest stage, even though they had finished the regular season with a franchise-record 64 victories.

"We played like we were happy to be there," Sloan said.

They lost badly in Game 2, before returning home to win the first two of three games at the Delta Center. They had a lead on the Bulls in Game 5, but Jordan put on one of the finest performances of his career, scoring 38 points while suffering from food poisoning to lead Chicago to victory and shove the Jazz to the brink of elimination.

Then came Game 6, and the confetti.

But the Jazz had worked too hard and too long to allow that to be the end of them. They had burdened themselves with too much hope and pride, and for too many years, to slink away and accept failing in their only chance at a championship. Too often they had heard the taunts of the critics, saying they were too old, or too predictable, or too fragile to win a title.

So while Jordan and the rest of the Bulls pranced around the United Center floor, basking in another round of glory and adulation, the Jazz showered and dressed in virtual silence. Their minds wandered back over the three losses by a total of eight points, over all the leads they had held but blown, and they realized how close they had actually come to winning. The thought hurt, certainly, but at the same time it fostered a sentiment that may have been missing from the deepest recesses of their hearts until that very moment:

The Jazz belonged.

They could do this.

They could win.

One by one, the players promised themselves they would do whatever they could to avoid feeling again the pain they felt right then. They made up their minds to keep the team together, and steeled themselves against the idea that they might fail. Wordlessly, they vowed their utmost effort to bring home a trophy—not just for themselves, but for all those players who had gone before them, as well as the fans who had encouraged them for so many years.

Finally, there in the locker room, in the wake of the most disappointing defeat in their history, the Utah Jazz had all the makings of a champion.

CHAPTER

2

Nobody was thinking championship back in 1979, when apathy and its attendant financial crisis conspired to create the Utah Jazz. Nobody could even have dreamt it. After all, John Stockton —skinnier than he is now, and shorter—still was worrying about where he might fit in on the varsity at Gonzaga University, and he had years to go before he would so much as make the acquaintance of one Karl Malone, who was then simply the most enormous of nine children in rural Louisiana and not someone the world would recognize by thick biceps and a catchy nickname. Jerry Sloan was only three years removed from his career as a player and had yet to try on a coach's suit and tie for the first time, and the collection of players who did pull on the Jazz jersey every other night was pretty much the laughingstock of the NBA.

Championship?

That was a punch line, not a possibility.

But as the Jazz opened training camp nearly two decades later, a championship was the only thing on anybody's mind. "Anything else will be a disappointment," said Malone.

Barely four months removed from their first trip to the NBA Finals, the Jazz found their resolve fortified rather than eroded by their six-game loss to the Bulls, on account of the improvement that their success had finally signaled. Three times in the five previous seasons, the Jazz had progressed as far as the Western Conference finals only to lose, the last time on a pair of failed free throws in the waning seconds of Game 7 against the Seattle SuperSonics in 1996. So, unlike many teams that used even the narrowest failure as a reason to dismantle the roster or fire the coach or "move in a new direction," the Jazz did not budge in the wake of their latest defeat. Instead, they continued a basketball tradition that seemed almost quaint, guarding against major changes and gathering their forces around Stockton and Malone to make another run at the title, as stubborn and determined as any doomed mythic figure who ever pushed a rock up a hill.

"There's nothing rewarding," said Sloan, "about coming in second."

That the Jazz could ever have grown so expectant only emphasized the scope of their quest, which had commenced almost unwittingly so many years earlier, and been fueled along the way by a blessed vision and twists of fate almost too propitious to believe.

The first was that the Jazz wound up in Utah at all.

Owner Sam Battistone wasn't married to the idea when he began scouting for a future home for his New Orleans Jazz only a few miserable seasons after they were born on the bayou in 1974 as the eighteenth member of the NBA. He just wanted to quit losing money.

In the five seasons they called New Orleans home, the Jazz won just 161 of the 410 games they played and never came any closer to the playoffs than a cat comes to a garden hose. They had obtained the legendary Pistol Pete Maravich as their first player in a trade with the Atlanta Hawks, but even he wasn't good enough to make up for a dearth of talent and a management team in over its head.

"We were mismanaged terribly," said Rod Hundley, a former player and longtime radio broadcaster who is one of only two men who've worked for the Jazz since their inception. "We had nonbasketball people making basketball decisions. That's one of the things that helped turn us around: When we moved to Salt Lake, we hired basketball people."

In New Orleans, for instance, the Jazz gave away two first-round draft picks in a 1976 trade with the Los Angeles Lakers to obtain aging star Gail Goodrich and, hopefully, some instant credibility. Goodrich played a little more than two seasons for the woebegone Jazz before retiring, and at about the same time he retired the Lakers used a draft pick they'd received in the deal to draft a guy out of Michigan State named Earvin Johnson. They called him "Magic."

"If we'd had Magic Johnson," said Hundley, "we'd have never left New Orleans."

Of course, the Jazz already had made plans to move by the time Johnson was drafted, but the point was valid: the Jazz had no magic, Johnson or otherwise. Their best record in New Orleans was 39-43 in their fourth year in the league, and the few fans who came to see them had to settle for Maravich's monster scoring games and occasional appearances in the All-Star Game instead of Jazz victories. That was the problem; because the team was so bad, it had an awful time drawing people to the cavernous Superdome, and that didn't sit so well with arena management. The Superdome bosses wanted to book more popular attractions, and they scheduled events that would have blocked out the Jazz for thirty-five straight days had the team stayed in New Orleans for the 1979–80 season. That conflict, and the endless evaporation of money, ultimately forced Battistone and fellow majority owner Larry Hatfield to search for a greener pasture.

That the Jazz settled in Utah may owe more to the greediness of Battistone's fellow owners than to any grand plan.

The Jazz had places other than Salt Lake City on their list of potential new homes, but Battistone's fellow owners around the league viewed most of those cities, Dallas among them, as ideal sites for expansion franchises. With the fees for expansion franchises worth millions of dollars to the league, the other owners would not have wanted to cut into their own profits by wasting a prime market on an exisiting team—especially a rotten one—that would not have to pay an expansion fee. Salt Lake City was one place the owners would not necessarily envision ever getting an expansion team, so they could agree to let the Jazz move there without costing themselves any future windfalls.

"It was an opportunity for Utah to have an NBA franchise," said Battistone. "And it maybe never again would have that opportunity."

The community had ultimately failed to support the Utah Stars of the American Basketball Association, who went belly-up amid a sea of red ink in 1975 even after winning a championship four years earlier, and it was hardly the kind of urbane metropolis that figured to be fit to embrace a major-league sports franchise.

Certainly, the NBA in 1979 was not what it is today; Magic Johnson and Larry Bird had only just begun their historic revitalization of the moribund league. But neither was Salt Lake City much more than a place planes occasionally stopped on their way out to California. And when Battistone and Hatfield announced their plans to move to Utah in the spring of 1979, many fans viewed the Jazz's relocation as merely a temporary experiment that would expire once something opened up in Battistone's native California.

Battistone conceded that geography was one reason he considered Utah. It was much closer to his Santa Barbara home, plus his wife's family lived there. But he denies that he had more devious schemes in mind; he recalled seeing in Utah a basketball zealotry not unlike Indiana's, and knew of the success of the state's major collegiate programs.

The NBA approved his move on June 8, 1979.

Leaving New Orleans wasn't easy, though. For all their desire to pack the arena with more profitable attractions than basketball, the Superdome owners answered the Jazz's plan to relocate with a charge that the team had broken its contract with them. Fearful that they would arrive with the moving vans only to find the arena padlocked, Battistone and Hatfield ordered trainer Don Sparks to surreptitiously remove the team's effects before the Superdome owners could stop them. Sparks made several late-night sorties into the locker room to retrieve uniforms and equipment and move them to a storage shed, to be hauled cross-country later. Eventually, the Jazz settled out of court with the Superdome and the myriad other entities that had charged them with a variety of offenses stemming from their leaving the city.

While *The Salt Lake Tribune* heralded the team's arrival in Utah and editorialized that the NBA "as a league, its teams and players, will surely be sincerely welcomed here," skepticism was the prevailing local sentiment. Many fans were still angry over the departure of the Stars, who abruptly folded without refunding season ticket deposits. Cynics wondered about the high ticket prices ($5, $7, and $9 for the opener) and who would support the Jazz. Others chided the team for keeping a nickname that was suddenly as appropriate as fishnets at a funeral, though the Jazz had hoped to maintain some continuity by maintaining their identity. (Plus, they were too broke to afford the new uniforms that a name change would have required.) It did not help at all, either, that the Jazz were so awful.

"We were just getting our ass kicked every year," said Hundley.

Slowly, however, things began to change.

Why?

"Very simple," said David Fredman, the other all-time Jazz employee who began in public relations and is now an assistant coach with the team. "A guy named Frank Layden."

*　*　*

Though he had a good reputation around the league, Frank Layden was nevertheless just another candidate for the Jazz's general manager job when he flew to Salt Lake City from Atlanta for a dinner interview with Battistone, about a month before the Jazz moved from New Orleans. Nobody knew that one day Layden would be remembered as a colorful, passionate, dedicated man who gave much of his adult life to the careful nurturing of the Jazz franchise. Years later, Battistone admitted he could not foresee how Layden's drive and unique philosophy would help build one of the firmest franchises in all of sports out of practically nothing. Layden simply had the coaching and administrative experience the Jazz wanted, and Battistone felt comfortable with him. The rest is a story fit for a screenplay.

"What Frank has meant to this franchise," said David Allred, the vice president of public relations, "cannot be quantified."

They were crazy years, those early ones, when the Jazz were constantly strapped for cash and Layden earned his reputation as something of a carnival barker, willing to do almost anything to get fans in the seats. He was known to stand outside the arena, overweight and shabbily dressed, and try to lure passers-by inside for a look at his basketball team. He sold and sold and sold, and made jokes about the quality of the team just to get some attention. One day, Layden liked to say, a fan phoned him in his office with a question.

"What time is the game?" the caller asked.

Answered Layden: "What time can you be here?"

Layden's first move as general manager was to name Tom Nissalke as the replacement for coach Elgin Baylor, and only a few months later he traded Spencer Haywood to the Los Angeles Lakers for high-scoring young forward Adrian Dantley, proving he had become a good judge of talent while working the previous three years as the director of player personnel for the Atlanta Hawks. What truly defined Layden, however, was his humor, energy, and vision.

"I had a philosophy, which I used to call the 'Catholic School Philosophy,' " he said, "that we'll win because we're the good guys. And I believed that. I always thought, 'If I do everything the right way, and I work hard and the players are good people, we'll win our share.'. . . I wanted to have fun, and I wanted to do it the right way."

Shortly after he was hired by the Jazz, Layden visited the Los Angeles Dodgers and the Dallas Cowboys, hoping to learn the secret to building a successful franchise. Stability, he learned, was a key ingredient, as was a good environment. Layden remembers the wisdom of Cowboys president Gil Brandt.

"He said, you can't always get good players," Layden remembered. "But you can get good receptionists. You can get good secretaries. You can get a good coaching staff. Good trainer. Get a nice gym. Do all those things. He said, 'Frank, do what you can do. Don't try to do the things you can't do. Be ready when the players come.' "

While he personally had his doubts whether he or the Jazz would last more than three seasons in Utah, Layden never shared his fears with the outside world. He simply tried to get Utah ready for when the players came.

"The first thing Frank told me," recalled Fredman, "was, 'They'll win a title here. Let's just hope we're around when it happens.' "

The early experiences were not promising.

For the Jazz's first game in Utah, against the Milwaukee Bucks on October 15, 1979, the team had offered a promotion through which fans would receive three tickets in the upper level of the old Salt Palace for each lower-level ticket they purchased. Even so, with NBA Commissioner Larry O'Brien in attendance, the arena was barely half-full for tip-off. Layden ran screaming to the exits.

"Throw open the doors!" he ordered the ushers. "Let 'em in for free! We have got to fill the seats!"

It didn't work—not that night, anyway. Only 7,721 fans showed up at the 12,000-seat Salt Palace to watch their new team lose, 131–107. It would be another week before the Jazz earned their first victory in Utah, a 110–109 triumph over the San Diego Clippers. And after its second win three days later, the team embarked on a fourteen-game losing streak that defined its first few years in Salt Lake City.

The only thing the Jazz had in shorter supply than victories and fans was money. Team officials turned down an invitation to enter a float in a local parade during their first summer in Salt Lake City because they could not afford the $1,500 entry fee. They advertised with cheap TV commercials in the middle of the night, because they could not afford decent production or better time slots. They bartered tickets for everything from sneakers to travel arrangements—once swapping 2,000 season tickets for life insurance policies on Dantley and some front-office personnel—and even asked employees to bring paper from home so they could print pregame notes for the media.

Armed with his unwavering philosophy, though, Layden began to build the franchise on the principles that would make it a model of stability and consistency. Instead of suffering through horrible seasons only to trade away the compensatory top draft picks (and because the Jazz had little money with which to dabble in the free agent market), Layden believed it better to build slowly, and with youth. He chose Darrell Griffith, the college player of the year at Louisville, in the 1980 draft, and signed Rickey Green out of the

Continental Basketball Association midway through the following season. Green and Griffith joined Dantley to form the nucleus of the team that would eventually rise from the cellar of the NBA's Midwest Division, though the transformation would take a few years to reach completion.

"There's no question that Frank Layden has had a tremendous impact on the success of the franchise," said Battistone. "He really adapted. He became such a great spokesman and a person who was able to join the total community of Utah together in supporting the team."

The Jazz finished 24-58 and 28-54 in their first two seasons in Utah, and were riding a four-game losing streak early in the 1981– 82 season when Layden fired Nissalke and took over as coach. Layden had gained his coaching experience at high schools and small colleges in his native New York, and had learned that he could use humor and distraction to deflect pressure from his players and bear it himself. Griffith recalled the night Layden took over the Jazz as one that cemented his reputation as a player's coach.

"He took over and told us, 'No plays. Just three passes and shoot. And have fun,' " said Griffith, one of the greatest players in Jazz history, whose No. 35 has been retired. "Then we beat K.C. by 20. I think that was his way of relaxing us."

Layden found ways to relax his players throughout his career, and his antics soon became legendary. He mocked Lakers coach Pat Riley by pretending to slick back his hair on the sideline, and made like he had fainted when Morganna the Kissing Bandit found him as a target. He once removed his Jazz shirt in the middle of a restaurant, so he could give it to a fan who had complimented his team. And one night at The Forum in Los Angeles (where the marquee advertised "Lakers vs. Jazz, Featuring Frank Layden"), he left the game in the fourth quarter, before the Lakers had finished stomping the Jazz.

"The restaurant in the hotel doesn't stay open after the game," he explained.

Fans began to come to games just to watch Layden coach—he once grabbed the halftime winner of a shooting contest to sit on his bench in the hope of inspiring his brick-launching players—and they learned to pay attention when he spoke. The one-liner became Layden's trademark.

"I have a great body," he used to like to say. "It's just hidden under this other one."

For all Layden's good humor, however, the Jazz still could not draw enough fans to make themselves profitable for Battistone. They drafted Dominique Wilkins out of Georgia with the third pick in the 1982 draft, but traded him to Atlanta for $1 million almost immediately because they needed the money to stay solvent. The Jazz also received John Drew and Freeman Williams in the trade; Drew would need eight weeks of drug rehabilitation, and Williams was released within four months of arriving in Utah.

Yet the 1982 draft was not without its reward for the Jazz: in the fourth round, they picked a lightly regarded 7-4 center out of UCLA named Mark Eaton, who'd played just 196 minutes in thirty games over two seasons for the Bruins, but wound up becoming the best shot-blocker in the history of the NBA and having his No. 53 retired to the ceiling of the Delta Center. Eaton was further evidence that Layden's plan was working. The Jazz finished 30-52 in Eaton's rookie season and then began their remarkable ascent as soon as they added forward Thurl Bailey out of North Carolina State with the seventh pick in the next summer's draft.

The Jazz added another piece to the puzzle that season, too, but in the front office. On the recommendation of future NBA Commissioner David Stern, then one of the league's executive vice presidents, they hired a twenty-six-year-old consultant named David Checketts to run the organization as executive vice president.

Checketts had grown up in Salt Lake City but was living in Boston at the time, and had recently completed a large project commissioned by the Boston Celtics to determine what elements are most important in producing winning sports teams. He found that stability, both in the front office and on the roster, was a major factor, and that put him in philosophical cahoots with Layden.

Checketts took the Jazz job in part because it afforded him a chance to move back home, where most of his family still lived. His wife thought he was crazy to trade his lucrative job and reputable firm for a pathetic basketball team nearly gone bust on the edge of the desert. But Checketts viewed the role as a challenge, and was spurred on, at least a little bit, by embarrassment at his hometown team.

"I thought if I could turn it around, I could do anything," he said.

The team made money for the first time in Checketts's first year on the job, and he grew to rate nearly as much credit as Layden for straightening out the Jazz.

Battistone had purchased Hatfield's share of the team around the time Layden fired Nissalke, then sold half to Dr. Gerald Bagley and his son, Thomas, before the 1983–84 season. Layden and the Jazz survived that ownership move all right, but the team still was on shaky financial ground. Team employees sometimes had to hold their paychecks until Dantley's—issued, by contractual obligation, in large sums and only six times a year—cleared the bank. The Bagleys sought and won approval for the right to play a few of their home games at the Thomas & Mack Center in Las Vegas, in the hope of attracting greater crowds and expanding the team's base of fans, but the experiment lasted only two seasons since it did little for the bottom line. Not only that, but it blew up in their faces when Kareem Abdul-Jabbar became the NBA's all-time leading scorer in 1984; he passed the milestone against the Jazz, but because the Jazz had scheduled the game in Las Vegas, they wound up depriving their fans in Utah of a historic basketball moment. The Jazz's sudden move toward respectability, then, could not have come at a better time.

The Jazz started the 1983–84 season as they had almost every other, with a losing record after seventeen games despite a lineup that included talented young players in Green, Griffith, Dantley, Bailey, and Eaton. But as the players adjusted to each other, they began to figure out what they needed to do to win. Near the end of November, about a month into the season, they took off on a streak in which they won thirteen out of fourteen games. By the time that stretch was over, Green and Dantley each had won NBA Player of the Week honors, Layden was Coach of the Month for December, and the Jazz sat in a pleasantly unfamiliar position— first place of the Midwest Division.

"We had a group of guys who were winners, who wanted to work hard and play hard to win," said Bailey. "We each accepted our roles and accepted the fact that A.D. was basically the stronghold of the team at that time. . . . We just got to the point where we understood each other."

The season was awash in landmark achievements. Layden coached the Western Conference in the NBA All-Star Game and won the J. Walter Kennedy Award for community service, while his team finished with its best record ever at 45-37. It won the Midwest Division, too, and became the first team in NBA history to have four players lead the league in four statistical categories.

After missing sixty games the previous season because of torn ligaments in his wrist, Dantley won the second of his two scoring titles by averaging 30.6 points per game, and won the Comeback Player of the Year award. Green led the league in steals, Eaton in blocked shots, and Griffith had the best three-point shooting percentage. Most important of all, the Jazz made the playoffs for the first time, and began to shed their image as interminable losers.

The Jazz secured that first playoff berth with a 106–96 victory over the Seattle SuperSonics at the Salt Palace on March 29, 1984, and celebrated as if they had just won the championship. Players hugged and shouted and shot champagne corks all over the locker room, and just as Layden began to exult in the scene, an usher grabbed him by the arm.

"They want you back out there," the usher said.

Layden was flabbergasted.

"The fans wanted us for a curtain call," he recalled. "I had never heard of that. It was something to see."

Layden won the NBA Coach of the Year award to go with his other honors, then pulled off the most notorious motivational ploy in the history of the franchise during the Jazz's first-round playoff series against the Denver Nuggets.

The Nuggets were leading the best-of-five series 2–1, and the Jazz, aside from having no previous playoff experience, hadn't distinguished themselves terribly well. Figuring a berth in the second round was a certainty for the Nuggets going into Game 4, Woody Paige of the *Denver Post* wrote a column predicting the Nuggets would advance easily that night, because the Jazz did not have the heart to come back.

Layden saw that, and he saw an opportunity. He had one of his friends, a surgeon at University Hospital who had pioneered artificial heart research, bring his entire staff to the Jazz locker room before Game 4—along with an artificial heart like the one revolutionarily implanted into Barney Clark.

"Here's your fucking heart, right here, baby," Layden said.

He passed the heart around while reading parts of Paige's column to the team. When he finished, Layden looked his players in the eyes and commanded, "Now go shove that heart up Denver's ass!"

Wedge it in, they did.

Dantley played one of the best games of his career, compiling 39 points, 8 rebounds, 7 assists, and 2 steals in leading the Jazz to a 129–124 Game 4 victory in Denver. The team then returned to Salt Lake City, where fans had caught on to the theme and waved signs with hearts on them, and beat the Nuggets 127–111 in Game 5 to advance to meet the Phoenix Suns in the Western Conference semifinals. The Jazz lost to the Suns in six games, but they proved they belonged in the postseason, and began a streak of playoff appearances that has yet to be broken.

"At that point, we knew we were on our way," said Layden.

That watershed season finally helped the Jazz grab more than cursory attention from the public. They set a franchise attendance record that year, and their success inspired *The Salt Lake Tribune,* the state's largest newspaper, to send a reporter to cover them on the road more than just occasionally. (Until then, a reporter usually would listen to the game on the radio and write a story based on Hundley's broadcast.) Because the Jazz made the play-offs, however, they did not get their usual high spot in the draft that summer. Utah was set to pick sixteenth—not usually a breeding ground for future superstars.

But the good fortune that landed Layden in Utah struck again.

The Jazz had noticed a kid named John Stockton.

Fans who had gathered at the Salt Palace to watch the 1984 draft on closed-circuit TV fell deathly silent when Layden announced the pick, because Stockton was so little known that they had to flip through their complimentary draft guides to find his name. It turned out that Stockton was an unassuming point guard out of tiny Gonzaga University in Washington, whose grandfather was an All-America running back and whose father ran a tavern not far from the college campus in Spokane.

Stockton was more of a scorer than a passer at Gonzaga, averaging nearly 21 points per game in his senior season while being named to the All-West Coast Conference team for the third straight year. He was a great shooter, with an intense will to win.

By the time the Jazz challenged for their first championship,

Stockton would be the league's all-time leader in assists and steals, a nine-time All-Star, and a veteran of the "Dream Teams" that represented the United States at the 1992 and 1996 Olympics. But as a rookie, he averaged only eighteen minutes per game playing behind an All-Star in Green while the Jazz went 41-41, and the idea that he would become one of the greatest point guards in NBA history did not seem the least bit possible. Even Layden did not care much for him.

"I thought he was a prospect," said Layden.

Compared to the previous season, the Jazz had all kinds of problems in 1984–85. Dantley held out for more money and played only fifty-five games, and Drew ran into drug problems again and earned a league suspension that contributed to keeping him out of all but nineteen games. The team was still struggling financially, too, and rumors again were afloat that the franchise was on the verge of being sold; a group in Minnesota was reported to be preparing to acquire the team and move it north.

Then fortune smiled again.

❖   ❖   ❖

Larry Miller was not a basketball fan. He preferred to watch football and baseball instead, and was something of a star pitcher on a nationally ranked fast-pitch softball team. In fact, the first few times the local car salesman used his dealership's season tickets to go watch the Jazz in person, he left the arena disgusted because the team was so bad. But as a businessman interested in contributing to his community, Miller continued to buy four seats a year to the Jazz games, and wound up on a mailing list of potential investors that the team had compiled as part of a plan to recapitalize by selling thirty limited partnerships for $100,000 apiece.

Already, the Jazz had tried raising money through a public stock offering. That didn't work. They had tried to connect with a local real estate developer, but he ran into financial difficulties for unrelated reasons and the deal fell apart. They even made an attempt to broker a deal with international arms dealer and billionaire Adnan Khashoggi, but he refused to disclose all his finances, which put an end to that flirtation.

So Miller found himself answering a phone call one March afternoon from a woman calling on behalf of Checketts, who was trying to find somebody—anybody—with enough money to help keep the team afloat. The woman was following up on the prospectus that had been mailed to Miller about the limited partnerships plan, and she asked if he had received it. Miller had, but he didn't think much of it.

"I'm interested in helping the Jazz stay in Utah," he said, "but I don't think a limited partnership is the answer."

Miller was speaking strictly off the top of his head, and had no particular ideas in mind. "But they were the magic words," he said. "I'm not kidding, in ten minutes—literally ten minutes, maybe five —Checketts was in my office and wanted to talk about this some more."

"The notion that anyone was interested was too much for me," said Checketts.

Checketts told Miller about the team's other plan, to sell half the team and not only recapitalize, but eliminate its existing debt altogether. Battistone and eight other investors had paid a $6.15 million expansion fee for the Jazz back in 1974, and since then had been able to make payments only on the interest of their loan. The principal was pratically untouched. That plan sounded to Miller more prudent than the partnerships, but since Checketts clearly was looking to him to make the purchase, Miller was worried about getting in over his head and keeping his car dealerships afloat in the event the team continued to founder.

Emotion, however, got the better of him.

"The further I got into that," Miller said, "I became very acutely aware that if the Jazz ever got out of town and went to another market—and there were a lot of rumors—that in my lifetime and probably my children's lifetime, they would never come back to this market."

Miller didn't care so much about the Jazz specifically, but he knew the positive influence a successful sports team could have on a community. Like Checketts, Miller had been around long enough to remember the ABA Stars, and the way they stirred the city's sense of pride when they won the league championship in 1971. Miller saw that the Jazz could serve the same purpose, and decided it was up to him to keep them from leaving town.

"It was an opportunity, I realized, to give to a community and to a state that I care a great deal about something that maybe nobody else could give them," he said.

Miller wound up buying the Bagleys' share of the team that year for about $8 million, and he purchased Battistone's half for another $8 million about two years later. The man who would rather watch football and baseball had saved professional basketball for the state of Utah. Outside, perhaps, of the team's fortuitous player acquisitions, Miller's purchase of the team ranks as the most significant event in its history.

Miller came to take an abiding interest in his team, too. He tried to treat his players like family, going so far as to negotiate big-money contracts on a handshake, and earned a reputation for weeping joyously at the slightest provocation because of his deep feelings about his investment. He took to shagging balls for the players in pregame warmups and joining them in the locker room for chats at halftime and after games. Even now, he sits with his wife in courtside seats at the Delta Center, wearing jeans or casual pants with a golf shirt and sneakers, and slaps hands with his players as they're introduced to the crowd. In the locker room, Miller has a stall that suggests he's just one of the players; the nameplate above it reads, "Larry Miller—9."

"If the question were, 'What do you want the Jazz to stand

for?' " said Miller, "I would want it to stand for good values. I would want it to stand for hard work still paying off and discipline still paying off and consistency still paying off. And I feel like, as a sports organization, we epitomize those things. . . . Those things still count for something."

But Miller had what might be called a downside. He was not the most sophisticated of businessmen, some thought, and he knew little about the business of pro sports when he plunged in with both feet in 1985. And as dedicated as he became to the team he saved, Miller had a competitive streak that could run wild when things did not turn out his way.

When the Jazz faced the Denver Nuggets in a 1994 playoff game at the Delta Center, Miller grew so angry that he screamed at Sloan to remove a struggling Malone from the lineup, and charged into the stands to grab an annoying Nuggets fan by the throat. News photographers captured the moment, and Miller awoke the next morning with his furious face all over the papers. That kind of impulsiveness also led Miller to almost provoke a fight with forward Elden Campbell of the Los Angeles Lakers in the middle of a game, and threatened to ruin the Jazz not long after he had saved them.

Late one night, a few days before Christmas in 1987, Checketts awoke to a phone call only a few hours after the Jazz had lost their fourth game on a five-game Eastern road trip. The voice on the other end was screaming.

"I can't even figure out who it is," recalled Checketts. "I figure it must be an obscene phone call. So I say, 'Who is this?' And he says, 'You know who this is!' By then, I'd woken up enough to realize, it's Larry."

Miller was furious that the Jazz had lost to the Nets that night. Already on the trip, they had allowed Larry Bird to score 38 points and beat them in Boston, lost by 24 to the Pacers in Indiana, and let Dominique Wilkins—their onetime draft pick—get loose for

46 in an overtime failure in Atlanta. Then, at New Jersey, the Jazz had entered the fourth quarter with an 11-point lead and wound up losing by 10. The team had one more stop on its trip, but Miller wanted Layden fired as soon as it arrived home.

"I want you to meet the plane when it comes in," Miller told Checketts. "Fire Layden, and I'm going to coach the team the rest of the way."

Checketts could not believe what he was hearing. He tried to remind Miller of what sports executives call the "Ted Turner Rule" —named for the owner of the Atlanta Braves baseball team, who embarrassed himself in his one-game attempt at managing the team in 1977—but Miller wouldn't hear of it.

"I don't care about any rule!" he blared. "We're not going to put up with this kind of effort!"

Checketts told Miller he was neither going to meet the plane nor fire Layden, and suggested Miller instead calm down and meet with Layden later, in a more rational way.

Still enraged, Miller hung up.

The Jazz beat the Cavaliers in Cleveland the next night, however, and when their flight returned to Salt Lake City neither Miller nor Checketts was there to fire Layden. Instead, Miller heeded Checketts's advice and called a meeting with Layden a few days later. At the meeting, Layden's job was spared, and the Jazz kept climbing.

(In part because of his differences with Miller, Checketts left the Jazz in 1989 to become a vice president with the NBA. He would go on to become president of the New York Knicks and then CEO of Madison Square Garden, but his impact in Utah would be felt for years.)

❖   ❖   ❖

Miller had only just learned that the NBA had approved the first half of his purchase of the team in 1985 when the Jazz faced another mid-round choice of eligible collegians in the draft. This time, they had the thirteenth pick, and that did not figure to bring them the kind of top-quality star for which they might have hoped.

But there was Karl Malone, still available.

He wasn't supposed to fall out of the top ten, not with the big body he had and the terrific numbers he'd posted in three seasons at Lousiana Tech. The 6-9, 240-pound Malone averaged about 20 points and 10 rebounds a game before leaving college early to pursue his career as a pro, and by then had been anointed "The Mailman" by a clever sports information graduate assistant at Tech seeking to win greater acclaim for his school's young star.

The name was conceived during Malone's sophomore season in Ruston, when Teddy Allen surmised that Malone always delivered. Until then, Malone had referred to himself as the "Rim Wrecker" and, as luck would have it, had shattered a backboard only the week before.

Coach Andy Russo still had the box into which he had swept the shards of the board, so Allen and a co-worker glued the pieces to index cards boasting of Malone's accomplishments, and sent them to 1,000 members of the media. "Special Delivery from the Mailman," the cards said.

The nickname did not really stick until a year later, though, when Tech played a game at Northeast Louisiana in nearby Monroe. A vicious ice storm had strafed the state and forced a postponement of the game, and when it finally was played the night after it was scheduled, Malone scored 29 points and grabbed 15 rebounds and led the Bulldogs to victory. Allen, who had since become the sports editor at the *News-Star World* in Monroe, wrote the next morning that the Mailman delivered and Allen's peers have been writing variations on the theme ever since.

Based solely on talent, Malone should have been off the board by the time the Jazz exercised their pick in the draft. He couldn't shoot, but he was big and strong and could rebound and score inside. A dozen teams passed on him, though, in large part because his coach had given him less than rave reviews, which contributed to the fear that Malone had an attitude problem. The Washington Bullets, who had the twelfth pick in the draft, opted instead for Kenny Green of Wake Forest. Yet the Jazz would not be dissuaded.

"We needed a body," said Layden.

A body they got.

Malone scored nearly 15 points per game in his rookie season and earned a spot on the NBA's All-Rookie team, showing an unparalleled willingness to work on his game as well as an uncommon devotion to the community in which he played.

Over the next dozen years, Malone grew into a local hero by accomplishing nearly everything an NBA player possibly could. He averaged more than 21 points per game every season after his rookie year, made 10 straight appearances in the All-Star Game (he was the Most Valuable Player in 1989 and co-MVP with Stockton in 1993 in Salt Lake City), played with Stockton on the two Olympic Dream Teams, became only the fifth player in history to score 25,000 points and grab 10,000 rebounds, and won the league's Most Valuable Player award after leading the Jazz into the Finals in 1997.

But in 1985, all that was still in front of him. Malone at the time was strictly an unrefined bruiser, big in the post, but unable to shoot from outside or even hit much more than half of his free throws.

"Just banging, that was my whole game," he remembered. "All inside. And of course, I wasn't a great free throw shooter. But I tried to work on those things. I tried, maybe the next couple of years, to start facing my guy up more in the post. And the next year, I stepped out further. And then the next year, I stepped out a little further."

Malone played every game of his rookie season and convinced the Jazz they would be able to survive if they traded Dantley. For years, Dantley had been the team's only real draw, and he was spectacular at getting the ball to the hoop. But he had grown into something of a cancer on the team, feuding almost constantly with Layden—who once fined Dantley thirty pieces of silver for being a "Judas"—and tending to ruin the team's attempts at finding an offensive rhythm by spending too much time setting up his moves down low. Dantley once told Malone to avoid diving for loose balls in practice, lest he suffer an injury that might curtail his career, and still has not had his Jazz number retired because of the hard feelings he inspired within the organization.

The 1985–86 season was not an overwhelming success, with a 42-40 record and a first-round playoff exit courtesy of the Dallas Mavericks, but it represented the start of a new era just the same. Stockton started to see more playing time behind Green at point guard, and he began to get a feel for Malone's inside game that would help forge the relationship that would land both of them in the basketball history books. That was Dantley's final year with the Jazz, too—the team traded him over the summer to Detroit for Kelly Tripucka, Kent Benson, and two draft picks—which meant that from that season forward, Malone would be the primary scoring threat.

The Jazz began to acquire a reputation for playoff failure, however, losing in the first round four times over the next five years following increasingly impressive regular-season finishes. At the same time, they provided flashes of brilliance. Having taken the starting point guard job from an aging Green, Stockton set an NBA record in 1987–88 by handing out 1,128 assists, and helped the Jazz survive an 18-22 start and claim a first-round playoff victory over the Portland Trail Blazers and a date in the second round with the defending champion Los Angeles Lakers.

Nobody thought the Jazz would be able to hang with Magic, Kareem, and the rest of the "Showtime" Lakers, and Game 1 of the series seemed to prove those suspicions right. The Jazz lost,

110–91, but managed to bounce back and steal Game 2, 101–97. The teams split the next two games at the Salt Palace, before a classic Game 5 at The Forum. With the Jazz playing much of the fourth quarter without Eaton, who had fouled out, the lead changed hands four times in the final minute, before Michael Cooper scored his only basket of the game with seven seconds left for a 111–109 Lakers victory and a 3–2 lead in the series.

Malone, then only twenty-five years old, guaranteed a victory in Game 6 back in Utah, and he came through with 28 points in a 108–80 win to force a deciding Game 7.

The Jazz had never played a Game 7 in the playoffs, and neither of the two they have played since even came close to carrying the same allegorical weight as the one against the Lakers did. The Jazz's sudden emergence against the first team since the 1968–69 Celtics who would win back-to-back championships validated their annual presence in the playoffs, and gave fans their first hint of what they might feel if the Jazz ever won a championship. Fans flooded downtown Salt Lake City the night of Game 6—celebrating, honking, and hoping with a fervor that would go unmatched until the team advanced to the Finals for the first time nine years later.

Alas, the Jazz lost Game 7, and would have to wait another four years before advancing to the Western Conference finals for the first time.

But the series against the Lakers helped the Jazz turn the corner, so to speak, and the events that unfolded over the next few months helped define it as the end of the good old days. The Jazz lost Green to the Charlotte Hornets in the expansion draft during the summer, leaving the point guard duties almost entirely to Stockton. Then, almost without warning seventeen games into the 1988–89 season, Layden walked into the locker room and told his players he was resigning as their coach.

"When he told us," said Malone, "I went into shock."

The announcement came on December 9, 1988, nearly seven years to the day after Layden replaced Nissalke, and sent shock waves not just throughout the organization, but throughout the state and the NBA.

Layden had transformed the Jazz from misfits into contenders, but had grown weary from the effort. The job was no longer fun for him, and he believed the referees were out to get him. So Layden handed the team over to the man he had groomed for it, his top assistant coach, Jerry Sloan, and stepped into a new job as president of the Jazz with the lasting dignity that he feared he might lose had he stayed on the job any longer. Layden's final coaching record was a mere 277-294, yet the team retired jersey No. 1 in his honor as a way of thanking him for all he had done.

"As he moves on and takes his one-liners and unpredictable behavior with him," columnist Lex Hemphill wrote in *The Salt Lake Tribune* the next morning, "he leaves a legacy as the NBA's comic coach. He leaves a legacy as the man who breathed life into a little pro basketball franchise in the mountains. But, more than that, he leaves . . . as a giver—a giver of his buoyant spirit to a community that can never repay him."

Sloan had known all along he would replace Layden, but was surprised when he was asked to do it in the middle of a season. Layden had rescued him from a job as coach of the Evansville Thunder of the CBA in 1984, giving Sloan another chance in the NBA only a few seasons after he was fired two and a half years into his tenure as coach of the Chicago Bulls. Sloan credited Layden with teaching him things like patience and perspective, which, while transcending coaching, helped make Sloan a better coach. Sloan believed strongly in loyalty, too, and he returned it to Layden time and again in gratitude for the faith Layden had demonstrated in plucking him from the CBA. Since joining Layden's staff, Sloan had turned down a chance to join his old friend and former coach · Dick Motta as an assistant with the Dallas Mavericks, and pulled out of negotiations for the head coaching job with the Indiana Pacers.

It was that kind of loyalty, too, that landed Phil Johnson in Utah for his second turn as an assistant to Sloan. Johnson's coaching roots, like Sloan's, can be traced back to Motta, a native Utahn and one of the winningest coaches in NBA history.

Johnson worked as an assistant coach under Motta at Weber State College in Ogden, Utah, in the mid-1960s, and replaced Motta as head coach when Motta left Weber in 1968 to coach Sloan and the Bulls. Johnson led the Wildcats to three straight Big Sky Conference championships and three straight appearances in the NCAA tournament, and earned his own shot at the NBA with another job as Motta's assistant in Chicago. After less than two years there, Johnson was hired as head coach of the Kansas City Kings, and in his first full season as coach, led them to their first playoff berth in seven years and won NBA Coach of the Year honors. The Kings fired Johnson during the 1977–78 season, and the next year Johnson joined Sloan's staff in Chicago, where the men coached together until they were fired in 1982. While Sloan fell into some scouting duties for the Jazz and his short-lived job in the CBA, Johnson latched on as an assistant to Layden before becoming the Kings' head coach again. When Johnson left Utah that time, Sloan replaced him under Layden.

Now, all of a sudden, they were together again.

"The organization is fortunate to get two very, very loyal guys like Jerry and Phil," said Scott Layden, Frank's son, who was an assistant coach, head scout, and director of player personnel. "When you're hiring an assistant, that's the most important thing. Certainly, you need talent and credentials and all that, but loyalty is the number one thing."

With Sloan's emphasis on defense and Johnson's offensive mind, the Jazz believed they had a perfect combination with which to mold their rising team. And though Sloan lost his first game as head coach, the Jazz won fifty games for the first time that season and finished 51-31. The only bad news was that the Jazz lost again in the first round of the playoffs, and rumblings persisted that the team was not long for Salt Lake City.

But the financial fortunes had begun to turn around, and fans who had made the Jazz a virtual pariah in the early years began clamoring to find seats in the Salt Palace. Stockton and Malone by then were household names, running the pick-and-roll with regularity and enough amazing precision that they would forever be linked by the thread of an ethereal pass. The Jazz sold out all but one game in 1988–89, and Miller put an end to the constant rumors of the team's departure by announcing plans to build a downtown arena for $66 million. That was the last of the monumental moves that allowed the Jazz to blossom into one of the finest teams in the NBA, and it was greeted with unbridled community enthusiasm.

"It takes someone special to build something special," said then-Governor Norm Bangerter.

Groundbreaking for the arena came on May 22, 1990, after the Jazz had completed a 55-27 regular season and, yes, lost in the first round of the playoffs. Construction began less than a month later, followed shortly by the first of several roster moves that imbued the Jazz with fantasies of at last reaching the NBA Finals.

Already the Jazz had solid contributors at almost every spot on the floor, but they needed a more dependable shooting guard, so they traded Bobby Hansen, Eric Leckner, and two draft picks to the Sacramento Kings for Jeff Malone. Malone had averaged more than 20 points per game in each of his five previous seasons with the Washington Bullets, who had sent him to Sacramento for Pervis Ellison, and was widely hoped to be the missing link to the Jazz's championship future. He uncomplainingly accepted his role as the team's third scoring option, in spite of the fact that it put a drain on his scoring average and kept him from ever making the All-Star team again.

With two Malones in the lineup, the Jazz went 54-28 and advanced to the Western Conference semifinals in 1991 (losing to Portland in five games) before finally making a breakthrough. In 1991–92, after another 55-27 season, the Jazz beat the Los Angeles Clippers in the first round of the playoffs, stopped Seattle in the second, and advanced to play the Trail Blazers in the Western Conference finals for the first time.

That was a big season for the Jazz; not only did they advance further in the playoffs than they ever had, but they opened the newly christened Delta Center and extended their consecutive sellout streak to 163 games.

The arena had been finished in just fifteen months and twenty-four days, and 6,000 invited guests joined Miller and his wife, Gail, for the dedication ceremonies on October 9, 1991. Miller arrived in formal attire, but tore off the uncharacteristic jacket, dress shirt, and tie to reveal a Jazz sport shirt underneath. Dignitaries, players, and church and business leaders all praised Miller for his contribution to the community, and Miller spoke of his dream that a child might pass the arena fifty years hence and ask his grandfather about the man who built it.

"I'd like the grandfather to say that Larry H. Miller was a friend of Utah," he said.

The NBA was sufficiently impressed, and announced it would hold its 1993 All-Star Game in Salt Lake City. Stockton and Malone were named that year to the team that would represent the United States at the 1992 Summer Olympic Games in Barcelona, Spain. Closer and closer the Jazz moved to greatness.

✿　✿　✿

It wasn't long after the Jazz lost to the Blazers in the 1992 conference finals that they promoted Scott Layden to director of basketball operations. It was a move made mostly on paper, since Layden had been the director of player personnel since 1988 and had been responsible since then for every transaction and draft choice the Jazz made.

Unlike his father, Layden did not crack many jokes or make himself a public spectacle. Instead, he tended to keep quiet and make his presence felt from behind the scenes, with deft personnel moves bent on finding just the right combination of players around Stockton and Malone.

Layden had traded Bailey to the Minnesota Timberwolves for small forward Tyrone Corbin early in the 1991–92 season, and after the Jazz went 47-35 in 1992–93 and lost again in the first round of the playoffs, he also traded center Mike Brown to the Wolves, in exchange for center Felton Spencer. Spencer was to take the place of Eaton, who was on his way to retirement because of a back injury, and help tutor 7-2 rookie Luther Wright, whom the Jazz had chosen with the eighteenth pick of the 1993 draft (the team also grabbed Bryon Russell out of Long Beach State in that draft, with the forty-seventh pick).

Wright, however, turned out to be one of the biggest mistakes in Jazz history. He had some promise as a big man, and actually started for the Jazz on opening night in 1993–94 after signing a five-year, multimillion-dollar contract with the first three years guaranteed. But it did not take long for teammates to start noticing his erratic behavior. Missed flights. Violations of team rules. He once bought a dog at a pet store while the Jazz were on the road and flew home with it on the team charter, and in January of that season infuriated Sloan by joining the musical band at The Summit in Houston for a set on the drums—in uniform, less than a half-hour before the Jazz played the Rockets. Wright did not play against the Rockets that night, and two nights later was picked up at 4:00 A.M. at a highway rest stop in the Utah desert for causing a disturbance by ranting and raving and swinging a five-foot stick. A police officer cited Wright for disorderly conduct, and took him into custody.

The episode was blamed on Wright's bipolar disorder combined with an overdose of the drug Ritalin, which had been prescribed for Wright to help combat a previously diagnosed condition of attention deficit hyperactivity disorder. He was hospitalized for weeks after the incident, and never played for the Jazz again.

Wright might have been the only big mistake Layden has ever made, and it was more than balanced a few months later when he dealt Jeff Malone to Philadelphia to get shooting guard Jeff Hornacek. Jeff Malone had not endeared himself to the other Malone, who in the days before the deal demanded the Jazz either acquire better players or trade him to a contender. Hornacek was younger than Jeff Malone and had more range on his jump shot, so his arrival was seen as another move in the right direction.

The Jazz made the conference finals again that year after finishing 53-29 in the regular season, but lost to Houston in five games. And amid the acquisitions of Adam Keefe, Chris Morris, and Antoine Carr, they won a franchise record sixty games in 1994–95, but lost yet again in the first round of the playoffs. After adding free agents Howard Eisley and Greg Foster the next year, they went 55-27 and fell to Seattle in 1996 when Malone missed those two free throws in the final ten seconds of Game 7.

The theme was growing painfully old.

With Stockton and Malone both having passed into the second decade of their careers, the Jazz's failure to get past the Sonics encouraged the increasing belief that the Jazz simply did not have what it takes to make it to the Finals, let alone win a championship, and that Malone, for all his other accomplishments, was a player who could not come through in the clutch.

But for the bazillionth time, the Jazz fought back.

Having drafted guard Shandon Anderson and traded away Spencer to make room for the budding talent of 7-2 center Greg Ostertag, they ripped through the next season with a franchise-record and league-best sixty-four victories, notched their first playoff sweep over the Los Angeles Clippers in the first round, and cruised past the Lakers in the second. It was against the Houston Rockets in their fourth trip to the Western Conference finals that the Jazz finally made their historic move, and they did it in the most dramatic way they could imagine.

The Jazz trailed by 13 points with just under seven minutes remaining in Game 6 of the series at The Summit. They led the series 3–2 but appeared destined to be forced back to Utah to play an all-or-nothing Game 7 at the Delta Center. By sheer force of will, however, Stockton changed all that.

He led the Jazz on a 17–8 run to cut the Rockets' lead to 98–94, then scored back-to-back layups to tie the game. Charles Barkley hit 2 free throws to reclaim the lead for Houston, but Stockton drove the lane and scored with 22.4 seconds left to tie it again at 100. They had trailed by 7 points only 100 seconds earlier.

The Rockets had the ball, then, but Clyde Drexler missed an unnecessarily hurried short jump shot, which Malone rebounded with about three seconds left. The Jazz called timeout to set up one final play, and they were going to use one of their favorites, with a new little wrinkle.

The Jazz lined up across the free throw line and facing Russell, who was to inbound the ball near the Jazz bench. But while the play usually called for Stockton to run straight at Russell before cutting up the sideline toward midcourt, Sloan wanted Hornacek to take Stockton's place, and have Stockton use a Malone screen to get open around the top of the circle.

The sellout crowd of 16,285 fans was nearly maniacal as Russell inbounded from the sideline. Only 2.8 seconds remained on the clock, and whoever caught the pass would have to catch and shoot almost immediately.

As the referee handed Russell the ball, the Jazz players did just as Sloan had asked. Hornacek broke toward Russell, forward Carr cut to the basket, and Stockton waited for Malone to set the pick. Perfectly, Malone stepped out and planted his huge body near the top of the circle, impeding Drexler's attempt to keep up with Stockton. Malone grabbed Drexler and put him in a bear hug for good measure, knowing that nobody was going to call that foul in that situation.

Barkley was guarding Malone, and should have switched with Drexler off the screen so the Rockets could have somebody defending Stockton, but Barkley was too late. By the time he even realized he should have rushed out past Malone, Stockton had the ball in his hands and was pivoting toward the bucket with the final seconds racing off the clock.

With no time to think, Stockton cocked the ball back behind his right ear and fired.

Time seemed to stop.

The ball floated gently from the tips of Stockton's fingers toward the basket some twenty-six feet away, carrying with it all the missed opportunities of games and seasons gone by. Every eye in the building locked on its course. Every breath was held. And when that ball finally swished miraculously through the web of white cotton twine to give the Jazz a 103–100 victory and a berth in the NBA Finals for the first time, the crowd went deathly silent and Stockton lost all the composure he had fought so long and hard to maintain.

Leaping high in the air, with a wide smile of undiluted joy crossing his normally placid face, he barely had time to swing his fist in triumph before Malone and Hornacek and all the others mobbed him at midcourt in a celebration as joyous as Utah had ever seen. Broadcaster Greg Gumbel punctuated the play perfectly for the millions of fans across the country watching on NBC-TV.

"John Stockton sends the Utah Jazz to the NBA Finals!"

Sweeter words had never been spoken.

"I'm just so glad it went in," Stockton said later.

Stockton had scored the Jazz's last 9 points to finish with 25 and 13 assists. He had waited so many years for such a moment, just as the Jazz organization had waited. But now, in the wake of Gumbel's proclamation, the little team risen from the ashes of debt and doubt and insecurity at the foot of the Wasatch Mountains had finally arrived.

Nearly 20,000 fans flocked to a private air terminal in Salt Lake City at 2:30 in the morning to cheer the arrival of their conquering heroes. They held signs and chanted "MVP!" and waved purple foam fingers declaring "We're No. 1!"

Malone stepped from the plane, and smiled like he had never smiled before. Stockton smiled, too—a miracle almost, twice in one day. Morris perched on the hood of his car as it inched its way through the crowd, and Carr wept as he slapped hands with fans through a restraining fence.

"We love y'all!" he told them. "You never let us down."

The city was rabid with excitement. Fans could not get enough Jazz news or Jazz merchandise. Tickets became runaway hot sellers. People planned parties around the upcoming Finals games, and placards taped to car windows and storefronts begged the team to "Show Me the Title."

It seemed nothing in the world could spoil the party. For a few days, after the trials and frustrations of nearly twenty tumultuous and sometimes desperate seasons, the state of Utah knew nothing but unfettered joy and peace and happiness and hope.

Then the Bulls showed up, and ruined everything.

*　*　*

As encouraging as it was for the accomplishment it represented, the Jazz's loss in the NBA Finals made equally evident their closing window of opportunity. Even though the Jazz had for years confounded the skeptics who kept predicting their end, they had just finished the best season in their history and still could not bring home the championship.

Malone had been as good as ever, averaging 27.4 points and upstaging Michael Jordan in a controversial vote to win the league's Most Valuable Player award for the first time, but Stockton clearly was slowing down. He hated to admit it—refused to, actually—but there was growing sentiment around the league that he wasn't quite the player he once was, and his statistics buttressed the argument.

Though he was responsible for the phenomenal shot that finally put the Jazz in the Finals, Stockton had spent the season compiling scoring and assist averages that had not been so low since before he became a starter some ten years earlier. To be fair, no other guard in NBA history had played with such effectiveness for so long, and Stockton was able to compensate for most of the slight physical shortcomings he had begun to develop with his veteran's intelligence and astounding mental toughness. The Jazz didn't need Stockton to carry quite as much of the load as he once did, either, blessed as they were with a deeper roster than in years past. But still, time marches on, and even the greatest players cannot pick-and-roll forever.

Miller felt the Jazz had perhaps two more seasons to make legitimate title runs before having to rebuild without their superstars, so in the weeks after the 1997 Finals, he opened his checkbook and set about cementing the key elements of his roster for at least that long. Six players had become free agents, and Miller managed to re-sign five of them.

Russell, the small forward who had been burned by Jordan in the Finals but who had grown into a versatile starter since being chosen deep in the second round of the 1993 draft, signed for five years and $20 million. Hornacek—his championship clock ticking in time with Stockton's—signed for two years and about $8 million. Young reserves Eisley and Anderson each latched on for two seasons at just over $1.2 million per, and Carr signed a one-year deal worth $1.6 million. Only Stephen Howard went unsigned, but he was the last reserve on the bench, and his roster spot had been taken when the Jazz chose point guard Jacque Vaughn out of Kansas University with the twenty-ninth pick in the draft.

Miller also was wary of losing Ostertag to free agency the following summer. Ostertag wasn't much to look at, but he had developed into a regular contributor during the playoffs and was possessed of the talent for blocking shots that the Jazz had long ago grown to cherish in their big men.

As a member of the rookie class of 1995, the first under the league's new collective bargaining agreement, Ostertag had the option to sign a contract extension before the new season, or wait until it was over and become a free agent. He had encouraged the Jazz with his performance in the playoffs and Finals, and Miller was concerned Ostertag might have an even better year and then command upward of $10 million per year like Bryant Reeves in Vancouver. So when Ostertag's agent called and said his client would prefer to sign a contract extension and stay in Utah rather than test the free agent market, Miller and the Jazz listened.

The agent, Jeff Austin, suggested a price range for a contract extension based on what he thought Ostertag was worth in the current climate, minus just a bit as a gesture of goodwill toward the Jazz, and it nearly matched the Jazz's own estimation of Ostertag's value. It wasn't long, then, before Ostertag signed a six-year deal worth $39 million that would go into effect a year later.

In all, Miller committed more than $70 million to keep his team together that summer, and everything was set. The man who had twice saved the Jazz for Utah was hailed again as a sporting hero, the Jazz were able to reload their roster with the ammunition of their choice, and everybody from the ushers to the towel boys was ready for the team to finally bring home the title.

But where Miller's enthusiasm had once caused him to make

negative judgments too quickly, it now led him to give praise too effusively and too soon. At the press conferences announcing the signings of Ostertag and Russell, the owner had declared them the key to the future of the franchise. This did not sit well with some of the players, especially one who was so much a part of the best of the team's past, present, and, he thought, future.

For Malone, the facade of team unity masked a growing sense of animosity. He was not the only player who felt insulted that Ostertag was about to start earning so much money without having proved himself, but he was surely the most important, and he was one of the few with the standing and security to say anything about it on this generally circumspect squad.

It did not take long after their first Finals appearance, then, for vanity to gain a foothold among the Jazz, and the insecurities bred by its collusion with jealousy threatened to destroy the team's next championship run—so painstakingly fostered over so many years —before it even had a chance to break from the blocks.

CHAPTER

3

The voice came from across the floor at The Forum, and reached Greg Ostertag as he wandered alone onto the court for the shootaround eight hours before the Jazz were to open the 1997–98 season against the Los Angeles Lakers.

"Hey, Ostertag!"

It was Shaquille O'Neal, beckoning.

O'Neal stood 7-1, weighed 315 pounds, and played center for the Lakers with a bad-ass snarl that matched his bad-ass game. A five-time All-Star, he was the most physically imposing player in the NBA, and probably would have been considered the best big man if not for his rotten free throw shooting and the fact that he had yet to win a championship. Ostertag, on the other hand, could most diplomatically be described as an underachiever, a 7-2, 280-pound doughboy who had yet to take his basketball career quite as seriously as the Jazz would have liked in the two years since he was a rookie. All the same, Ostertag and the Jazz were the most recent reason O'Neal wasn't wearing a championship ring.

Not five months earlier, the Jazz had beaten Los Angeles 4–1 in the Western Conference semifinals, a series that served as a launching pad for their most successful postseason ever. O'Neal led the Lakers in rebounds in each game of that series, and averaged 26.9 points in spite of being slowed by a knee injury and furious Jazz double-teaming. But in the series finale, Ostertag blocked 9 shots and rendered O'Neal practically invisible in the Jazz's 98–93 overtime triumph. Then, by virtue of the victory and all those blocks, Ostertag saw fit to talk a little trash when he was asked to compare O'Neal to his upcoming opponent, Hakeem Olajuwon of the Houston Rockets.

"Hakeem's a classier guy," Ostertag said. "Nobody thinks I've done anything all year, especially Shaq. But I guess that's why he's playing golf and I'm going to the Western Conference finals."

Ostertag was flying high. He had emerged as a legitimate force in the playoffs after two years of up-and-down performances and the almost constant derision of local critics, who thought he looked like Baby Huey and moved only about half as well. His performance against O'Neal cemented the Jazz's belief that they wanted to hang on to Ostertag as an anchor for the defense, and it paved the way to make the team's $39 million off-season investment look reasonably prudent.

Ostertag's incendiary words found their way back to O'Neal, who hardly shied away when the issue resurfaced in the days before the season-opener.

"I'm not worried about Ostertag, he can't hold me," said O'Neal. "Ostertag is a scrub. My knee was hurting me. I had that big brace. But that's okay. He blocked some shots. That ain't real life. Real life is here."

And yet it wasn't.

O'Neal had strained a muscle in his abdomen during the preseason and would not be able to play in the opener. Forward Elden Campbell was scheduled to start in his place, and the rematch between the big men with the big mouths would have to wait.

Unless . . .

"Hey, Ostertag!"

Ostertag answered the call—heard his name and started across the floor toward O'Neal. Since the Lakers had just finished their workout and the Jazz were several minutes away from beginning theirs, few people were on the floor to witness what happened next. By all accounts, though, words were exchanged as Ostertag drew near.

"I just told him, 'Hey, yo, watch your mouth and just play.' You don't gotta talk," O'Neal recounted months later in an interview with *ESPN Magazine*. "He said, 'Fuck you.' I said, 'Oh, fuck me?' Okay."

And just that fast, O'Neal smacked him.

One shot, with a cupped left hand, to the side of Ostertag's buzzcut head, and the big lug went down in a heap. Stayed down, too. While O'Neal fairly puffed out his chest and prepared for the fight, Ostertag simply lay there, waiting for the threat to pass and then looking for his contact lens, which had been knocked out of his eye and onto the floor.

"I didn't swing at him," said O'Neal. "I didn't punch him. It was a mush, you know, a push. Maybe it was like a testosterone reflex. I'm in my house, and he tried to jump in my house, and just had to show him he really wasn't that tough."

A few Lakers who'd been lingering nearby joined O'Neal's bodyguard in sparing Ostertag the additional indignity of having to curl up in the fetal position by ushering O'Neal into the hallway, his point made.

* * *

"Damn! Did you see that?"

Karl Malone couldn't believe it when he heard about it, and neither could the rest of the Jazz, most of whom had yet to leave the locker room when O'Neal struck. But word traveled fast. Several broadcasters were among those at The Forum at the time, and thanks to the miracle of modern cell phone technology, they disseminated the news even before the hubbub subsided enough for the Jazz to start their practice.

Since so few people had witnessed the incident, however, many reporters spent the next little while trying to verify through the principals precisely what happened. They knew players fought during games and practices and occasionally in bars, but nobody could recall trouble breaking out at a shootaround. A group of reporters managed to catch up with O'Neal as he left the Lakers' dressing room, but he offered little in the way of an explanation.

"Words were said," he said. "That's all I have to say." Then he launched into a bizarre lecture to children about being careful that night on Halloween.

Ostertag wasn't talking before the game either, and he wound up playing that night as if he was having flashbacks. It turned out that not even Campbell could play because he had muscle spasms in his neck, so Ostertag found himself facing backup Sean Rooks while O'Neal watched from the bench in street clothes—but even that, apparently, was too close for Ostertag.

Ostertag seemed petrified as the Jazz took the court, and he missed seven of the first eight shots he took. He grabbed a number of rebounds, but most of them were off his own misses—and he still managed just one basket in ten minutes on the floor. With about two minutes left in the first period, coach Jerry Sloan had seen enough: he sent in Adam Keefe to replace Ostertag.

The Jazz finished building a 16-point lead while Ostertag sat on the bench, and led by 14 with 3:20 left in the second quarter, but the Lakers held them scoreless over the next three minutes while young Kobe Bryant and Nick Van Exel combined for 11 of the Lakers' 14 straight points to tie the game. Howard Eisley hit a running jumper with only a few seconds left in the quarter, and Utah went into the locker room leading only 45–43.

Sloan allowed Ostertag to start the third quarter, but he did not perform any better than he had in the first. Ostertag missed all 3 shots he tried—the last one was viciously rejected by 6-6 Lakers guard Eddie Jones—and flattened a Laker for an offensive foul. Disgusted, Sloan sent Keefe back in, and Ostertag did not play the rest of the game. The Jazz lost, 104–87.

"I played like shit tonight," said Ostertag.

Sloan did not disagree. "We quit screening," the coach complained. "We quit doing a lot of things. I'm not happy with that at all."

Their first season-opening loss in five years gave the Jazz something important to worry about, but their thoughts kept coming back to O'Neal's attack on Ostertag.

Having spent the off-season cultivating an image as his team's mature new leader, O'Neal took a lot of heat in the press and earned a $10,000 fine and a one-game suspension from the league. Yet few perceived Ostertag as a hero who had taken the moral high ground in the conflict. Instead, he was portrayed nationwide as a stooge and a coward for staying down and not fighting back.

Naturally, fans in Utah preferred to believe the worst about O'Neal and the best about Ostertag, but the Jazz themselves fell more in line with the national average. While Malone did defend Ostertag against heckling fans during the game, and Sloan said O'Neal's attack "shouldn't be a part of basketball," both men probably would have rather seen Ostertag stand up for himself than let himself be embarrassed.

A rugged man who grew up poor and learned the value of a

good counterpunch long before the worth of a well-spoken word, Sloan probably would have jumped O'Neal himself, even at age fifty-five, had O'Neal tried to fight him. Sloan, after all, used to knock down opposing players if they "embarrassed" him with fancy dribbling tricks, and he once stood up to Wilt Chamberlain during a game, even though Sloan was eight inches shorter and about sixty pounds lighter.

"Wilt told me he was going to knock me on my butt," Sloan recalled. "So I told him something you can't print. He might have knocked me out or killed me, but I told him I'd step in front of him any time I could get an offensive foul on him out of it. I guess I was crazy and didn't know any better."

Chamberlain won that 1973 playoff game for the Lakers over the Bulls, but Sloan won the war: he won respect. That was one thing that was in seriously short supply in the Jazz locker room in the wake of the opening debacle.

"Biggest pussy in the locker room, right there," mumbled Bryon Russell, with a nod toward Ostertag. "And they're paying him all that money."

It was ironic, perhaps, that Russell referred to Ostertag's paycheck, since Russell had scored only 2 points against the Lakers after having secured his own multimillion-dollar deal over the summer, but his remark reflected precisely the sentiment on the team. If Ostertag's teammates had ever had much respect for him, it seemed to have evaporated by the time the opener was over.

When Ostertag finally spoke to reporters about O'Neal after the game, he made himself appear as enfeebled as he had in his original surrender. Ostertag said he was "shocked" at what happened, suggesting he was either too naive or too dumb to foresee trouble when O'Neal called him over. Then he fairly gushed about O'Neal's game, like a child worried that the schoolyard bully might come back for more.

"I don't want to take anything away from him," Ostertag said. He called O'Neal "one of the best players in the league" and "one of the top fifty players in the history of the game," and refused to discuss the incident any more than that. Reporters left the locker room commenting that Ostertag would probably wet his pants the next time he saw O'Neal.

The Jazz played their home opener the next night, and Ostertag bounced back from his miserable 2-point performance against the Lakers by scoring 10 points and grabbing 11 rebounds in a 102–84 victory over the Denver Nuggets at the Delta Center. When he finally wandered out of the shower area in the clubhouse after the game, wearing a T-shirt and shorts and complaining about a "humongous zit" on his forehead, Ostertag drew a crowd of reporters as he sat down in his locker stall.

"Anything about the game," he said, meaning no Shaq questions.

Just then, forward Chris Morris wandered past on the way to his locker, next to Ostertag's.

"So, Greg," he said in mock reportorial tone, "how does it feel when Shaq slaps you upside the head?"

The Jazz already had begun to find out.

The Ostertag embarrassment was only the most literal of slaps upside the head that the Jazz had endured by the time the ball went up to start the season, and the team's vital duo was not exempt from the problems. Malone had publicly assailed his teammates—primarily Ostertag—for failing to stay fit over the summer, and John Stockton had suffered the first serious injury of his career, which was expected to keep him out of the lineup for up to three months. It was a hell of a way to start a season, and the championship that looked so reachable that June night in Chicago suddenly appeared to be as much of a dream as it had been when the Jazz were sloshing around the swamps of New Orleans.

Malone himself had landed the first blow to the Jazz's tranquillity on the day before the team started preseason workouts, by calling certain teammates "fat-asses" for not staying in shape over the summer.

"A damn shame," he said. "It's literally a damn shame that we were so close to winning and guys didn't take their off-season serious enough about getting in shape. That is a disgrace as a professional athlete. It's a disgrace that Coach Sloan will have to say something, or he'll have to run some of us because other guys have been fat-asses all summer. Those same people like to talk about how good they are, so I'm pissed off right now."

No surprise there.

Anger was an emotion that would characterize Malone throughout the season, and one that, in some ways, defined his entire career. At once both uncomplicated and complex, Malone had long since come to be understood as a man who fought with his emotions as much as he surrendered to them.

Born the eighth of nine children in Summerfield, Louisiana, Malone was raised in a two-bedroom house by his mother, Shirley Malone Turner, after his father committed suicide when Malone was three years old. (The similarity to Sloan's childhood is striking: Sloan was born the youngest of ten children, and also grew up fatherless after his dad died as a result of a farming accident when Sloan was four.)

Malone learned to play basketball under the sweltering Louisiana sun, on an earthen field dotted by clumps of weeds, and though he was quite a hell-raiser, he was also no stranger to hard work or the ways of properly respecting his elders. But he also developed a need to be respected, to feel admired for what he could do, and those who Malone believed withheld that satisfaction from him risked eternal scorn.

To wit: even as he proclaimed his happiness at having the Jazz draft him by saying he was eager to play in "the city of Utah," Malone was memorizing the list of the twelve teams that had the chance to take him but did not, never to be forgotten. He complained in recent years of not receiving the proper deference from "knucklehead" young players, and once scored 52 points against Charlotte to prove a point to the Hornets' Armon Gilliam, whom Stockton said had trashed Malone in a TV interview before the game. (Only thing was, nobody had trashed Malone; Stockton had made the whole story up.)

By his own admission, Malone is motivated by fear, and can barely stand to take a day off now that he had turned his body and his game into textbook specimens. "I'm afraid it won't come back," he said.

His fear had served him well in most respects, providing the inspiration to transform himself from a glowering ruffian who could make barely half his free throws into the greatest power forward the game has ever seen. But it was that same fear that may have been the reason Malone went into this season still in search of that treasured championship ring.

He admitted to not being able to shake the thought of millions of people watching as he attempted free throws near the end of Game 1 of the 1997 NBA Finals. He promptly missed both shots, and the Jazz lost—just as they had in 1996, when Malone also missed two late free throws that cost the Jazz a chance at winning Game 7 of the Western Conference finals.

Fear alone does not begin to explain the tapestry that is Karl Malone.

He loves hunting, fishing, country music, and taking his Harley-Davidson motorcycle for long, meditative rides—things few other NBA superstars enjoy. He seldom frequents nightclubs or seeks celebrity for its own sake, yet indulges his attention-grabbing occupational whims: Acting. Merchandising. Truck-driving. Pro wrestling. Malone has tried them all.

He is admired for his charity. He gives away his shoes and wristbands after nearly every game, and once handed a $100 bill to a legless transient near an Atlanta arena with the admonition to keep it out of his cup, lest it get stolen. Those close to Malone say he does things like that all the time. At the same time, however, Malone bemoans autograph-seekers who never seem to care how he's doing.

Malone married a former Miss Idaho, Kay Kinsey, has four children with her, and speaks in praise of the family while doting on his kids. Without the companionship of TV cameras, he regularly visits sick children at a Salt Lake City hospital, and practically adopted a twelve-year-old leukemia victim he met there in 1995; the boy, Danny Ewing, died shortly after the 1995–96 season, and inspired Malone to create the Karl Malone Foundation for Kids to aid needy children.

Yet Malone settled paternity suits involving three children born before he was married, and so completely ignored all three of them—not even speaking to them when by chance they crossed paths in Summerfield—that nobody outside Louisiana was aware they existed. When Malone finally acknowledged those children (in the wake of an article in *The Globe* tabloid newspaper that "outted" him), he contacted the seventeen-year-old fraternal twins by one mother but not the fourteen-year-old boy by another, inciting hurt feelings in the boy and arousing suspicions around Summerfield that Malone was aiming to take credit for the increasing basketball prowess of the other two.

He boasts of not trusting agents, yet complains about his contract; he is extremely sensitive to criticism, though he claims not to care what others think of him. And through it all, he remains one of the hardest-working players in the NBA, giving the Jazz everything he has, every single night, and offering no excuses if he fails in some small respect.

It may be just that litany of vagaries that makes Malone appealing, his public demonstration of so many human frailties making him emotionally accessible to fans. After all, who can't relate to having to keep plugging away at life after getting angry, or after saying something stupid at the wrong time, or after watching a lazy co-worker get the big reward from the boss?

Nobody needed Ostertag's acknowledgment to certify that he was on Malone's preseason rip list; Malone already was known to have to ride herd on Ostertag to stay in shape and work on his game, and Ostertag had arrived at camp looking as if he'd spent his summer in a deli instead of a gym. He was nearly twenty pounds over his optimal playing weight of about 265, and his body fat percentage had skyrocketed. It was clear he had done little all summer except sit on the couch. That infuriated Malone, who already harbored a fairly deep resentment about being one of the lowest-paid superstars in the NBA. (Malone was scheduled to make about $5.1 million for the coming year, ranking him thirty-fifth in the league.) By contrast, after watching the Bulls parade around the United Center as champions, Malone had retreated even earlier than usual to his ranch in Arkansas to begin his legendarily strenuous summertime training regimen.

Malone took only a few days off after the Finals, and had offered his teammates the chance to join him in Arkansas and work themselves into even better shape for the upcoming season. None of them took him up on it. So Malone worked out on his own—up at 6:00 A.M. for an hour on the StairMaster, followed by sprints at the local school track, weights in the gym, and more StairMaster—to make sure he would once again be able to carry his teammates when the situation demanded it.

Malone had advised Larry Miller against signing Ostertag to a long-term contract because he thought the team would get more out of Ostertag if he were playing for a new deal. He grew disgusted when he saw how much the team was willing to pay an unproven player—two, actually, counting Russell—especially after it had asked Malone many times to forgo a big payday in order to help it maintain a reasonable financial balance. And when Malone heard Miller, at separate press conferences, praise Ostertag and Russell as the future of the franchise—and the two players echoed the owner's belief that the team would belong to them once Malone and Stockton retired—that pushed Malone over the edge.

"You want to be the man?" he snarled. "Be the man now. Step up. Maybe then I can play four or five more years."

With his "fat-ass" remark, Malone was also indicting veteran Antoine Carr, who had reported to work considerably out of shape, and, like Ostertag, violated the weight and body fat stipulations in his contract. Carr's measurements were not as outrageous as Ostertag's, but his poor condition would later contribute to a hamstring injury that limited his action in training camp.

"A disgrace," Malone kept saying.

Malone was not in a good mood in the first place, since Miller had decided to move training camp from southern Utah for the first time in a dozen years so he could show off the Jazz 300 miles north in Boise, Idaho, the home of his eight newest auto dealerships. The players thought that was ridiculous, not only because it needlessly ruined a routine that had worked well for them in the past, but because it meant they were going to have to sign more than a few post-practice autographs. Malone and Stockton both complained to Miller about the move, but while Miller said he understood their concerns, he refused to change his plans; Miller already had scheduled a scrimmage at Boise State University that was open only to his new employees and their families, with a mandatory autograph session afterward.

That was one sure way to annoy Stockton; he might not hate anything in the world more than signing autographs.

On his way to the team bus one day during training camp, Stockton mistakenly went out the wrong door of the hotel and found himself clear on the other side of the building from the bus. Instead of simply going back inside and taking the shortcut through the building, though, Stockton walked quietly all the way around the outside of the hotel, so he would not have to run the gauntlet of autograph hounds that had gathered in the lobby. And when finally he was corraled into signing during the post-practice session that Miller had arranged, Stockton sat stonefaced and silent, never looking up from his hands while signing items and holding them out blindly for their owners to reclaim. Signing and returning, over and again, with neither a word nor a smile until he was allowed to leave.

Stockton had long been known for his cautious demeanor toward reporters and his disdain for special attention (he learned long ago that he could duck a lot of interviews by hiding out in the Jazz's training room, which is off limits to the media), but that grew out of a simple belief that he had a right to keep his life private. The ceaseless and often ridiculous demands of the press and over-zealous fans—a woman once screamed at him for not signing a bagful of trading cards—drove Stockton further away from the typically public life of a superstar, but he remains, in private, the kind of person everybody would like to know.

"He kind of comes across as this stoic, unemotional guy," said Miller. "But he's a great person. People ask, 'How is John Stockton?' And I tell them, 'He's exactly what you hope he is. He will not let you down.' And if they knew his heart and how he feels about people, and the lengths to which he goes . . . they would understand."

Stockton's legend among family and friends extends far beyond his charming public legacy of returning each off-season to his hometown to live in the house next door to the one in which he grew up, where his parents, Jack and Clementine, still reside. The folks back home know him as the kid who cultivated his competitive spirit in breakneck pickup games against his older brother in the family driveway, and who beat out all but one senior to make the Gonzaga Prep varsity as a sophomore.

Growing up attending Catholic schools in a small town, Stockton had an idyllic childhood. His entire life was comfortably ensconced in a few square blocks, which included his neighborhood, his schools, and the now-famous tavern, Jack & Dan's, that his father operates with one of Stockton's former college teammates. Stockton even married his high school sweetheart, the former Nada Stepovich.

One of four children, with two sisters and an older brother, Stockton was the one whom everybody noticed as particularly focused and driven. He was small, and that helped instill in Stockton a sense that he always needed to work harder, to play smarter, and to play more than everybody else just to keep up with them. One mistake, and a guy his size was sure to be shooed away. So it was that early on, Stockton developed the intensity and focus that years later would define one of the best point guards in the history of the NBA.

The library of Stockton stories is no match for Malone's, and that's the way Stockton likes it. He enjoys spending time with his wife and three children and aspires to be a good parent more than an athletic icon. Watching him play, fans would never suspect Stockton's wry sense of humor. At a Jazz awards dinner early in his career, guest speaker Bob Lanier praised Malone for a fine season, but then suggested, with a nod toward Stockton, "You ought to give a couple of hundred thousand dollars to that little white boy over there."

Stockton got up and gave Lanier a one-man standing ovation.

Within the privacy of the locker room or team bus, Stockton routinely chides his teammates for just about anything—the way they're dressed, their hair, their hometowns. He makes fun of Malone for liking to hunt, and jokingly tells Sloan that other teammates are making fun of him.

"Coach?" he'll shout. "Shandon says 'nice hat.' "

Nearly every joke he makes comes complete with a deadpan delivery, no smile necessary. He was taking extra jump shots a couple of hours before a game against Los Angeles one night when the Lakers' Jones happened down to Stockton's end of the floor and started stroking three-pointers. After watching Jones drill about five in a row, Stockton caught Jones's ball as it snapped through the net.

"You about locked in?" he asked. "You about locked in at this height?"

Jones nodded.

"Because it's about an inch and a half short right now," Stockton said as he threw the ball back. Jones erupted in laughter, while Stockton simply turned around and walked the other way, stifling a grin.

Training camp was not nearly as amusing; all the Jazz did was run drills and scrimmage twice a day in an empty gym. Stockton was hardly practicing because the team was trying to go easy on his aching knees, and with just about everybody back from the previous year, only the possibility of a late draft pick or nonroster invitee beating out a veteran for a job qualified as a subplot. (That was a phenomenon for which the Jazz were becoming renowned. Russell had beaten the odds and stuck after the Jazz made the former Long Beach State star the forty-seventh pick of the 1993 draft, and quiet workhorse Shandon Anderson followed in Russell's footsteps after being made the fifty-fourth pick out of Georgia in 1996. But aside from Jacque Vaughn, a personable rookie point guard from Kansas, no newcomers had much of a prayer of displacing any of the Western Conference champions.)

Meanwhile, Malone's tirade was generating big news back home. Guessing at Malone's targets became a water-cooler pastime, and Malone made it worse for himself when he couldn't keep quiet after hearing of Miller's supposed reaction to his rant.

The way Malone heard it, Miller said he did not take Malone's comments seriously because they were simply one of the ways Malone motivated himself for the season, and added that Malone had "lost a step." Malone had not actually spoken to Miller, however, or heard his reaction firsthand; he was told of the remarks by family members in Louisiana.

While Miller did, in fact, downplay the seriousness of Malone's remarks, he did not accuse his star of slowing down. What Miller did say was that even if Malone had lost a step, he would never admit it. But since perception often ranks as reality, Malone was steamed just the same.

In Malone's mind, his boss should have agreed with him about the "fat-asses" instead of dismissing Malone as he did, and Miller certainly shouldn't have even raised the specter of his losing a step. Malone was better with half a step, he would insist later, than the rest of the league was with a full one. He was so mad that he erupted again, this time complaining about feeling disrespected and suggesting that he might leave the Jazz after his contract expired.

"You call my bluff," he dared. "We'll see. . . . We'll see what happens."

That was heresy, as far as many fans were concerned. Because Malone was such a fine player, fans had learned to live with his quirks, but hearing him complain about being unappreciated when he pulled down more than $5 million a year and practically walked on water in Utah was just too much for many of them to take.

The newspaper columnists in town took aim with both barrels, and the folks at the sports radio stations had a field day. Listeners called in ceaselessly to accuse Malone of being a crybaby, and to mock him for trying to come off like a working stiff just trying to feed his family. The radio hosts at one station in Salt Lake City were in the middle of dumping on Malone the next morning when another in the parade of phone lines lit up.

The first-time caller?

Mrs. Karl Malone.

And she was not happy.

Kay Malone had been driving her children to school in Salt Lake City that morning, and had to turn off the radio because the fusillade of anti-Malone opinions was so angry. She dropped off the kids, turned the radio on again to hear more, and couldn't help but reach for the phone once she returned home.

"I just felt really sick to hear everybody be so negative" about Malone and his salary, Kay Malone said on the air. "Players are getting paid a lot of money, but I think if the Jazz are going to look at it, I think they should see what he has accomplished . . . and plus what he does for the community and Utah. Maybe that doesn't mean nothing to nobody, but to me I think it does, just because role models are such a big thing for children. They look up at Karl and what he does. . . . If Karl was like a Dennis Rodman, then, yeah, I wouldn't want to pay him crap. But the thing is, Karl is trying to set examples for children and yeah, he's making money, but my God, half the money he earns, he does give a lot to charity. And I don't think people know that. But the thing is, what upsets me, is when people call and say negative things about my husband, and just kind of say things that they don't even know. I think that's really wrong."

She went on like that for six minutes, an eternity in radio time. And by the time she had finished, it was clear that Kay Malone was speaking her husband's mind as much as she was speaking her own. And the perception that Malone was complaining about his contract again was a huge problem for him. He hated being cast in the same lot as the NBA's more notorious malcontents, or being portrayed as the same kind of money-hungry petulant that he'd always claimed to despise. He knew how devastating such a distraction could be if it were allowed to fester into the season, so he did the only thing he could think of that would allow him to bury the issue once and for all:

He invited the media to his home.

Invitations were delivered over the phone by Malone's personal assistant, Roxanne Hasagawa, on the final morning of training camp. She said Malone wanted each of the three newspaper beat writers to join one representative from two radio stations and each of the four TV stations in town to meet him at his new home in the foothills above Salt Lake City as soon as the Jazz returned from Boise.

The 27,000-square-foot Malone house was not quite a monument to modesty. Built of wood and river rock to affect a hunting lodge sort of coziness, it featured four bedrooms—each opening to a log deck that runs the length of the house and overlooks the Salt Lake Valley—a backyard pool, a playground, half of an indoor basketball court, a shooting range, a weight room to rival any spa, and much, much more. The kitchen was enormous. The garage? Huge, with enough room for Malone's famous motorcycles. The driveway circled in front of the house under a roof, like a hotel, and running parallel to the entry hall was a babbling brook built into the wall about waist-high.

And it turned out that Malone hadn't been exaggerating when he'd said, upon winning the MVP award the previous season, that he already had picked out a special place at the then-under-construction home to display the trophy. Indeed, the bronze model of a basketball player running upcourt sat on a ledge above the fireplace in the main family room, much closer to eye level than the two enormous deer heads that watched over the room from farther up on the wall.

Similar mementos of Malone's great career were everywhere. His letter jackets from Summerfield High and Louisiana Tech hung in frames on the wall at the bottom of the stairs that led to his entertainment room, and glass cubes housing autographed shoes and basketballs sat around like potted plants. Several walls were covered with photographs and press clippings of Malone's more impressive achievements, and in the rec room—just off the entertainment room, with its full bar and movie screen that descends from the ceiling—Malone had on display the autographed uniform of every member of the 1992 Olympic Dream Team. He said one day he'll donate all of his memorabilia to the city for a museum.

Once the media arrived, Malone sat on a couch near the front door behind a coffee table loaded with a dozen microphones. The eighteen reporters and cameramen who showed up formed a rough semicircle around Malone's makeshift podium, and there was some hope among the more vulturous that Malone would just say to hell with it, my wife was right, and damn straight I want to leave Utah. But Malone hadn't spent his professional career slaving away just to screw up his best opportunity for the big reward, and the first words out of his mouth that night were, predictably, repentant ones.

"I want you guys to stop reporting that I'm unhappy with my contract," he said. "I want to squash that right now. I'm fine with my contract."

That's as far as the contrition went. Malone spent about thirty minutes on his sofa that night, and after his few-sentence spin on the contract angle, he used most of the time to complain even more.

"It's not about money," he insisted. "I was disappointed that Larry said I was just spouting my mouth off. That showed me no respect. It should have been, 'I agree with him.' I didn't get that support from him, and that pisses me off."

Malone explained how much it angered him that the organization, while signing six of his teammates to new contracts or contract extensions in the off-season, frequently referred to the days in the not-too-distant future when Malone and Stockton would retire.

"To talk about retirement," said Malone, "is a lack of respect."

Malone also refused to take back the comments he made that started him on the path to controversy in the first place. All that "fat-ass" stuff, that stood.

"I meant it," he said.

That having been said, Malone stood up and smiled, shook hands with the reporters and led them on a tour of his house, allowing the Jazz and the community to direct their full attention to the preseason—for all of about three days.

That's all the time it took for the Jazz to beat Charlotte at home in the exhibition opener, beat Dallas on the road, then watch hopelessly as the fates reached down and unceremoniously ripped their heart out.

❖   ❖   ❖

The news arrived like a punch in the stomach.

Stockton had undergone knee surgery, and would be lost to the Jazz for as much as three months.

"I'm in disbelief," said Malone.

So was the whole state. Stockton had missed a grand total of four games in his thirteen-year NBA career—two to a sprained ankle and two to a viral infection, all in 1989–90—and owned the league's third-longest streak of consecutive games with 609. But that wasn't the half of it: Stockton never missed practice either. Never missed a workout. Never even missed a pickup game, if he could help it.

Perhaps everybody should have seen something serious coming when Stockton did not play in the Jazz's second exhibition game of the season, against the Dallas Mavericks in El Paso, Texas, on October 13. But even then the Jazz doctors were holding out hope that the pain that had been so nagging Stockton's left knee could be cured with a little extra time off and a lot of ice.

Stockton had played twenty minutes in the exhibition opener against the Charlotte Hornets two nights earlier, but his knee swelled so bad that doctors had to drain fluid from it before the Mavericks game. That convinced them they ought to conduct a magnetic resonance imaging exam when the team returned home the next day, just to be sure nothing was structurally wrong.

Something was; a tiny piece of cartilage had become separated from the underlying bone in the knee, resulting in a grinding sort of pain and the swelling. The team's orthopedic surgeon, Dr. Lyle Mason, knew surgery would be the best way to correct the problem, but convincing Stockton of that was another matter.

The last thing Stockton wanted was to go under the knife. He inquired about other options, other treatments, but Mason impressed upon him that without surgery, the injury would get worse and eventually might render him incapable of playing for even short stretches.

Reluctantly, Stockton agreed. He had the operation that night at Columbia Lakeview Hospital in Bountiful, a suburb just north of Salt Lake City, and Malone spoke with him by telephone hours later.

"I'll see you in two weeks," Stockton promised.

"No," answered Malone. "You just sit your little butt down."

Mason had not been certain of the severity of the injury until the surgery was under way. He had hoped Stockton would miss only about three weeks, but once he saw the extent of the damage, Mason knew it would take at least eight before Stockton was ready to suit up again. Stockton took great pride in his constitution, and that bit of information took a hard swing at his psyche.

"It's fair to say he's lower than a snake's belly," Mason told reporters the morning after the surgery, on the lawn of the Jazz's practice facility at Westminster College in Salt Lake City. "I couldn't get two words out of him at first. Yes. No. One-word answers."

Mason had brought with him a plastic model of a knee joint, and while TV cameras rolled, he explained how he had removed the kidney-bean-sized chunk of cartilage that had come loose in

Stockton's knee. The result, he said, was something like a pothole in the road.

Since cartilage does not contain blood vessels, it cannot regenerate, so Mason also drilled tiny holes into the part of the bone left exposed by the removal of the cartilage—the technique is called microfracture—which would allow blood to flow into the area and encourage the growth of scar tissue. That scar tissue, though not as good as cartilage, would serve at least a little bit as a replacement, Mason said.

The catch was that the process was a long one. Mason said Stockton would miss between eight and twelve weeks, and if he came back too soon, as a fierce competitor like Stockton might feel inclined to do, he could tear loose the growing scar tissue and force the process to start all over again.

"He asked me if that was the worst-case scenario," said Mason. "I told him it was *the* scenario."

Mason could not say for sure whether Stockton would be able to return to his old form, nor could he promise that the injury would not threaten Stockton's career. "You just kind of have to wait and see how he responds," said Mason.

Nobody was quite certain when Stockton had originally hurt himself. Stockton told doctors of an incident during a pickup game in Spokane over the summer in which his knee buckled, but he doubted that was the cause of the injury, even though that was the explanation Mason gave to the media.

"I mentioned it," Stockton said. "But it was such a tiny thing, it couldn't have caused this big of a thing. . . . My guess is, I did something to it in the past and it just hadn't shown up before."

That explained why nobody envisioned a serious problem when Stockton's knee began to swell during the early stages of training camp. "Swelling happens all the time," said Stockton. "You just try to let it settle. When it didn't this time, that's when there was a reason for concern."

Stockton had sat out many of the camp workouts in deference to the knee, and was disgusted at having to ride a stationary bicycle set up along the baseline of the court at the Boise State University Pavilion while his teammates ran drills and worked on the offense.

"Oh, it's great," he cracked one day while pedaling. "Can't beat doing what you love."

The Jazz already had planned to go easy on Stockton, since, at thirty-five years old, he did not need to suffer any extra wear and tear and did not need camp to get himself into shape. The team had brought to camp three other point guards—Eisley, Vaughn, and rookie Troy Hudson—with the idea of letting them battle on the floor while giving Stockton a bit of a break. It turned out to be a fortuitous consideration.

Most of Stockton's teammates did not learn of his surgery until the morning after it happened, when the Jazz announced it, and they were as shocked as anybody to hear they would have to start the regular season without him for the first time in a decade. At the same time, they tried to remain stoic, behind the lead of Coach Sloan.

"I feel bad for John," he said. "But it gives some of our other guys a chance to see what they can do. Everybody knows how important John has been to this franchise and knows what he has done for us, but life goes on."

Eisley and Vaughn promised they would be ready.

A twenty-four-year-old journeyman, Eisley had played two seasons in his second stint for the Jazz after being cut twenty-six preseason days into his first in 1995. Chosen early in the second round of the 1994 draft by the Minnesota Timberwolves, he had been cut by the Wolves and the San Antonio Spurs, and played a short stint with the Rockford Lightning of the CBA, before landing with the Jazz and developing into one of the more reliable backup point guards in the league. He had really proven himself during the previous season's playoffs by shooting 50 percent, making all but one of his 28 free throws, and helping fans forget all about the days when Stockton would leave the game for a breather and take the Jazz's offensive efficiency to the bench with him.

The last in a long line of backups to Stockton, Eisley fit the Jazz in a way none of his predecessors could quite manage. He was good (unlike Jim Les and Delaney Rudd), deferential (unlike Eric Murdock, who put off the Jazz with an attitude too big for a rookie), young (unlike Jay Humphries, who was thirty by the time he played for Utah and wound up forced into retirement by knee injuries), and able to stick around (unlike John Crotty, who signed as a free agent with Cleveland before the 1995–96 season). Eisley turned down an off-season offer from the Los Angeles Clippers to become their starter, because he wanted to stay with the Jazz and make another run at a championship rather than run the show and win only thirty games, regardless of the money.

"It's a good thing for us that Howard didn't sign with someone else," said Jeff Hornacek.

Eisley was quiet, too, and so shy that he had a hard time looking up from the tops of his sneakers when he talked. Of course, he spoke so softly he could barely be heard, making it hard to believe that he had majored in communications at Boston College, with designs on one day becoming a sportscaster.

Eisley was a bit overwhelmed by all the attention suddenly thrust his way. Every day, the Stockton question came hurtling at him from one direction or the other, and though he had the confidence of his teammates, as well as their promise to be patient while trying to adjust to him, it did not take Eisley long to get sick of answering about the comparisons.

"More John Stockton questions?" he asked one day. "Man, no more."

For Eisley, that qualified as histrionics.

He had a point, though, and his teammates backed him up on it every day: Eisley was not Stockton and never would be Stockton, so there was no reason to expect that he (or anybody else) could play up to Stockton's historic standards. That didn't mean that he could not do a good job, but it did mean that Eisley shouldn't have to bear the burden of trying to live up to a player who one day will grace the Hall of Fame.

"I'm not going to go out and try to be John," Eisley said.

It wasn't just concern for Eisley, either; there was as much about Vaughn, who was being asked to step in immediately and play fifteen to twenty minutes per game as the backup.

When they drafted Vaughn, the Jazz said they couldn't pass up a player of his ability at such a low draft spot, and they planned to use him in a three-guard rotation at point to cut down on Stockton's minutes. Now they looked like prophets, however unfortunate that appearance might have been.

"The first thing I said when I got here is that when my name and number is called, I want to be ready," said Vaughn. "This is that opportunity. Unfortunately, it comes because our best point guard is injured, but Howard and I need to step up our games."

Malone said the same thing, that he was ready to shoulder a greater burden and "pick it up a notch," but evidence of his teammates following suit was a long time in coming.

✤ ✤ ✤

After winning those first two exhibition games in less than spectacular fashion, the Jazz lost three games on a four-game road trip looking most of the way like a team too shell-shocked to care much about trying hard. They shot poorly, rebounded only on occasion, and if anybody ever went to the floor for a loose ball, it was entirely by accident. Guys weren't hustling, and Sloan railed away game after game about lackluster effort and absent desire. He said the Jazz were feeling sorry for themselves because Stockton was gone.

"We have to decide if we want to play or if we're going to do a lot of talking," Sloan said. "Nobody's going to fall out of the air and help you. There's no magic wand or anything."

Malone was the only one playing well, really; everybody else was either inconsistent or downright awful. Ostertag was still fighting to get into shape, and was shooting like he was blindfolded, while Russell seemed to have acquired a bad attitude to go with his fat contract. After losing to the Hornets on that road trip, Malone heard Russell say he didn't care about shooting 1 for 5 from the field because it was only the preseason, and that his shots would start falling once the regular season began.

That did it.

When the team returned home for a day between road games, Malone convened a players-only meeting after practice, and his lecturing in the basement locker room at Westminster College could be heard on the stairway, through two closed doors. Again, he let his teammates have it. Time was growing short on a championship, he knew, and the Jazz had little room to fool around.

"I don't care if it's the preseason," Malone said later. "You get ready to play in the regular season during the preseason. Even if you don't play a lot of minutes, it's when you get ready to play. I don't want to hear that 'When the regular season starts, we'll be ready.' Don't give me that stuff. How many years have we been saying that?"

While some of his teammates at least offered vague accounts of and agreements with Malone's latest tantrum, Russell emerged unwilling to speak with reporters about anything. He maintained his silence even after scoring 16 points and grabbing 8 rebounds in forty minutes of the Jazz's next preseason game, a win over the Portland Trail Blazers. The Jazz won their final preseason game against the Phoenix Suns to finish 5-3, but they had improved little since the day nearly a month earlier when Malone had implored them to do so; prospects for the new season had dimmed significantly.

They had yet to play a cohesive game under Eisley and Vaughn, and Sloan was each game growing more disgusted with the lack of effort the players were showing. The season-opener against the Lakers was supposed to be a good chance for the Jazz to show the NBA they were ready to challenge again for the title, but the opportunity was lost when Ostertag lay down and the Jazz came apart at the seams. A team that had been so close only months before instead was bickering and sulking.

It was a horrible time for Stockton to be gone.

The Jazz were to spend that first month of the regular season playing teams from the Western Conference almost exclusively, which would give them a chance to see how they measured up against their competition for playoff berths. The Jazz felt strongly that they needed to secure home court advantage throughout the playoffs to have their best chance at winning a title; over the previous ten seasons, they had the largest home-court edge in the NBA, as measured by comparing home and road winning percentages. To secure that extra home game in every series, the Jazz needed to finish with the best record in the league, something that would be much more difficult if they didn't get off to a good start.

The early schedule wasn't padded with patsies, either. The Jazz had a whole stack of contenders on the list in the season's first month. After the Lakers, they played the Spurs—both in San

Antonio and in Salt Lake City—the Suns, the Sonics, and the Timberwolves. All those teams had improved themselves in the off-season, either by acquiring new players or rehabilitating old ones, and figured to be serious contenders for division titles and playoff spots.

The Lakers had perhaps the most raw talent in the league with Shaquille O'Neal and Nick Van Exel, Rick Fox, Eddie Jones, and Kobe Bryant, and the Spurs had landed number one draft pick Tim Duncan to complement All-Star center David Robinson after their injury-plagued season of a year before. The Suns had perhaps the deepest team in the league (as well as the shortest), and the Sonics had swapped disgruntled Shawn Kemp for the smooth Vin Baker to make themselves better. The Jazz went 11-2 in November 1996 on their way to their franchise-record 64 victories, but with Stockton out, a repeat looked almost impossible.

Reality needed but a week to catch up with appearances.

In their third game of the regular season, the Jazz lost for the second time, 90–86, to the Washington Wizards on the Delta Center floor to end a fourteen-game home court winning streak, and followed that with a 106–84 loss at Phoenix the next night. Each game was offering some heretofore unseen problem: against the Wizards, the Jazz made only 23 of 38 free throws, and against the Suns they shot only 36 percent and scored just 33 points in the first half. At 1-3, the Jazz were off to their worst start since 1991.

The slump took its toll on the players, even so early in the season. Karl Malone was just barely speaking to the press, preferring to give monosyllabic—and often profane—answers on his way off the practice court or to hide out in the off-limits training room after games until the media gave up and went home. Greg Ostertag wasn't talking either, since he was shooting about 30 percent and growing increasingly worthless during his time on the floor, and Bryon Russell practically ran from reporters one day after practice.

"I'm struggling," he said over his shoulder. "What else do you want?"

Everywhere the Jazz went, too, fans and the media wanted to know about John Stockton.

How was he doing?

When would he be back?

Can the Jazz survive without him?

Russell saved the Jazz in their next game against the Nuggets by making a late three-pointer to ensure a 91–89 win in Denver, and he was all smiles afterward. But Russell's accomplishment was more cautionary tale than cause for celebration, considering that the Nuggets were one of the worst teams in the league and that Russell's big three was only his second of the season against 12 misses. In fact, there was growing suspicion that Russell had let the money go to his head.

The year before, he'd built a reputation as the team's best perimeter defender and maker of three-point shots in crucial situations. "He really buried some teams," recalled coach Jerry Sloan. But through the preseason and the first five games of the regular one, he'd shown almost none of his previous tendencies, and looked sluggish after proclaiming in training camp that he wanted to make the All-Star team.

The Jazz then lost their first meeting with the revitalized Spurs, 87–80, when the Spurs committed 45 fouls and the Jazz set franchise records by making only 19 baskets and attempting only 58.

"I don't think we've shown enough toughness to even warrant playing against teams," groused Sloan. "The most important thing is to find somebody for us to come out and compete. Obviously, we've got guys who aren't competing quite hard enough. . . . Then you don't have a chance."

It was early, but the Jazz were averaging more than 10 fewer points per game than they had the previous season, and were shooting far below the level that had earned them the best percentage in the league for three years running. Sloan had to make a move, or risk falling hopelessly behind in the race for the league's best record. So he benched Ostertag and Russell, who combined were shooting barely 30 percent, and replaced them in the starting lineup with Greg Foster and Adam Keefe.

"Maybe somebody else is going to come in and give us a lift," said Sloan. "At least act like you want to play. It's kind of frustrating when you have guys who aren't really focused in on playing."

Russell was relieved, having asked (to Sloan's silent disgust) to relinquish his starting role for a less pressure-packed one coming off the bench. But Ostertag's demotion seemed to crush his spirit even more than O'Neal had. Still, Sloan needed more offensive production from his starting lineup, and he got it.

Keefe had always been a hard worker and gave the Jazz a tenacious force inside, while Foster was the perfect complement, since he had a nice outside touch for a man 6-11; he often floated around the perimeter, allowing Keefe and Malone more room to maneuver inside.

With the new starting lineup, the Jazz won three straight games, beating Vancouver and Seattle at home, 98–80 and 114–110, and the Mavericks, 85–77, in Dallas. It wasn't an awe-inspiring stretch, but at least it loosened up the players a bit. They were showing signs of improvement, however slight, and just in time.

Next on the schedule was the rematch against O'Neal and the Los Angeles Lakers.

O'Neal was healthy again, but was looking less inclined to make any more trouble with Ostertag. Word out of Los Angeles was that O'Neal regretted his attack on Ostertag, at least in part because it did so much damage to his image, and the Lakers arrived in Salt Lake City on an 8-0 season-starting winning streak that matched the one by their 1987–88 championship team as the best in franchise history. The lure of 9-0 kept the Lakers on their best behavior, and O'Neal eventually came around to issuing what he considered an apology for slapping Ostertag.

"Maybe it was wrong and maybe it wasn't wrong," he said. "I want it to be over with, and it will be over with. . . . Do I regret it? I realize I made a mistake, but I'm at peace with myself."

Ostertag seemed set against another confrontation, too.

"I have a job to do on the court," he said while dodging direct answers to Shaq questions. "I'm going to do my best—or try to do my best—to help this team win. It's important to me."

What might have appeared to be Ostertag's leaning toward the high road, however, was to some minds simply blind fear. "He was scared shitless," opined one member of the Jazz staff.

Neither Ostertag nor O'Neal showed any emotion when they took the floor for the shootaround immediately before their November 18 game at the Delta Center. O'Neal was anchored to the free throw line, trying to improve his miserable percentage, when Ostertag first ambled out of the Jazz locker room and onto the other end of the floor; in the short time the men shared the floor they made neither visual nor physical contact. For the game, more than 20,000 fans showed up to cheer the Jazz and to jeer O'Neal, and many of them armed themselves with clappy little noisemakers —"Shaq-Slappers," they were called—distributed by a local radio station. Signs dotted the arena, bearing messages like "Slap the Shaq" and "Slap This!," but their holders, it turned out, would be sorely disappointed.

As had been Sloan's habit in the three games since he began bringing Ostertag and Russell off the bench, Ostertag did not enter the game until the final ninety seconds of the first quarter. When he did, O'Neal was not in the game. But both men were in the lineup when the second quarter began, and the fans, perched on the edges of their seats, held their breaths and waited.

And waited.

And waited.

But nothing happened—not in the second quarter, not after halftime, not ever.

The game passed without a confrontation. The big men barely came into contact, for that matter, playing simultaneously for only about ten minutes, and less than that actually head-to-head: O'Neal was assigned defensive responsibility on Antoine Carr when Carr replaced Malone early in the second quarter, and Elden Campbell guarded Ostertag.

Not that there was much to guard.

He was running up and down the court with O'Neal no more than a few arm-lengths away, but Ostertag still was suffering from the trauma of being smacked nearly three weeks earlier. He bobbled passes, and couldn't hit a free throw. Some who knew him off the court wondered if the slap hadn't changed Ostertag as a person, if O'Neal hadn't robbed his soul. Ostertag scored 6 points and grabbed 3 rebounds against the Lakers—which, sadly for him, soon would pass for a good night.

Even worse, the Jazz blew the game again. They'd led almost the whole way, and by as many as 10 points. But just like in the opener, they shut down at the end. Part of the problem was that Howard Eisley could not control the tempo of the game and the temperament of his teammates the way Stockton could, and too many of his teammates were screwing around and not playing as a team.

The Jazz did not score in the final 2:28 against the Lakers, while Los Angeles scored 9 straight points over the same span to emerge with a 97–92 victory that helped exorcise the ghosts of the previous season's playoffs. Young Bryant was the hero, with 19 points off the bench and a block and dunk at the end, and the Lakers danced off into the locker room while the Jazz retreated, again, to try to figure out what had gone wrong.

They discovered only more questions.

*   *   *

While Stockton had progressed far enough in his rehabilitation that he was able to take some gentle jump shots before the Lakers game—his workouts had grown to five hours a day by that point—the rest of the Jazz had seen little consistent improvement.

They needed more than two minutes of their next game at Sacramento to score their first basket, and they fell behind by 18 points to the Kings, one of the worst teams in the NBA. The Jazz hadn't lost to the Kings in nearly four years, a span of fourteen games, and yet there they were at Arco Arena, straining to get back into the game after another horrible shooting effort. They managed it, but only by virtue of Malone's 24-point second half and the Kings' hideous free throw shooting; Corliss Williamson missed 8 of 10 and sank his team's average to 16 of 38, and Utah trailed only 97–95 when Mitch Richmond missed a jump shot with ten seconds left.

After a timeout, the Jazz inbounded at midcourt with a pass to Eisley. Malone set a screen at the top of the key and rolled to the basket, but two defenders followed him. That left Eisley to drive the lane, and he got a good look at the basket as he pulled up for a jumper over Terry Dehere.

His shot hit the front of the rim, and then it hit the back. Then it landed in the hands of Sacramento's Olden Polynice. Game over.

"I don't think guys really showed up and played a physical game like Sacramento played," said Eisley.

Same old story.

In the first eleven games the Jazz had played without Stockton, they'd lost six of them, and the games they did win came mostly against weak teams like the Mavericks, the Grizzlies, and the Nuggets (twice).

They could be thankful, however, that none of their competition in the Midwest Division had raced out to the same kind of start as the 11-0 Atlanta Hawks in the Central Division. The Spurs won seven of their first ten games but then began to fade, the Timberwolves were 6-4, and everybody else trailed the Jazz in the division standings. Spirits picked up a bit when Utah exacted revenge with a 103–74 whipping of the Spurs in the Delta Center, then beat Minnesota, 133–124, in overtime two days later.

And the next morning, Stockton showed up in T-shirt and shorts and practiced with the team for the first time in six weeks. Players even laughed a little bit on their way out of the gym.

Maybe everything would be okay after all.

❖   ❖   ❖

Stockton could not help but feel a little edgy, sitting on the bench wearing his Jazz uniform for the first time in months. He was about to be introduced to a capacity crowd at the Delta Center that was rocking the rafters in anticipation of witnessing his return from knee surgery against the Indiana Pacers. Stockton kept telling himself to stay calm; he'd done this hundreds of times before. But really, he hadn't. The injury he'd suffered several months earlier was the first serious one of his career, and how his tightly wrapped left knee would respond under game conditions was anybody's guess.

"There were a lot of things going through my head," he confessed later.

Yet even as the public address announcer introduced the rest of the Jazz players and the fans turned up the volume on their cheers, the expression on Stockton's face never changed. His mouth sat in a flat line across his face, and his eyes seemed to be focused not on anything in particular, but on some point just vaguely in the future. And when his name finally came across the sound system at nearly 100 decibels and the crowd went out of its mind with adoration, Stockton simply blocked out the anxiety and the emotion, slapped the proper hands on his way through the gauntlet of his teammates, and ran to the center of the first pregame huddle of the rest of his surgically repaired life.

"I was just really concentrating on listening in on what was happening to me out there from a physical standpoint, and listening to what coach wanted us to do," Stockton said. "I had plenty on my mind with that."

It was December 8, eight weeks to the day since Stockton lay on a table while surgeons removed bits of torn cartilage from his left knee, and in the time he'd been gone, the NBA seemed to have started to implode

Injured superstars littered the landscape. Aside from Stockton, O'Neal was missing time with the same strained abdominal muscle that kept him from the opener against the Jazz; Miami's Alonzo Mourning missed twenty-two games with a knee injury; Houston's Hakeem Olajuwon was out till the All-Star break with a knee injury of his own; and Chicago's Scottie Pippen hadn't played all season because of an injured foot and was vowing to never play for the Bulls again because of his differences with management.

Scoring and attendance were down in spite of new rules designed to encourage offense, and the league was being portrayed as a fashion fascist for fining several players who wore their shorts too long. (Russell was the only Jazz player the NBA found to be in violation of the rule, which stipulated that shorts not hang any lower than one inch above the knee. He avoided a fine by hemming his drawers after a warning.)

On top of all that, Golden State's Latrell Sprewell had given the league its biggest black eye in a long time only a week earlier, by attacking Coach P. J. Carlesimo at practice and threatening to kill him.

The fallout from the Sprewell incident was tremendous. The Warriors terminated the remaining three years on Sprewell's four-year, $32 million deal, and the NBA suspended Sprewell from playing with any team for an entire year. It was that suspension that sparked the hottest debate; the players union filed a grievance, saying the punishment was far too harsh, even though most of America seemed to believe that Sprewell should be shipped off to an uncharted desert isle somewhere. Yet while everybody else in the NBA weighed in with opinions on the attack and suspension, the Jazz kept themselves out of the firestorm, in large part because many of them believed Sprewell was a thug and that the league did the right thing by banning him for a year. They did not, however, want to open themselves to reproof by expressing opinions that would suggest a philosophical chasm in the union to which they all belonged.

"I don't need that," one of them said.

Some did observe, though, that a situation similar to the one at Golden State would never arise with Sloan.

"No one on this team wants to mess with Jerry," said Jeff Hornacek. Team president Frank Layden agreed: "Nobody fights with Jerry because you know the price would be too high," he said. "You might come out the winner, at his age. You might even lick him. But you'd lose an eye, an arm, your testicles in the process. Everything would be gone."

All of the controversy over Sprewell and the cynicism over the Jazz's rough start had melted away, though, by the time news leaked out that Stockton would start and play as many as twenty minutes against the Pacers and their new coach, Larry Bird.

The Jazz had managed to go 11-7 without Stockton, largely by virtue of a six-game winning streak that had worked wonders for the team's confidence in spite of its construction against some of the worst teams in the league. In the two weeks before Stockton's return, the Jazz added to their wins over San Antonio and Minnesota by beating Golden State (three days before the Sprewell incident), the Los Angeles Clippers, New Jersey, and Toronto. Only the Spurs, Wolves, and Nets could be considered respectable, yet Russell was so emboldened after scoring a season-high 19 points against the 1-15 Raptors that he practically dared the rest of the league to take its best shot.

"Once we're playing well, we'll be the best team in the West," he declared. "Those teams that beat us better watch out. We're coming back to get them."

Naturally, then, the winning streak ended in the next game, a disastrous 94–77 loss to the Trail Blazers in Portland. The Jazz barely had time to sulk about it, though, before they learned Stockton was coming back.

When Stockton took the court against the Pacers, the maniacal cheering at the Delta Center grew even louder. He wore a canvas brace on his leg, just to be on the safe side, but if anybody thought its presence portended the debut of a more susceptible Stockton, they were sorely mistaken.

The Jazz won the opening tip, and not ten seconds had ticked off the clock before Stockton got the ball in his hands and passed to Hornacek on the right wing. At the same time, Malone ran from the low post to the free throw line, and set his hard body directly in the path of Indiana point guard Mark Jackson.

As if he'd never been away, Stockton took the cue and squeezed past Malone, leaving Jackson to thump against Malone's expansive chest while dashing unsupervised toward the basket. The Pacers' defense rotated, but it was too late; Hornacek zipped the ball in to Stockton, Stockton flipped it up off the glass and in, and even picked up the foul when Jackson finally caught up enough to crash into him.

The crowd went crazy.

"Things were pretty revved up," Stockton said. "I didn't expect that to happen that quickly. But Jeff made a great pass and Karl set a great screen. It was like a broken record as far as that goes. Those guys are tremendous."

Stockton made his free throw, and that play alone probably would have qualified Stockton's return as a success, but Stockton was far from finished. A minute after his triumphant layup, he registered his first assist since the injury—and the 12,171st of his career—when he fed Malone on the right side for a jump shot. Then, on a fast-break twenty-five seconds later, Stockton looked one way and threw the ball another, finding Foster cutting to the basket; Foster caught it, cocked it, and threw it down with as much attitude as he could muster for a 6-point Jazz lead.

Indeed, Stockton was back.

"It was good to see him," Jackson said after the game.

Not everybody thought so. Even at 6-11 and 230 pounds, Indiana forward Dale Davis was feeling picked on that night. Not only did he have to guard Malone, which was never easy for anybody under any circumstances, but he also had to put up with Stockton constantly setting screens in the paint by planting himself hard and throwing his forearms into Davis's rib cage. Setting screens on big guys is something the Jazz guards always have done under Sloan —Hornacek had taken about a half-dozen David Robinson elbows to the back of the head for his efforts against the Spurs earlier in the season—and Stockton never showed any fear doing his duty down there with the giants of the NBA. He was, in fact, notorious for his enthusiasm.

"Stockton sets the hardest screens of anybody in the league," said Orlando's Rony Seikaly. "He's so small, but he comes at you with his elbows locked up, and he ends up hitting you right in your spleen. I would rather have Shaquille O'Neal set a pick on me than John Stockton."

Stockton was playing against the Pacers with his traditional intensity, too, recovering knee or not. His abandon had led his face inadvertently into the elbow of 7-4 Indiana center Rik Smits early in the game, and Stockton played a good bit of the first half with a tissue jammed up his nostril.

"I don't think there was any question I was in an NBA game," said Stockton. "I had a bloody nose. But that was good. You don't have time to think about your knee or anything else. You just go play, and that was probably a plus."

By the second half, Davis was plenty frustrated at having Malone pushing on him from one side and Stockton giving him the business on the other. So when Stockton came charging into the lane with his elbows up, ready to lay another one on Davis midway through the third quarter, Davis simply threw out his enormous right arm and plowed Stockton to the floor. None of the referees blew their whistles, and Stockton was red-faced and furious. He chewed out the officials as much as he could with the game still going on, and spent the entire trip downcourt screaming to no avail that he'd been fouled.

So, like the cantankerous player he was, Stockton charged right back into the key on the Jazz's very next possession to set another hard pick on Davis. This time, Davis clobbered him even harder, sending Stockton sprawling to the floor between Davis's legs.

Whistles went off like crazy this time, and as Stockton scrambled around trying to get out from the tangle of size 17s, Davis appeared to kick at him. The place erupted. Fans jumped to their feet in anger as Malone shoved Davis and Jackson pushed Malone, and Sloan leapt from the bench and raced to the other end of the floor in a frenzied search for some Pacer ass to kick.

No punches were thrown during the scramble, and Jazz assistant coach Phil Johnson caught up with Sloan in time to help keep him from getting his hands on anybody. Johnson escorted Sloan back to the bench as the scrum died down, but Sloan was still enraged. He never grew any more angry than when he perceived Stockton was being bullied.

"You gonna throw [Davis] out?" Sloan yelled at the official. "He kicked him, you gotta throw him out!"

Standing on the sideline nearly at midcourt, Sloan turned to Rod Hundley, the Jazz radio broadcaster, who sits in the front row of the press section and who has a view of a TV replay monitor.

"He kicked him, right?" Sloan asked Hundley.

Hundley, wearing his headset and in the middle of his broadcast, nodded.

Sloan, his righteous outrage now reinforced, turned back toward the refs. "He kicked him!" he screamed again.

The officials decided on a technical foul on Davis, and once everything was sorted out and the free throw was made, the Jazz led 68–66 and had the ball.

With Davis guarding him, Malone called for the ball, got it, and ran right over Davis on his way to the basket. The refs made no call, and the layup scored. That inspired Indiana's Reggie Miller, on the Pacers' next possession, to show a little solidarity and try laying a hard pick on Malone, which is about like a palm frond deciding to set a screen on a fire hydrant.

Still, Miller set the screen, Malone crashed into it, and both men sprawled away and heard the referee's whistle. When official Jim Kinsey pointed toward Miller, Miller went berserk. He needed only about five seconds of screaming at Kinsey to earn his first technical foul, and maybe another ten of sticking his nose in Kinsey's face and pointing at his chest before getting his second, along with the ejection and $1,000 fine that automatically comes with it.

The crowd?

Absolutely bonkers.

Once Miller left the court, Kinsey approached the scorer's table and clarified: he had called three seconds in the key on Davis, not an offensive foul on Miller, as Miller had thought; he was pointing at the lane where Miller lay, not at Miller himself. Hornacek then turned Miller's mistaken outrage into 2 made free throws, Malone gathered up a loose ball and turned it into a dunk on the ensuing possession, and Foster made 2 free throws. Just like that, the Jazz led 76–66, and the Pacers were playing without their best player —all because of Stockton, who was headed to the bench for an ovation and a rest.

That was the second time in the game that Stockton had helped the Jazz build a double-digit edge before taking a seat to rest his knee. And this time, like the last, the Jazz blew the lead; as soon as Stockton came out, the Pacers went on a 12–2 run that tied the game at 78–78, and the teams traded the lead until Stockton returned with 6:56 left in the game. Utah led 92–89 at that point, which turned out to be the end for Indiana. Stockton was finished with his own heroics, but he helped Malone score 10 of his 31 points in the final six minutes, and the Jazz won, 106–97.

"What can I say that hasn't already been said?" said Malone. "Everybody in the world knows what it means to have John back. Every time he suits up, guys are going to go at him, whether he's 100 percent or 50 percent. But he has a way of protecting himself. He came out and did a great job."

After the game, the Jazz corraled Stockton into a press conference, mostly because that way he could get all of those interviews done at once. He ambled out of the locker room, wearing his warmup jacket and a bulging bag of ice on his knee, and climbed into a chair set up on a podium in a room down the hall. Reporters packed the room, and the first question was the most obvious one.

How did the knee feel?

"Good," Stockton replied. "Everybody has been real careful with me. They weren't going to let me play if they didn't feel good about it."

They felt good about it, all right. Everybody did. Now the Jazz could put their troubles behind them and get on with the task of securing home court advantage, whisking through the playoffs, and earning the repeat appearance in the NBA Finals that the whole state had been so anticipating.

And if there was somehow any lingering fear that Stockton might have emerged from his ordeal a different person than he was during all those years of piling up steal after steal and assist after assist, it was erased during that postgame news conference. Stockton declined to speak specifically about his rehabilitation schedule, answered most of the questions in his typically vague and stand-offish way, and even shot a reproachful glance at one reporter who had the temerity to ask Stockton's wife if Stockton had been difficult to live with during his recuperation.

Yeah, it was the same guy, all right.

Same old Stockton.

CHAPTER

5

It had long since become clear that nothing was going to come easily for the Jazz in their effort to get back to the NBA Finals, and even the afterglow of John Stockton's return to the lineup didn't last but a few hours. The night after beating the Pacers, the Jazz lost again to the lowly Sacramento Kings, 113–101, in the 1,000th game of Karl Malone's career, and within hours of that faced their newest crisis.

Antoine Carr wanted to retire.

"Let's put it like this," Carr said the next day after practice. "I'm very close to doing it."

Closer, even, than he would admit. By the time he broke from practice that morning, Carr had told at least one teammate that his retirement was a sure thing, that it was nice to have played with him but that he'd had enough and was hanging up his sneakers after thirteen seasons in the NBA.

Carr had distinguished himself in his three seasons with the Jazz largely by his colorful persona as the "Big Dawg." He always wore sunglasses on account of a once-lacerated eyeball that no longer adjusted well to the light and caused migraine headaches, and he woofed for the crowd as if he was part Labrador. Carr signed with the Jazz as a free agent after his mother, while watching Carr play for the San Antonio Spurs against the Jazz in 1994, implored Malone during the game to find her baby a spot on the Utah roster. Malone heard her, amazingly enough, spoke briefly with Carr, then phoned him after the season to discuss the possibility. A week before the 1994–95 season, the Jazz signed Carr to a contract.

With his gregarious personality, Carr quickly became a fan favorite, even if he was no longer quite as productive on the floor as he once had been.

Carr was quite a scorer in his prime, averaging 20.1 points per game while playing for the Kings in 1990–91, but age and an expanding waistline had begun to conspire against him. His scoring average and playing time had gradually decreased in the seasons since signing that first deal with the Jazz, but Carr still played an important role in providing fifteen to twenty minutes per game of relief work for Malone or whichever center the Jazz were employing at the moment. He hadn't played particularly well, though, since suffering the sting of Malone's preseason rant and injuring his hamstring during training camp.

The thought of retirement had first crossed Carr's mind near the beginning of the season, because he wasn't enjoying the game as he once had. He longed for the halcyon days when "basketball was basketball," he said, when "part of the job was traveling, part of it was being with your teammates all the time, walking through the airport, going out and having dinner together." He bemoaned the way NBA veterans had come to be treated vis-à-vis the hotshot young players who, despite all their potential, had not done anything in the league before securing multimillion-dollar contracts.

Sincere as they were, those sentiments were largely a smoke screen for the source of Carr's real dissatisfaction: Carr did not know whether the Jazz viewed him as an important part of the team or simply as a mop-up guy now that Greg Ostertag had signed his big contract. That feeling of uncertainty was fostered by Jerry Sloan's criticism, which was as constant as it was caustic. The coach seldom gave his team much credit in public, and in private he could be downright cruel to players who failed to meet his expectations. He swore at them, called them names, suggested they were too lazy to be any good. It was his way of fending off complacency, but it didn't work on everybody.

As mean as he could look with his bald head and goatee, Carr was a peaceful man with a sensitive soul, and he was one of the Jazz players—along with Ostertag, Greg Foster, and Chris Morris —who sometimes visibly had difficulty coping with Sloan's intensity. Carr hated to argue, and the strain of enduring Sloan's interminable disapproval had started to wear on him. He didn't want to say too much, though, since Sloan took the greatest umbrage at those who made the team look bad by violating the sanctity of the locker room. Carr had already pushed the envelope far enough by saying the Jazz had some "internal issues" that needed to be resolved, though he refused to elaborate.

"I don't want to get into all that," he said.

Carr had not spoken with Sloan or the other coaches about his pending decision, and said he was not certain if he would be in uniform for the Jazz's next game, two days later against the Dallas Mavericks. Carr suggested he might travel to Europe instead, not to play basketball as he had in Italy in his first season out of Wichita State University, but just to get away for a while.

"I need to get with my agent and my family and see what I'm going to do," he said.

Quite often, only a few writers showed up to attend the Jazz's daily practices; the local TV and radio stations tended to send representatives only when they needed to stockpile sound bites in advance of the Jazz leaving town on a road trip. Spurred the next morning by a newspaper story that said Carr might be gone by that day, however, every media outlet in the area sent a reporter and cameraman to practice, eager to learn what the thirty-six-year-old had decided.

Meanwhile, Sloan had learned of Carr's possible retirement from a reporter, and had called Carr into a private meeting before practice. Carr told Sloan how he'd been feeling adrift, and uncertain that the team still needed him.

"If I'm not part of the team," Carr said, "then why am I here?"

Sloan was angry that Carr had spoken to the media about his plan to retire without speaking to him first. But the coach also knew that Carr was an important part of the lineup, and that the Jazz would have precious few options at center in the middle of the season if Carr were to quit. He talked Carr down from the ledge, assuring him that the Jazz needed him if they were to make another championship run. The coach then called a team-wide meeting aimed at clearing the air.

The players took turns discussing what they perceived to be their roles on the team and the roles of others, and Carr was pleased to learn that everybody was generally in agreement. That unity, however, had been fractured by the criticism and pressure that had accompanied the team's rough start without Stockton, and only now was being voiced for all to hear.

By the time the Jazz opened the gym doors after practice (they had closed workouts to reporters for the first time only weeks earlier), Carr had been pacified and the news crews had to settle for a happy ending rather than anything terribly salacious.

"I've decided to stay," Carr announced. "I hope everyone understands it isn't a matter of a team thing, this is a personal thing. I sat down and talked to my people and I'm going to play."

Knowing the Jazz very much preferred to keep their inner workings to themselves, Carr did not want to anger Sloan a second time by explaining all the details behind his retirement threat. So he emerged from practice intent on only vaguely explaining how he'd changed his mind, and agreeing to every reporter's suggestion of possible reasons.

Shooting a career-low 42 percent as he was, Carr said he had been upset over his own poor play, and added that he'd felt frustration over a number of issues around the NBA. He mentioned the Sprewell incident, and suggested that the fractious reaction to it around the league made him feel less united with his fellow players than he once had. It took quite a bit of prodding before Carr would acknowledge the biggest reason he thought about quitting—that he felt like nobody wanted him around.

And those internal problems?

"The internal problem was my own things," Carr said. "I don't think we have a bunch of problems. . . . Everything has been said and done, and I think you're going to see a difference in our play."

*　*　*

Carr missed all 4 shots he tried and grabbed only one rebound in fourteen minutes of the Jazz's next game, a victory over the Mavericks. His performance went almost unnoticed, however, thanks to the bizarre strategy adopted by Dallas coach Don Nelson.

Only a few days removed from the firing of coach Jim Cleamons, the Mavericks were not much good in the first place, and they were missing 7-6 center Shawn Bradley because of a calf injury and starting point guard Robert Pack because of torn ligaments in his thumb. Several reserves were hurt, too, leaving Nelson with not nearly enough talent to compete with the Jazz in a standard, up-and-down-the-court NBA game.

So Nelson decided that the Mavs would hold the ball on each possession until only about six seconds remained on the shot clock before even considering an offensive move. Point guard Khalid

Reeves stood dribbling near the top of the circle while his team-mates lined up along the baseline and watched the clock. The idea was to limit the number of chances the Jazz would have to score, but the jeers from the crowd were not long in coming.

"C'mon, Nellie! Play ball!"

"Knock it off already!"

But Nelson wouldn't, and his players showed remarkable restraint in executing their game plan. Not once did they lose their cool and sprint off after grabbing a long rebound, or get suckered into pushing the pace. Possession after possession they stood around, dutifully waiting for the clock to run down before casting off whatever shot they could manage. Quite often, too, those shots fell; Dennis Scott made the first 5 three-pointers he tried, 4 of them as the shot clock expired, and the Jazz did Dallas some favors with their inability to hang on to the ball. Utah wound up committing 19 turnovers—Sloan later extrapolated that to equal 30 or 36 in a regularly paced game—and by the time the game reached its final two minutes, the Mavs found themselves trailing only 65–64.

That's when their wheels came off.

The Mavericks missed shots and failed to get rebounds on back-to-back possessions, and though Hubert Davis stripped Jeff Hornacek with thirty-four seconds to go, the Mavs proceeded to stand around just a bit too long on their next possession, and failed to get off a shot before the twenty-four-second clock expired. That left them no choice but to foul the Jazz to stop the clock and get the ball back, and Hornacek made a pair of free throws with 3.6 seconds left to put Utah ahead 67–64. Erick Strickland threw up an airball on the Mavs' last attempt before Bryon Russell corraled the rebound and made a free throw after being fouled. The final score was 68–64, the lowest-scoring Jazz game in history, the fifth-lowest score in the NBA's shot clock era.

The Jazz credited the Mavs with a plan that almost worked. But while it might not have been pretty, a win was still a win, and the

Jazz were taking whatever they could manage. They were 13-8, and leaving two days later on their first big road trip of the season, Antoine Carr in tow.

The trip was to cover five cities in eight days, and the Jazz were approaching it as a good chance to get back on the right track. Though it's more difficult to play on the road than at home in the NBA, Sloan said leaving Utah for a while would give his team a better chance to improve because the players would not be occupied by home life and Christmas shopping and all the other distractions that can take over during the holidays. That was Frank Layden's philosophy when he began routinely scheduling the Jazz's pre-Christmas trip more than a decade earlier: while their opponents would be busy worrying about decking the halls and inviting friends over for parties, the Jazz would be bonding, focusing on basketball all the time, and learning to rely on each other in one hostile arena after another.

"We need to get four or five wins out of this road trip," said Shandon Anderson. "Hopefully all five."

That seemed a bit too much to ask. The Jazz had lost two of their last three and were facing five teams—the Wizards, Heat, Magic, Cavaliers, and Hawks—that all could make the Eastern Conference playoffs. The trip began on a sour note, too; broadcaster Ron Boone had his Jeep Grand Cherokee smashed by an automatically closing gate at the airport less than an hour before the Jazz's flight was scheduled to leave. The Jazz hoped that would not be any sort of omen.

The first stop was Washington, for a rematch with the Wizards. They had beaten the Jazz in the second game of the season to stop the Jazz's fourteen-game home winning streak, and they were playing now in the comfy confines of the new MCI Center downtown.

The Wizards hadn't lost in four games at MCI, even though

they were trying to recover from the scars left by a fight between teammates Rod Strickland and Tracy Murray. Apparently, Murray had made disparaging remarks about Strickland to some woman in Los Angeles, who taped the conversation and played it back later for Strickland. Only hours before the Wizards played at Charlotte the week before the Jazz game, Strickland attacked Murray at the team hotel. The Wizards had been playing well when the incident occurred, but predictably found their synchronicity screwed up.

By halftime, however, it was the Jazz who were screwed up.

Late in the first quarter, Ostertag failed to block out on the boards and allowed Washington's Chris Webber to grab an offensive rebound. Then, when Webber went back up for a shot, Ostertag fouled him, but not nearly hard enough to prevent Webber from making the basket. The double dose of inadequacy infuriated Sloan, who immediately sent Carr into the game for Ostertag. As Ostertag arrived at the Jazz bench, Sloan laid into him about his pathetic effort.

"You big guys gotta get in there and compete!" he yelled.

For once, Ostertag showed some spine. Hearing Sloan chastise him, he spun on his heels and screamed back, "I was competing!"

The outburst might have taken Sloan by surprise, but it did not convince him of anything. The coach continued to berate Ostertag, and Ostertag finally grew so frustrated that he blew up. Enraged, he kicked a chair along the Jazz bench, glared over the heads of the rest of his teammates and demanded of Sloan to "put me back in there!"

Sloan did no such thing. Instead, he ordered Ostertag off the bench and back to the locker room.

"We're not going to make it a circus out there," Sloan said later.

Ostertag reappeared on the Jazz bench for the second half, but played only forty-four more seconds. Meanwhile, the Jazz fought back from an 11-point deficit and occasionally led the Wizards, but could not pull away. And after falling behind in the fourth quarter, Malone missed a wide-open jump shot from the top of the key with six seconds left that would've tied the game.

Stockton missed a three-pointer at the horn, and the Jazz lost, 88–86.

The Jazz certainly could have found better ways to start the trip, and all of a sudden they were back to complaining about the ailments that had plagued them all season long.

"Going into training camp, I said this should be the easiest coaching year [Sloan] has had, because we've been there and guys know what it takes," said Malone. "We shouldn't be fighting battles on the sidelines. That's kid shit. We have to be together, on the same page all the time, and let the coach coach the team."

It was not the best time for Sloan to be forced to deal with the various frustrations of guys like Carr and Ostertag, either, since for perhaps the first time in his professional life, basketball was the least of his concerns.

❖   ❖   ❖

Bobbye Sloan had always been the healthy one. She didn't smoke. Barely drank. She ran and watched what she ate. It was her husband who abused himself.

Jerry Sloan smoked to set records. He drank to win. Sleeping was not high on the priority list.

"People die in bed," he said.

So when the tests came back and told Bobbye Sloan that it was indeed cancer that had burrowed its way into her chest and given her that painful jab the night the Jazz lost the NBA Finals, she was left with one ironic thought in particular.

"I'm the one who gets this?" she said. "Not him? It wasn't fair."

Bobbye Sloan had allowed her husband to learn of her disease only after several trips to the doctor on her own and one with their son, Brian, in which a biopsy certified that Bobbye had intraductal carcinoma, one of the most common types of cancer that strike women. Brian Sloan had flown to Salt Lake City from Indianapolis, where he was in residency at a hospital emergency room, to be with his mother, since she had allowed Jerry to leave for their summer at home in McLeansboro, Illinois, before she visited Dr. Russell Shields, the Jazz's team internist. Bobbye could not bear to deliver her news to the family, so the task fell to Brian.

"I found his notes after he left," she said. "He had notes about the things he was going to tell people, especially Jerry. He told Jerry he's got to lift his attitude because my spirits were good. He couldn't come home with that typical Sloan long face."

Sloan did his best, and was by his wife's side throughout three surgeries and four chemotherapy sessions. The good news was that Bobbye had caught the cancer early, and her chances of survival were excellent. She had always been the healthy one, after all. But the anxiety over his wife's condition seemed to be taking a toll on her husband.

Bobbye endured the last of the four chemotherapy treatments only days before Stockton made his return to the lineup. Few people knew about her condition, or the strain it was putting on her husband as he tried to hold his team together while not betraying the painful details of his personal life.

Jerry and Bobbye Sloan met in 1957, as students at McLeansboro High School in southern Illinois, where Sloan grew up poor and fatherless on a hard patch of land called "Gobbler's Knob" that only technically qualified as a farm. He lived a rough life as a child, and learned that nothing was going to come easily for him. That bred a brand of toughness that meant keeping his mouth shut and his feelings to himself. Complaining didn't do any good.

When Sloan was four years old, his father died as the result of a farming accident that had rendered him mostly bedridden for the last nine years of his life. As the youngest of ten children, Sloan was left a consistent diet of hard work and sacrifice just to avoid going hungry.

"Poverty was a level higher than what they were used to," said Dick Motta, Sloan's former coach in Chicago and a close friend.

Sloan worked a variety of odd jobs around the farm, and as he grew older he found work in the nearby oil fields. He attended a one-room schoolhouse for eight years before heading off to McLeansboro High, sixteen miles from his home. He did a lot of walking.

"Eight miles on the hard road," he recalled, "and eight miles off the hard road."

Sloan was small growing up, and stood only 5-6 when he met Bobbye Irvin while they were both high school freshmen. She stood 5-9, and was the class president. He was vice president. She refused the first time he asked for a date because he was too short, but eventually relented. Right away, she regretted her decision.

"I'll never go out with him again," she complained to her mother after their first date. "He didn't say two words all night."

Sloan and Irvin did not have a whole lot in common, either. Sloan was a shy, quiet "sporto" who hung out with a dubious crowd —"his friends were the guys who stood on the street corner and chewed tobacco," she recalled—while Irvin was a gregarious girl who enjoyed music and played in the school band.

But Sloan grew, eventually to 6-5, and he grew on Irvin. He became a handsome fellow after all, and a gentleman.

"You've heard of pheromones, right?" she said.

Eventually, the two began dating regularly, and after graduating high school they became engaged. Sloan went to the University of Illinois on a basketball scholarship, but felt swallowed up by the size of the school and dropped out almost immediately. He wanted to move home and simply start a family, but Bobbye had just begun a nursing program at Washington University in St. Louis, and did not want to quit. She told Sloan the engagement was off unless he found something to do with himself.

So Sloan enrolled at Evansville College in Indiana, only eighty miles from McLeansboro, and sat out the 1961–62 basketball season as a transfer student. The engagement was back on, and the couple were married the following year, just as Sloan was beginning the basketball career that would be remembered as one of the most passionate the game has ever seen.

Sloan averaged more than 15 points and 12 rebounds per game in three seasons for the Purple Aces, and led them to the Division II national championship during his senior year in 1965. An All-America, he was selected by the Baltimore Bullets in the second round of the college draft, and played one season with them before going to the Chicago Bulls in the expansion draft in 1966.

In Chicago, his career blossomed.

Fearful his career could come to an end any second, Sloan played each game as if it were his last. He turned the fans on with his headlong style, and damn near frightened coaches and teammates with the seething intensity he brought to the court. He arrived four hours early for games to tape his own ankles—he refused to let anybody else do it—yet never went onto the court to warm up, because he did not want to become friendly during the shootarounds with the men he needed to hate in order to defeat.

"He'd just sit in the corner and smoke a cigarette," said Motta.

When the ball went up, Sloan was an animal. He was named to either the first or second All-Defensive team six times in his ten-year career with the Bulls, and teamed with Norm Van Lier to form one of the most intimidating backcourts in the NBA during the early 1970s. Opponents grew to loathe the way Sloan would grab their jerseys and pull them down on top of him to get offensive fouls called, and knew better than to try to intimidate him.

Sloan wasn't afraid of anybody, and he seldom let go of the games even when they were over.

Johnny "Red" Kerr, who played with Sloan in Baltimore during Sloan's rookie year in 1965–66, then coached him for two seasons in Chicago before Motta took over, remembered returning to his hotel room late one night after postgame pizza and beer.

"The room was dark except for this small orange glow in the middle of the room," Kerr wrote in his book, *Bull Session.* "It was Sloan, sitting on the bed, smoking a cigarette. After I closed the door, he said, 'Red, you know that play in the middle of the third quarter . . .' He started reviewing the whole game, almost play-by-play, and he hadn't left the bench all night. Finally, I said, 'Hey, rook, give it a rest. The game is over.' That intensity impressed me."

It impressed everyone, except Sloan. From his perspective, he simply needed to be that intense to stay in the league. He thought of himself as virtually talentless (though until Michael Jordan, he was the only guard to lead the Bulls in rebounding), so he believed he had to work twice as hard as anybody else to be successful. He figured that he could give his team a 17-point advantage without ever taking a shot, simply by denying the other team possessions by snatching a certain number of loose balls, grabbing rebounds, drawing charges, and making free throws and steals. Coaches, teammates, and fans all loved him for it.

Sloan's glory days ended in 1976, when a severe groin injury forced him to retire. He soon accepted the job as head coach at Evansville, only to quit several days later. Sloan has never publicly discussed his reasons for quitting, but the decision might have saved his life.

When Sloan walked away from his alma mater, the university turned to a man named Bobby Watson and hired him to coach the Purple Aces instead. So it was Watson, not Sloan, who was aboard the team's chartered airplane with twenty-nine other coaches, players, and boosters one stormy night a few months later, when it tried to take off from Evansville for a flight to Nashville, Tennessee. From there, the Aces planned to take a bus to their game in Murfreesboro.

The plane took off on December 13, 1977, amid rain and heavy fog, into which it made a sharp left turn almost as soon as it was airborne. Within five minutes, the plane emerged from the fog and plunged to the ground, bursting into flames as it crashed into a ridge near some railroad tracks east of the airport. Everyone on board was killed.

The headline in the *Evansville Courier* the day after the crash read: "The Night It Rained Tears." The victims of the crash have been memorialized at Roberts Stadium with photos and news clips in a display case not far from Sloan's retired No. 52 jersey.

"There isn't a day goes by that I don't think of that circumstance," he said. "That changed my entire perspective on basketball."

It made him realize there are more important things in life than basketball. And now, his perspective was being altered again, in much the same way, nearly twenty years after that tragic night in the Indiana fog.

◊   ◊   ◊

Despite his wife's illness, Sloan was still smoking, still drinking, still staying up until all hours of the night. His fellow coaches had begun to fear for his health.

"He was getting down," said assistant Kenny Natt.

And in the middle of it all, Sloan was having to put up with players screaming back at him on the sideline in the middle of games. After the loss to the Wizards, Sloan publicly downplayed his confrontation with Ostertag, saying, "We just got into a situation there where he needed to go in the locker room and cool off. It was the best place for him at that time."

It looked like that might be about the end of Ostertag for a while, given his problems and Sloan's historical willingness to keep a player, no matter how well paid, on the bench if he couldn't do his job. Chris Morris was a perfect example; he had signed a three-year deal worth $9 million two years earlier, yet never really endeared himself to Sloan because of the lackadaisical way he played defense. The thing that saved Morris was his superior athleticism, which Sloan ultimately drew on during the 1997 playoffs, when the Jazz faced more versatile teams that could give them trouble with all their physical talent. Ostertag did not have that going for him, although he did have the benefit of his size and shot-blocking ability.

Even so, Sloan put Ostertag in the rotation for the Jazz's next game, in Miami; the even bigger surprise was that he benched Greg Foster and gave Carr his first start since he was a member of the Kings some seven years earlier. Though he fouled out in seventeen minutes, Carr grabbed 7 rebounds, and Stockton played his best game since his surgery with 14 points and 4 assists in 27 minutes of the Jazz's 103–95 victory. Ostertag played better, making all 3 shots he tried, although Malone kept up his pressure on the Jazz's centers by praising more highly his friend and former teammate, Isaac Austin, who had become a hot prospect with the Heat.

Austin didn't play terribly well in the game against the Jazz, but he had made himself an increasingly valuable commodity by losing the weight that got him released from the Jazz four years earlier and performing well in the absence of injured Heat center Alonzo Mourning. Austin was making $388,000 for the year, and figured to be asking for an awful lot more when he became a free agent after the season. But Austin said he would love to rejoin Malone in Utah, and Malone failed to see any reason that couldn't happen.

"I have a birthday wish," he said, "and I hope it comes true."

The Jazz beat the Orlando Magic, 85–73, two nights later, but after the game, Morris broke the team's 12:30 A.M. curfew and was suspended for the next game at Cleveland. Then, after the Jazz lost to the Cavs, 106–101, they encountered airplane trouble that kept them waiting on the runway for two hours before deciding to return to a hotel for an extra night in Cleveland while mechanics fixed the plane.

If it wasn't one thing, it was another.

Finally, the Jazz beat the Hawks in Atlanta, 101–99, when Malone drilled a jump shot after ducking under a hard-charging Christian Laettner with thirty-three seconds left at the cavernous Georgia Dome, and the Jazz had themselves a 3-2 trip. That was not quite up to Anderson's expectation, but it was better than the 2-3 effort the previous season, when the Jazz went on to win 64 games. What's more, at 16-10 they had moved a half-game in front of the Houston Rockets for the lead in the Midwest Division for only the second time all season. (They had been a half-game ahead, briefly, after beating New Jersey and Toronto at the end of that six-game winning streak in early December.)

Still, the Jazz were dissatisfied.

"We had an opportunity to win all five games," said Howard Eisley. "It gets tough on the road, and we let two games slip away that we were definitely capable of winning. That's hard to take. But you just have to look forward to the next game."

"Not a bad trip," said Hornacek. "It's nothing to celebrate about, but it's nothing to get down about, either."

So many things had changed, too, even since the first game of the journey. Ostertag had gone from being kicked off the bench to playing twenty-nine minutes against the Hawks, Carr had gone from nearly retired to starting center, and Foster had gone from being a starter to seeing almost no playing time. Stockton was improving each time he played, and was cleared after the trip to play as many minutes as Sloan wanted him. And Keefe had begun to wonder when his wife, former Olympic volleyball player Kristin

Kleine, would deliver the couple's first children—twin daughters. They were due anytime.

The Jazz came home to a Christmas Day date against the Houston Rockets, and while most of the players weren't thrilled with the idea of working on the best holiday of the year, the game turned out to herald the arrival of a whole new team.

Center Hakeem Olajuwon was still out, nursing his knee injury, when Stockton put together his most masterful performance since beating the Rockets in Game 6 of the Western Conference finals the year before. He made 10 of 16 shots, scored 24 points, and single-handedly pulled the Jazz away from the Rockets in the final two minutes to give Sloan his 500th victory as coach of the team.

"I couldn't care less," said Sloan, "other than we got the victory."

Before Stockton could take over entirely, however, Ostertag provided perhaps the most memorable moment of the season to that point. With the Jazz leading 99–96, Houston's Charles Barkley made a steal and flung a pass downcourt to point guard Brent Price, who was streaking the length of the floor for what figured to be an easy layup to cut the Jazz lead to one.

Somehow, though, Ostertag caught up to Price and swatted his would-be layup out of harm's way. "I just turned on the Carl Lewis speed," he said. Price was left in a puddle of humiliation, and Ostertag was allowed to hear some good-natured criticism for a change.

"I feel like I've already seen the replay in slow motion," joked Keefe, "but that was the first time."

The owner by then of 18 points, Stockton took care of the rest. He scored the next 6 points for the Jazz, blowing past Price for an uncontested layup, answering a Houston bucket with one of his own at the top of the key, and hitting 2 free throws to make it 105–101 and render the last 17.6 seconds academic. The Jazz won, 107–103.

"We're starting to gel a little bit," said Russell. "Now we all know what we're doing. Stock's back in the lineup, so everyone is playing a little more freely and not worrying about anything, knowing Stockton's there."

Within days of that victory, Sloan returned home from another of his nights out, smelling like cigarettes and booze. The scene had repeated itself hundreds of times before during the Sloans' long marriage, but as much as Bobbye Sloan disliked it, she had grown weary of struggling to get her husband to stop—particularly with the smoking. She had tried and failed with every manner of persuasion years before, and "had reached a point in our lives where I simply stopped saying anything about it." For years, she had absorbed herself in raising the couple's three children, and her life with her husband had grown into something closer to distracted tolerance than marriage.

But now, here she was, ravaged by chemotherapy and only days away from the reconstructive breast surgery that would signal the end of the worst of her ordeal and begin five years of waiting to make sure her cancer never returned. She had watched herself shrivel into a shell of her former self, but had kept fighting and fighting to save her own life. And there was her husband, coming home from three packs a day and a late night at the bar, just like always.

She summoned the courage to confront him.

"Here I am, fighting for my life," she said. "And you're snuffing yours out."

She stormed off, just like she always did, and for a long time was unaware of the impact her words had finally had on her husband.

❖ ❖ ❖

An hour before the Jazz's first game of the new year, Carr lay alone on his back in the Jazz locker room at the Delta Center with his right leg propped up against the wood partition of his locker stall.

"Just trying to get this thing ready," he said.

The thing was his hamstring, which he'd somehow injured a few hours before during the team's pre-shootaround workout, and it was so tight that Carr feared he would not be able to play against the Atlanta Hawks. It was the same muscle Carr had had some trouble with in training camp, and at his age, it wasn't healing quite like it used to.

That wasn't so good. The Jazz had won six out of eight games since Sloan inserted Carr into the starting lineup, and despite losing again to Portland, 102–91, after the win over Houston, they had brought two straight victories into 1998 by beating Vancouver, 89–88, and Denver, 132–99. They also had managed to hang on to first place in the Midwest Division while the rest of the NBA calmed down from its tumultuous beginning.

During their holiday surge, the Jazz had begun to shoot much better than they had to start the season, and after wallowing around near the bottom of the league in scoring for the first few weeks had also increased their productivity. Yet while the game against the Hawks appeared in the standings to be a good measuring stick of how far the Jazz had progressed since the end of that big road trip, it didn't really turn out that way. Atlanta was 19-11, but point guard Mookie Blaylock was still battling the injured groin that had kept him out of the teams' previous meeting, and without him the Hawks were in the middle of a six-game slide that was ruining their 11-0 start.

"They're a totally different team on the floor without him," said Keefe.

Keefe himself had been an Atlanta Hawk after the team made him the tenth pick of the 1992 draft, out of Stanford University, where Keefe was a three-time Player of the Year in the Pac-10 Conference. He played two seasons for the Hawks before they decided Keefe wasn't developing quite like they'd hoped and traded him to the Jazz for forward Tyrone Corbin before the 1994–95 season. And while players sometimes carry chips on their shoulders when playing against former teams, Keefe had been traded so long ago that it was not even an issue anymore. Besides, he was still too busy waiting for those babies, so he could join the ranks of the Jazz fathers.

Combined with Carr's unexpected injury, the Hawks' recent impotence gave Sloan a chance to put Ostertag back into the starting lineup without subjecting him to an overwhelming amount of pressure. Yes, he'd be matched against 7-2 Dikembe Mutombo, but the Jazz would have advantages in other areas. Plus, Ostertag had been playing more like himself in recent games, which is to say his adequacy occasionally intruded upon his ineffectiveness, and his confidence had grown to the point where he said he was ready to become a starter again. All this, only two weeks after the shouting match.

Ostertag did not learn of his assignment until nearly game time, since Carr lay on his back and stretched and jogged up and down the hall as long as he could before concluding his leg simply would not loosen up. But when the opportunity came, Ostertag seized it. He came right out and made a short jump shot barely forty seconds into the game, and proceeded to play another thirty-six minutes of the Jazz's 97–82 victory. By the time it was over, Ostertag had made 7 of the 8 shots he tried, scored 15 points, grabbed 10 rebounds, blocked 4 shots, and accepted a hug from Malone on his way off the court. It was the kind of performance the Jazz expected out of Ostertag more than once a month, and it also was the kind that prevented the team from giving up on Ostertag when he suffered through bad stretches.

"I've been playing pretty well," he said. "I started off cruddy this year and I'm starting to come around."

Reporters in the locker room pressed for a deeper explanation.

"Earlier in the season," Ostertag explained, "that wasn't me. That was my evil twin. I was kidnapped by aliens, and they ran all kinds of crazy tests on me."

"Did they probe you?" somebody asked.

Thank God, Ostertag did not say.

Much of Ostertag's improvement stemmed from his increased fitness. He had been spending a lot of extra time after practice with the Jazz's new strength coach, Mark McKown, working on his strength and aerobic conditioning. Even after the Jazz finished a rigorous workout, McKown would put Ostertag through another one with running drills, medicine balls, and sit-ups. Ostertag complained about it at every opportunity—he was the first to admit he was lazy and hated working to stay in shape—but he participated nonetheless. His effort seemed to be starting to finally pay off.

"He got a couple of dunks," Sloan said after the Hawks game. "And he hasn't had many dunks all year long. That's a sign of his conditioning."

Said Stockton, "His concentration is getting better, and that's the whole key for him. We're a better team when he plays like that."

Carr, meanwhile, spent the next few workouts riding the bike instead of practicing basketball on account of his hamstring. He missed the Jazz's next two games, a 98–95 overtime victory over the Philadelphia 76ers and a 116–109 win over the Milwaukee Bucks in the Delta Center, and probably had seen the last of his starting job, since Ostertag blocked 11 shots and grabbed 9 rebounds against the Sixers and pulled down 10 boards to go with 6 points against the Bucks. Ostertag also averaged nearly forty minutes per game in that stretch.

The Jazz traveled to Houston on January 10 for the first of only four road games in January. It was the Jazz's first visit to The Summit (which had been renamed the Compaq Center in the off-season) since Stockton's shot, and somebody asked him on the way off the team bus if he felt like he owned the place now.

"Not hardly," he said. "Feel like I've lived here, though. Spent a lot of time here."

Appropriately, then, the next three hours felt like three days, because the Rockets were without nearly all of their starting lineup. Olajuwon was still out, Barkley was suffering from a hematoma on the middle toe of his right foot that was going to keep him out at least a few more days, Clyde Drexler had a sore right shoulder that he thought might require surgery, and Matt Maloney had a sore right elbow. The only starter who wasn't hurt was Mario Elie, and because of all the injuries he would be teamed with Price and rookie Rodrick Rhodes in the backcourt, with Othella Harrington and Kevin Willis up front. Though Elie was solid and Willis had been playing exceptionally well in Olajuwon's absence, the Rockets hardly figured to have much of a chance against the experienced Jazz.

The Rockets were, in fact, worried if they'd even have enough players against the Jazz, since veteran Eddie Johnson was questionable, too, because of his own sore elbow. So instead of risking the possibility of jogging out for the tip-off with only eight healthy players, the Rockets put Drexler on the injured list about an hour before the game so they could activate Joe Stephens, who had played all of four NBA games. It turned out Johnson was able to play, but for all the good it did, he might as well have rested his arm.

Given the critical condition of the home team, the fans at the Compaq Center hardly reacted to the introduction of Stockton; they were too busy bemoaning their injury problems. One bunch had draped a banner over the railing on the upper level, working a pun on the town's self-addressed nickname as "Clutch City." Flanked by red crosses, the sign read: "Crutch City."

Alas, the remaining Rockets were not even that good. They stayed close to the Jazz for the first half thanks to a mediocre Jazz effort and the rebounding abilities of Harrington and Willis, who worked the Jazz over on the glass so completely that Sloan gave his players a halftime lecture that made them think they were losing rather than winning.

Inspired, the Jazz shot out of the locker room for the second half and scored the first 12 points of the third quarter, and extended their run to 24–7. They made 15 of their 25 shots in the third quarter, forced 9 Rockets turnovers and stretched their lead at one point to 28 points. About halfway through the deluge, the remaining Rockets gave up.

"All you can do is keep your head up and stay positive," said Willis. "Things are bound to get better for us. There are better times ahead for this team, once we get our guns back."

With the victory, the Jazz matched their previous season's pace at 23-11, and the talk in the locker room after the game focused on their prospects of equaling their 1997 accomplishment of winning forty-one of their last forty-eight games. If the Jazz could beat the Cleveland Cavaliers at the Delta Center two nights later, they would actually be ahead of their 64-win pace. And that much was quite possible, for while the Jazz were beating the Rockets into submission, the Cavaliers were losing.

At home.

To the Toronto Raptors.

And the Cavs' luck did not improve once they arrived in Utah, where they lost, 106–99, in one of just seven games all season in which Malone was not the Jazz's leading scorer; Hornacek had 23 points. After the game, Sloan greeted the media and described what he saw as his team's resurgence in the four weeks since Carr's retirement threat prompted that team meeting.

"We're improving," he said. "There's more togetherness now, more sense of purpose. Earlier in the year, there were a lot of little things going on. Guys struggling. Now, they're stepping up. I'm thrilled with the team. We held together better than I thought after losing John. We're getting there. That's the thing in this business. That's how you win. And winning is the only reason I'm in this. You win by trying to get better.

"We can't win as a bunch of individuals," he added. "We're not that kind of team. We have to do it together. We have to execute on offense, set screens, pass, run our plays, and, for the most part, we now are doing that. We have to get good play out of all our guys. But what will make or break this team is defense. We can get so much better. We've had stretches where we just kind of hang out. You have to put yourself in a position to win. Consistency comes from defense. Confidence comes from defense. When guys feel like they're shooting well, like they can't miss, it usually comes from playing well defensively. Confidence comes mostly from hard work. . . . When you work hard, everything is better. You even look better. There's no easy way, not that I know of."

The Jazz's winning streak had reached seven games, their longest since a fifteen-game cruise that spanned the end of the previous March and the beginning of April, and Sloan had reached an epiphanous moment. Unbeknownst to everybody except those closest to him, he had finally taken his wife's advice seriously. Like the plane crash in Indiana so many years before, the words she hurled at him that night after Christmas had reached his heart, and he realized she was right: if he did not change his ways, he was going to wind up in worse shape than the courageous woman who was fighting off a killer.

So with the help of Dr. Shields, team psychologist Keith Henschen, assistant coach Phil Johnson, and the prescription drug Zyban, Sloan went on a program to quit smoking. He quit drinking, too, since for him the two went together, and soon found himself breaking free from the shackles of habit that had held him for years. And as Sloan found himself needing fewer and fewer cigarettes, and fewer and fewer bottles of beer, he began to rediscover a connection with his wife.

"It changed our whole relationship," said Bobbye Sloan. "I could see he was trying to do something that, in the past, would have been virtually impossible."

They began to talk more, and once Bobbye began to recover and feel like herself again, to take long walks together. Within a couple of months, Bobbye would join her husband on road trips, a practice she had long since forsaken for the strain it caused their marriage. Sloan could be found less and less at the hotel bar with his fellow coaches after games, and more and more out dining quietly with his wife of thirty-five years. He hated to talk about the particulars of his transformation—he'd learned to keep his feelings to himself, remember—but deep down, Sloan was incredibly proud that he had made it.

"We're as happy as we've ever been," he said.

Now, he was the healthy one, too.

CHAPTER

6

All year long, the Jazz and Bulls had been on parallel paths, and the similarity in their seasons grew only more striking as their Super Bowl Sunday rematch approached.

While the Jazz had played the first month of the season without John Stockton and amid the chaos created by Karl Malone's criticisms, the Bulls had played the first two and a half months of the season without forward Scottie Pippen and amid the concern that this would be their final season together. Management had proclaimed it would not rehire Coach Phil Jackson for the following season, and that had inspired Michael Jordan to say he would retire if Jackson was not the coach. And Pippen, who was out all that time with a foot injury, declared he would never play for the Bulls again because he said the team treated him poorly and didn't accord him the respect he deserved.

The Bulls won only twelve of their first twenty-one games, and like the Jazz suffered embarrassing losses to lesser teams. While the Jazz had lost twice to Sacramento and could not seem to figure out Portland, the Bulls had fallen to the Boston Celtics on opening night and failed against the mediocre likes of Washington, Cleveland, and Orlando.

Pippen had gone so far as to demand a trade, to either the Phoenix Suns or the Los Angeles Lakers, but the Bulls never cut a deal. Eventually Pippen's stance softened, and by the time the Jazz beat Cleveland on January 12, Pippen was back in a Bulls uniform and Chicago was back on the winning track. Just one day later, the 26-11 Bulls had reclaimed the best record in the Eastern Conference by clobbering the Seattle SuperSonics, who, at 29-8, still had the best record in the NBA.

"This might be a preview of the Finals," said Sonics forward Vin Baker.

The Jazz did not agree. Their victory over the Cavs had moved them back to the top of the Midwest Division at 24-11, which was one game ahead of their previous season's record pace. They had begun to talk about their prospects of winning 41 of their final 47 games, like they had the year before, even though conventional wisdom said the task would be much more difficult the second time around.

At the same point the year before, the Jazz had only one more long road trip on their schedule, and only one other trip as long as three games. They also had a stretch of seven straight home dates in February, and had already played the defending champion Bulls twice. (The Jazz won at home and lost at the United Center.) This season, while they had the same number of home and road games remaining as last year, the Jazz still had to make two five-game road trips in March, a month in which they would play twelve of seventeen games away from the Delta Center. They had only one stretch of home games that lasted as long as three games, and they had yet to play the Bulls at all.

What's more, the Jazz still could not be counted on every night. For all their recent success, they hadn't beaten any top-quality teams in a while, and occasionally struggled against bad teams.

"We're not there yet, but we're starting to get back to last year's form," said Malone. "We go through periods where we're just lackadaisical on defense as well as offense. When we're aggressive on both ends of the court, we play better."

The Jazz followed their Cleveland victory with a third straight loss to Portland, 96–86, before beating Orlando, 107–93, Detroit, 98–89, and Golden State, 98–85. That gave them ten wins in their last eleven games and a 27-12 record, but considering the victims, who knew what that really meant?

That's why Super Bowl weekend loomed so large for the Jazz; it would give them a chance to reestablish their legitimacy among title contenders and show they could beat good teams on the road. They would meet the Bulls after taking on the Indiana Pacers two nights earlier in Indianapolis, then would come home to play the Seattle SuperSonics. That was three of the top four teams in the NBA within a week, and the combination would give the Jazz a good sense of where they stood among the league's elite.

"You never really know what your best is until you play the best teams," said Jeff Hornacek.

Promptly, then, the Jazz lost to the Pacers.

It was one of those games—like the losses to Sacramento or collapses against the Lakers—that made you think, no way is this team going to win a championship.

The final score was 106–102 at Market Square Arena, and the Jazz wilted in the second half to achieve it. Malone and Stockton were typically outstanding, scoring 26 and 18 points, respectively, and the Jazz built a big lead in the first half, but they allowed a 29–14 scoring run in the third quarter that earned Indiana an 81–80 lead entering the fourth.

The Jazz pulled away a bit to lead 94–89 with 5:38 remaining in the game on a tip-in by Ostertag, but could hardly grab a rebound against the worst offensive rebounding team in the league. What was worse was that Ostertag was being abused all night by the Pacers' Rik Smits.

Smits had scored 10 points in the first quarter, and had shown an eagerness to get the ball against Ostertag that the Jazz had seen a lot from other centers around the league. Even Vancouver's Bryant Reeves, whose big contract paved the way for Ostertag's, couldn't get the ball fast enough against Ostertag in the Grizzlies' last game against the Jazz, which they lost by just 89–88 at the end of December.

After the Jazz got their 5-point lead against Indiana, Smits took over again, and wound up scoring 8 of the Pacers' last 10 points. He also grabbed the rebound of Malone's last miss with seventeen seconds left to seal the victory, before Chris Mullin hit a pair of free throws for the final margin.

Malone refused to speak to reporters after it was over. That was far from a rare occurrence, but it usually happened more often at the Delta Center, where Malone (and Stockton, for that matter) had the convenience of the training room adjacent to the locker room that was off-limits to the media. There, players could wait until deadlines had passed and reporters had given up hope of an interview before finally emerging. On the road, though, the Jazz rarely had the luxury of a separate training room, leaving all the players to dress in the locker room, which by NBA rules is open to the media ten minutes after every game. And while Malone most times was cooperative with the press, he occasionally turned surly if the game hadn't gone his way.

After the Jazz lost at Portland a week earlier, for example, Malone found himself pulling on his shirt and icing his feet while a few reporters waited to ask him some questions. He was in a foul mood already; the loss had been the Jazz's third in a row to the Trail Blazers, and Utah had been so manhandled in every one of them that coach Jerry Sloan had arrived at the conclusion that "they're just better than we are." That remark prompted a reporter to broach the same topic with Malone.

"Coach Sloan said the Blazers are just a better team than you are," he began.

Malone interrupted.

"Talk about something else," he said, shaking his head. "Don't give me that bullshit."

"I'm just telling you what coach said," the reporter offered.

"Well I don't give a fuck what you're telling me," Malone snorted. "I don't want to talk about that shit." He paused a moment, then declared: "I'm done. I'm done. Because of assholes. See you guys."

The reporter stammered again that he was simply repeating Sloan's remark.

"I don't give a fuck what the coach said," Malone repeated. "Just leave me the fuck alone."

Perhaps, then, it was just as well that Market Square Arena had a training room adjoining the visitors locker room. That's where Malone stayed for a good long while after he and his teammates gave up 5 offensive rebounds in the fourth quarter and allowed 60 points in the second half to blow their seven-game winning streak against the Pacers. Almost all of Malone's teammates had showered and dressed and cleared out of the locker room to board the bus when reporters saw assistant trainer Terry Clark emerge from the training room, remove the clothes that hung in Malone's locker stall, and duck safely back into the confines of the training room. That meant Malone planned to get dressed in private, then stalk right past everybody holding a pen or a microphone on his way out of the arena.

But Malone would need one more tactic to make it onto the bus without talking that night, and he relied on one of Stockton's old standbys: the diversion.

Stockton generally sequestered himself in the training room even more often than Malone, and he frequently waited until one of his teammates had attracted the attention of the media and was surrounded by all the microphones and cameras. Then Stockton would slip past, quietly and unnoticed, and board the bus before anybody knew what had happened. That's what Malone did in Indiana, and, adding a touch of irony, he used Stockton as his decoy.

* * *

With Pippen seven games into his comeback from foot surgery, the Bulls had won six times and reclaimed the lead in the Central Division with a 30-12 record by the time the Jazz pulled into town on a cold, gray Saturday, and they were sounding a lot like the guys from Utah, too.

"I don't think we should sit around and pat ourselves on the back, because we still have to improve as a team," Jordan was telling the Chicago media. "We're not the caliber of team that we were last year at this stage. . . . We're getting closer. We don't want to play our best now because it doesn't mean anything. I still think we can improve our overall game."

Until the same day the Jazz lost to the Pacers, life had been increasingly sanguine for the Bulls. They still were dealing with the talk of a last go-round, but Pippen was back and the losing had stopped and even Dennis Rodman had been a model citizen.

Known as much for his tattoos and dyed hair as for his considerable rebounding talents, Rodman had been nearly a paragon of virtue all season long. He'd missed fourteen games to suspensions and been fined more than $32,000 the previous season for transgressions ranging from missing workouts to kicking a courtside photographer to head-butting a referee during a game, and the Bulls were so concerned about his destructive outbursts that they nearly did not sign him to a new contract when he became a free agent over the summer.

Ultimately, the team and Rodman agreed on a one-year deal heavily weighted with incentive bonuses for good behavior. For the first forty games of the season, it appeared to be working. But after missing his first game of the season against the Charlotte Hornets with the flu, Rodman failed to show up for the shootaround the morning of the Bulls' game against the Nets in New Jersey; when Rodman finally did arrive at Continental Airlines Arena later in the day for the game, a disgusted Phil Jackson sent him home to Chicago.

And the circus began anew.

The *Chicago Tribune* declared the next morning that "The Bad Boy Is Back" and media reports placed Rodman at various unsavory locations until as late as four in the morning before the Nets game. The *Tribune* suggested Rodman had been gambling at an Atlantic City casino; SportsChannel said he'd been cavorting at a strip club in New York City.

The Bulls won their game against the Nets, 100–98, without Rodman, but they needed overtime and a controversial goaltending call on the last play of the game to do it, in part because they were so badly beaten on the boards. And considering how much trouble the Jazz had in that same department in their loss at Indiana, they certainly could have used the advantage if Rodman were to miss another game.

But when the Bulls opened practice the next day at the Berto Center in suburban Deerfield, Rodman was there, and his attendance inspired Jackson to assure him he would play against the Jazz; he might not start, the coach said, but he would play. The team fined Rodman an undisclosed amount—though by players union rules it could not exceed $2,500—and said the matter was closed. Rodman, for his part, had a simple explanation.

"I messed up, and that's it," he said. "It's as simple as that. . . . People should know that Dennis Rodman is a person who loves to do what he wants to do any time, any day. I'm not trying to hurt anybody's feelings or make anyone look bad. I apologized to my teammates and to my coaches, but this is just one of those deals that happened. It's not like what President Clinton is going through right now. That's a guy who's having a bad damn week."

Clinton was suffering the first days of his sex scandal involving White House aide Monica Lewinsky. Come to think of it, Rodman never did confirm where he'd spent his Friday morning.

While Rodman was attracting a crowd at the Bulls' practice, a matter more pressing to the Jazz was playing out at their workout in downtown Chicago. After hurting his back during the loss to the Pacers, Adam Keefe did not practice with the team and was not certain he'd be able to play in the game against the Bulls. If Keefe couldn't play, Bryon Russell would start in his place, and the Jazz would be one player thinner at a position that was particularly important against the Bulls.

Russell had been in the starting lineup exactly once since the seventh game of the season, and that was when Keefe missed the January 19 victory over Detroit to be with his wife while she delivered twin daughters Caitlin Suzanne and Michaela Joann. (Those kids were certain to be bionic, given their parents' athletic credentials.) Russell had played pretty well in that game, but said afterward that he didn't care whether he started or came off the bench.

Still, the Jazz wanted Russell back in the front five by the time the playoffs rolled around, mostly because he was a better perimeter defender than Keefe and complemented Malone's and Oster-tag's inside play more with his three-point shooting, absent though it mostly had been to that point.

Russell figured to be a better fit against the Bulls, too, and there was some speculation that Sloan would use the opportunity of Keefe's injury to put Russell back in the starting lineup for good. If Keefe were to start—given the obvious matchups of Malone on Rodman or Jason Caffey, Ostertag on Luc Longley, and John Stockton on Ron Harper—he would have to guard Pippen while Jeff Hornacek guarded Jordan. That seemed like a mismatch in the Bulls' favor because Pippen was more athletic than Keefe and could play anywhere on the floor, while Jordan . . . well, Jordan could kill anybody. It seemed to make more sense for Russell to guard Jordan, as he had in the Finals the previous season, and let Hornacek try to handle Pippen. Though that remained a mismatch in the Bulls' favor, it did not seem as egregious as the first one.

Sloan disproved the whole theory.

When the Jazz took the floor that afternoon at the United Center, Keefe was right there with them, limbered up and ready to check Pippen. He did a pretty good job, too. But the Bulls came out strong and forged a 49–43 lead in the final minute of the first half, and the Jazz needed a fortuitous turn of events to stay in the game.

Angered by an official, Pippen threw the ball at him and picked up a technical foul with 37.1 seconds left. Hornacek made the free throw for the Jazz, and nine seconds later Malone hit a jumper from the wing that cut Chicago's lead to 49–46. The teams exchanged possessions, and with only a few seconds left Hornacek heaved up a three-pointer from the top of the arc that he hoped would tie the game but instead didn't even hit the rim.

As luck would have it, Malone was waiting beneath the basket;

he caught Hornacek's shot, and, with his back to the basket, flipped the ball back up toward the rim while being pushed from behind. The shot fell, and as Malone walked smiling to the free throw line for the shot that would tie the game, Hornacek asked him a question that could easily be read on his lips.

"Like my pass?" he said.

At the break, Malone had 19 of the Jazz's 49 points on 8-for-14 field goal shooting. Jordan had 17 points for the Bulls, Pippen had 14, and Rodman was on his way to 16 rebounds. Neither team had led by more than 6. It figured to be a fantastic second half.

Having scored the last 5 Jazz points of the first half, Malone picked up where he left off to start the second. Starting with a 3-point play early in the third period, Malone scored 6 straight points and 12 of 22 to help Utah build a 77–73 lead going into the fourth quarter. Keefe added 6 points in the final six minutes of the quarter, and despite his bad back was really putting the clamps on Pippen, who did not score in the third period before managing just one basket in the fourth, while having the ball stolen twice.

On his way to 14 points in one of his best games of the year, Howard Eisley started the fourth quarter by burning Bulls backup guard Rusty LaRue with back-to-back baskets, while Russell drilled a couple of three-pointers to lead a fantastic charge from the Jazz bench as Utah moved ahead by 13.

Jordan, however, was still Jordan.

He scored 9 of his 32 points in a four-and-a-half-minute span that cut the Jazz's lead to 98–91 with 1:30 to go, and Utah led only 98–94 when Stockton drove to the basket and tried a layup that looped over the hoop with 37.9 seconds remaining.

Stockton recovered the rebound on the other side of the basket four seconds later—and after the shot clock had been reset—but referees stopped the game amid the Bulls' protests that the ball had missed the rim. If that had been the case, the shot clock should have been allowed to run, and the Jazz would have had only about two seconds left with which to work.

Instead, the officials conferred at the scorer's table and let the play stand after hearing from ESPN radio man and former coach Jack Ramsay, who had seen a TV replay and told them the ball had indeed hit the rim. The Bulls were disgusted.

"It changed the momentum of the ball game," said Jordan. "It certainly shouldn't have done that."

The Jazz inbounded the ball, and the Bulls were forced to foul Stockton rather than risk a 6-point deficit with only about twelve seconds to go. Stockton stepped up and made one of 2 free throws for a 99–94 lead, and the Bulls did not score again. The final: Jazz 101, Bulls 94.

Malone finished with 35 points to overshadow Jordan and help the Jazz end Chicago's thirty-eight-game home winning streak against teams from the Western Conference. The Bulls also had won seventeen straight at home against all teams, and four straight overall, and acknowledged that allowing the Jazz to win in the United Center could prove fatal down the road.

"That could hurt us in the long run," said Jordan, who envisioned the Jazz as the top contender in the West. "Utah still has the upper hand. Sure, physically, Seattle's better, Los Angeles is better and maybe San Antonio is better. Houston is on the same page, although maybe they're not as healthy. I still see Utah coming out of the West."

Coach Jackson agreed with Jordan, as did NBC-TV's Isiah Thomas, but the Jazz wanted nothing to do with talk like that. To a man, they proclaimed the victory no big deal—"It's all hype, anyway," said Antoine Carr—and said that in no way did their regular-season victory make up for losing the NBA Finals.

"Revenge had nothing to do with it," said Malone.

All the same, the message had been sent: the Jazz could win in Chicago.

That meant a lot, considering the Jazz had lost their last five games there, including all three in the Finals. Perhaps now, if the teams wound up meeting again in the championship round, the Jazz would feel a heretofore unknown confidence.

What the Jazz were concerned about at the moment, however, was improving their record enough to secure home court advantage so they wouldn't have to worry quite as much about playing well on the road. To that end, the win over the Bulls meant little, since the Jazz had lost to the Pacers.

"It would be a big deal if it were for the championship and we won," said Carr. "Then it would be a big deal."

It became even less of a big deal three nights later, when Vin Baker erupted for 28 points and 10 rebounds and the Sonics snapped the Jazz's seven-game home winning streak with a 101–93 victory at the Delta Center. Even with the advantages of a couple of days' rest and the home crowd, the Jazz could not cut into the Sonics' three-game lead in the Western Conference play-off race.

"I guess we felt good about playing Chicago," Sloan said, while most of the players hid in the training room. "Everybody likes to play in a tuxedo, with a nice little tie on all straight and pretty, when they don't have to get dirty. We played that way."

Sonics coach George Karl said he still considered his team, the Lakers, and the Jazz the favorites to win the West, but Sloan and everybody else who had been watching the Jazz couldn't be sure what to expect. The big week had ended with the same amount of uncertainty with which it began, and the Jazz continued their maddeningly uncertain play by doing as they were supposed to and whipping Dallas and Golden State, 104–94 and 115–88, before losing to the lowly Los Angeles Clippers, 111–102.

And then, as if to keep everybody guessing over the five-day break for the All-Star Game, the Jazz beat the Bulls again—101–93 at the Delta Center for their first season sweep since 1994.

"When we play, we're as good as anyone," Malone explained. "When we don't play, we're mediocre."

Welcome to Team Schizophrenia.

CHAPTER

7

It had been a long time since Karl Malone enjoyed the NBA's All-Star Game. He remembered enjoying the experience the first few times, but after about his fourth trip to the league's mid-season extravaganza he began to view it as more hassle than it was worth. The game itself was usually a drag, he thought, and in addition, he had to put up with all the crowds and cameras and interviews. He would rather spend the days off from the regular season at home with his wife and kids, and this season was no different. In fact, Malone had even less desire to attend the game this season, since it was being held in the media fishbowl of New York City and without John Stockton.

While Malone had received more votes than anybody else in the Western Conference and therefore been elected to start the forty-eighth annual game—his eleventh in a row—Stockton was neither voted in by fans nor chosen as a backup by coaches because he had missed the season's first eighteen games. It would be the first time in a decade that Malone and Stockton were not teammates for the West.

"It's weird," said Malone. "It's definitely weird that he's not here. I don't think he'd ever admit it . . . but I think it's one of those things where he's probably more disappointed than anything because he has been here every year, and even though he started off injured, he still wanted to be here. It's unfortunate; considering what he does for our team and what he does for the game, I think he should be here."

Stockton wasn't the only star veteran who was missing. Houston's Hakeem Olajuwon, Chicago's Scottie Pippen, and New York's Patrick Ewing also had been injured much of the first half of the season and were not chosen for the team, leaving as teammates for Malone many of the young players he had famously derided as "knuckleheads" the year before. Nick Van Exel of the Los Angeles Lakers was one of them, and he was the guy who essentially took Stockton's spot. That was a hard pill for Jazz fans to swallow; Stockton was one of the greatest players of all time, while Van Exel was perceived in many circles as a thug who had embroiled himself in a public feud with his coach during the Lakers' playoff series against the Jazz in 1997.

But Malone showed up anyway, and managed to be more diplomatic about his reluctance to attend than he had been in Cleveland; fans there booed Malone mercilessly the year before, because they thought that his desire to skip the All-Star Game meant he didn't like their city.

"People say I hated Cleveland and that's not the case at all," said Malone. "It's not a knock against any state or anything, it's just that I'd rather be at home. That's all.

"I just don't think I'm really cut out for All-Star Games," he added. "I'm not a guy who's going to do anything flashy or nothing like that. I just go out and play. I do the best I can. I'm not looking to play a lot of minutes. It's an honor to get voted in, but could I have used these five days to do something else? Absolutely. But I'm here and I'll make the most of it."

That wasn't easy, either. Malone said the hotel room the NBA provided for him was about the size of his son's room at home. He said he could "turn the TV on with my toes," and that he awoke at seven in the morning two days before the game to jackhammer construction on the floor above him. So Malone checked out, and found a room at another hotel where he said he paid his own way.

"Let's just say that Donald Trump came up big for us," said Malone.

The game itself had as much dramatic tension as could be expected of an All-Star event, mostly because of Michael Jordan and Kobe Bryant. Jordan's threat to retire meant that this could be Jordan's final All-Star Game. Bryant, meanwhile, was a nineteen-year-old from the Los Angeles Lakers playing in his first All-Star Game and gracefully enduring the speculation that he was the one who would take up the basketball throne once Jordan abdicated. And if that wasn't enough, along with the All-Star Game returning to Madison Square Garden for the first time in thirty years, Jordan missed practice the day before the game; the NBA said he was sick with a 101 degree temperature, and was "uncertain" for the game.

But while Jordan was constructing his own theater and enduring his public feud with Bulls management, the Jazz had, in the final few days before the All-Star break, become embroiled in troubles of their own.

About a week before the break, Jerry Sloan uncharacteristically confided to a newspaper columnist that he was perplexed that the Jazz and owner Larry Miller had yet to offer him his usual contract extension.

Sloan had been working in recent years on a three-year contract, which the Jazz typically extended by one year every summer. But nearly halfway through the new season, Sloan still was under contract only through the following year. That was unusual enough, but what was more unusual still was that Sloan said something about it publicly; that was not his style.

"I get the idea Larry isn't going to do anything at all," said Sloan. "When you've been around ten years, maybe it's time to move on. Maybe that's the way it should be."

Miller hadn't been heard from yet, but it didn't take a genius to figure that if he was entertaining the thought of starting over with his team—and it had to happen sometime—perhaps this would be how he'd choose to do it: allow the contracts of his superstars to expire at once and move in a new direction with a virtually brand-new bunch in two years. After all, Sloan's wasn't the only contract set to expire after the following season; Malone's was up then as well, along with those of Stockton, Jeff Hornacek, Greg Foster, Howard Eisley, and Shandon Anderson.

That notion occurred to Malone, too, who walked into the interview session two days before the All-Star Game intent on securing a little leverage for his beloved coach.

The interview session was held in a ballroom at the Hilton Towers in New York City. The NBA had set up tables to accommodate each of the two dozen or so participants in the weekend's activities—which included not just the All-Star Game but the rookie game, the three-point shootout, and the inaugural 2ball competition—as well as the members of the media. The NBA had issued more than 1,800 press credentials for the game, and it seemed that almost all of the credential holders were jammed into that ballroom.

Jordan was not there, of course; he traditionally accepted the $10,000 fine and skipped the media session to go play golf. But there were plenty of other targets for the swarm of microphones.

Each of the tables had atop it a placard identifying which player was to be sitting there, and no fewer than sixty reporters were already crowded around the one marked for Bryant some fifteen minutes before he even arrived. New Jersey's Jayson Williams was a hot interview, too, given his standing as the only local player involved and the one with the best personality. Very few reporters surrounded Malone's table, and even after he arrived no more than twelve or fifteen stopped by at any one time to listen to what the league's reigning MVP had to say. Of those who did stop, many wanted to know what Malone thought about Jordan's threat to retire.

"We got a similar situation happening in Utah," Malone said.

And off he went.

Malone drew parallels between what was happening in Chicago and what was happening in Utah; he said the Jazz had approached Sloan about a contract extension, but went back to the coach and said they'd changed their minds. He also alluded again to the team's signing of unproven young players like Greg Ostertag and Bryon Russell while not similarly rewarding its veterans for all their years of hard work.

"They give you the sad story about, 'We don't want to jeopardize this organization' and 'We don't want to put them in a financial bind.' Then they go pay these players the money they're paying them," said Malone. "They tell you, basically, 'Help us out and secure this franchise.' And you go out on a limb and you do that, and they give you a pat on the back and say, 'Hey, good job. Good game.' And the guy that they're giving all the money to just kind of shows up whenever he wants to. It's the same way [with coaches], just a different level."

Indeed, Sloan had done everything the organization had ever asked him to do, and remained loyal through a change of ownership and the retirement of one of his mentors, coach Frank Layden. He was the longest-tenured coach in the NBA, and was on the way to moving into thirteenth place on the all-time list of coaching victories. There seemed no reason for Sloan to be forced to worry about his contract, or to be one of the lowest-paid coaches in the league.

"I think what's happening with Coach Sloan and Jazz management is bullshit, that's what I think," said Malone. "If it ain't broke, don't fix it.

"Next year is my last year and John's and Hornacek's, so maybe they're trying to tell us something," Malone added. "It's hard enough to win. I'm not going to make any waves as far as a contract, but the coach? What is that telling you as a player? Whether I want to come back or not, do you think I want to come back if Coach Sloan's not there? Absolutely not. We started something here and I want to finish it with him. I'm not washed up after next year, so we'll see what happens."

Malone remained less than excited about the All-Star Game, too; he said his ambitions extended only as far as playing a few minutes, getting a rebound or two and not spraining his ankle on his way back to the bench, and he added that he would not be hurt if coach George Karl didn't use him at all.

Malone had no interest in answering questions about his participation in the inaugural 2ball competition. That was the attraction the NBA had conceived to replace the Slam Dunk Contest, which most perceived to have run its course.

In 2ball, an NBA player was teamed with a player from the WNBA, and together they tried to score as many points as possible in sixty seconds while shooting from designated spots on the floor. Each of the seven spots was assigned a point value—a layup was worth one; a three-pointer worth eight—and the players had to alternate shots.

Malone was probably the most high-profile player in the contest, and he was teamed with guard Tammi Reiss of the Utah Starzz. Their strategy certainly was an amusing one: Given Malone's expressed desire to avoid an injury, he camped out at the eight-point spot just beyond the three-point arc and did not move.

Ever.

When his and Reiss's turn came on All-Star Saturday Night, Malone hoisted the first shot and missed, and Reiss chased down the rebound. Then she ran to a spot, made her shot, chased the ball down again and passed to Malone. He missed again. Reiss chased after another rebound, ran to another spot and made another shot. Malone missed. Over and over again they did this. The poor woman was running herself ragged, and there was Malone, perched out on the line and lazily lofting three-pointers. It looked ridiculous.

But it worked; Malone wound up hitting a couple of the eight-pointers, and Reiss made six of her seven shots as they advanced from the original field of eight teams to the final round of two. They lost in the finals to Houston's Clyde Drexler and Cynthia Cooper of the Houston Comets, but still took home $10,000 for second place, even if they had to endure a little ribbing from the media.

"Karl," a reporter asked, "are you winded from your 2ball experience?"

"We had a game plan," said Malone, seeming to take the question with more gravity than had been intended. "Tammi approached me when we worked in Salt Lake and said, 'I want you to stay on the eight and let me do all the running around.' I don't want all the women's lib people saying, 'Oh, look at him, he didn't do nothing.' We had a game plan and we stuck with it."

Hornacek had a strategy, too: slow down.

The Jazz's shooting guard was entered in the three-point shootout for the first time since losing in the first round seven years earlier, and he'd decided that he needed to take a split second more time and make sure he followed through on his shots. Not that he cared a whole lot about how the contest came out; he was happy to have been included for the sake of his wife and family, who'd been pestering him all season about getting in so he could take them to New York City.

"I wasn't counting on anything," he said.

Hornacek scored 17 points to advance out of the first round, and scored 15 to tie with Seattle's Dale Ellis and force a twenty-four-second tiebreaker in the second. Hornacek won that, 11–9, then had an easy time in the finals after Dallas's Hubert Davis scored only 10 points. Hornacek put up a 16, and took home a check for $20,000.

"I just wanted to get in it so we could come to New York and have a little family vacation," said Hornacek. "We'll take the win, too, I guess."

The Hornaceks stayed to see a Broadway show on Sunday afternoon, then skipped the All-Star Game entirely and headed home.

With some reporters joking that Jordan's 101 degree temperature reflected how hot it was on the golf course he played in Las Vegas, the Bulls' star recovered well enough to make tip-off. And his battle with Bryant turned out to be an intriguing one, if only for three quarters.

Jordan made the game's first basket fifteen seconds in, but Bryant got even fast. He hit a jumper at the 10:27 mark and missed an alley-oop attempt from Seattle's Gary Payton a minute later, but halfway through the first quarter got loose for a 360 degree breakaway dunk and a give-and-go slam from Minnesota's Kevin Garnett that brought the sellout crowd of 18,323 to its feet.

Then Jordan dunked.

Two minutes later, Jordan spun on the baseline and drained a fallaway jumper in Bryant's face. Bryant tried to match Jordan but missed, and Jordan worked him again on the East's next possession. Bryant even fouled him on that one, and Jordan, calm and composed as can be, made the free throw.

While Bryant was trying so hard to upstage Jordan, the West

was getting its butt kicked. It trailed by 12 at the quarter break, and Malone had touched the ball precisely one time, when he missed a baseline jumper in the game's first three minutes. He sat out the final sixteen minutes of the first half, and the East led 67–58 at intermission. Jordan had 13 points. Bryant had 10.

The show continued after halftime.

After Malone made his only two baskets of the game, a pair of jump shots from the wing midway through the third quarter, Bryant and Jordan went at it again. Jordan pump-faked Bryant into the air and ducked under him along the baseline, only to have Bryant's Lakers teammate Shaquille O'Neal swat the ball away and get called for goaltending.

On the next trip down the floor, Bryant stuck a three-pointer, and a minute after that performed a move so astonishing that it was bound to be replayed on every highlight film of the year: stealing a pass from Miami's Tim Hardaway at about midcourt, Bryant dashed off toward the basket to find himself face-to-face with Atlanta's 7-2 Dikembe Mutombo. As he raced past the right side of the free throw line, Bryant dribbled behind his back—toward the middle of the court and Mutombo, not away from them—took one more step, and, as he sailed toward the baseline, lofted the softest little right-handed hook shot you ever saw. It seemed to float in the air forever, as thousands of throats gasped for the air that would propel their vocal astonishment if it fell.

And it did.

Swish.

The place went crazy, and Bryant was feeling the love.

On the West's next possession, he felt so good that he launched a twenty-four-foot three-pointer from the left side. That fell, too, and Bryant, the teenager who had skipped college to enter the NBA draft out of a high school in Pennsylvania, was showing up the greatest basketball player who ever lived on the hallowed floor of Madison Square Garden in the NBA All-Star Game.

But Bryant's glory did not last long. He came out of the game with about two minutes left in the third quarter, and never did return. He had 18 points. Jordan had 17.

Karl said later he kept Bryant on the bench because the game was a blowout, though the East led only 101–91 after three quarters and fell behind more disastrously only when East coach Larry Bird put Jordan back in the game early in the fourth. That's when it began to look like the NBA All-Star Game was being governed by the same people who choreograph pro wrestling.

While Bryant sat on the bench with a towel draped over his head, Jordan took the court and was allowed every opportunity to win the game's MVP award. He reentered the game with 9:27 left, and within thirty seconds had taken a wide-open three-pointer that gave him 20 points, and later scored a nifty layup and a free throw that put him at a game-high 23 to finish. He had also handed out 8 assists and grabbed 6 rebounds in the East's 135–114 victory, and the trophy belonged to him almost as if it had been planned that way.

NBA Commissioner David Stern presented the award, saying, "I'm only going to allow him this trophy if he promises to come back and do it again."

Jordan simply smiled.

Malone, meanwhile, was not in a mood to even do that. Malone was angry, though not at sitting on the bench for thirty-one of the game's forty-eight minutes and scoring only 4 points, his lowest output ever in an All-Star Game. It was the knuckleheads again.

"As far as I'm concerned, this is the worst All-Star Game I've been in," said Malone. "Everybody was going one-on-one. I went to set a pick for a guy and he told me to get out of there. . . . Like I said, I'm not cut out for All-Star Games."

It turned out that the guy who waved off the screen was Bryant, who had angered not only Malone, but several of the other Western Conference veterans with his selfish play. That was the real reason Karl kept Bryant on the bench in the fourth quarter.

The flight back to Salt Lake City the next morning was delayed an hour, but Malone did not care. Nor did he mind that he had to wait in the uncomfortable chairs of the terminal with everybody else. He was simply relieved at being able to leave the noise and congestion and traffic behind and get back to Utah.

"I'm happy," he said.

And why not? Now he could put the foolishness behind and get back to the important business of winning a championship, with a team that had won sixteen of its last twenty-one games and seemed to be drawing ever closer together.

CHAPTER

8

G reg Foster and Chris Morris said they never saw it coming.
When the trade winds first starting blowing out of Orlando
shortly before the Jazz were to tip off against the Charlotte Hornets at the Delta Center on February 15, Morris was working up a
sweat in the pregame shootaround and Foster, having finished his
pregame routine, was sitting idly in his locker stall perusing some
statistics.

"I haven't heard a thing," he said.

He hadn't heard a thing, that is, about his role in a trade that
was rumored to be on the verge of coming down. It was six o'clock,
three days before the NBA trading deadline, and the Orlando
Magic already were under way in their game against the Hawks in
Atlanta. That's what started the rumor: the Magic had held center
Rony Seikaly out of the game because of the rule that prohibits
teams from using players about to be involved in a trade with

145

another team. Seikaly wasn't hurt, at least as far as anyone knew, and he just sat there stewing in street clothes while the Magic beat up on the Hawks. He had yet to learn his destination.

"I can't believe it," he said before the game. "I've played hurt. I've flown to New York at four in the afternoon to meet the team for one game. I gave up a lot of money to make the deal work here, and this is how they repay me? It just goes to show there's no loyalty in the NBA."

Word had filtered back to Salt Lake City that the Magic were shipping Seikaly to the Jazz in exchange for Foster, Morris, and a first-round draft pick. It hardly seemed believable; Morris was stuck at the end of the bench and hadn't played meaningful minutes in ages, and Foster was not the kind of front-line player who figured to be of equal value in a trade for a player like Seikaly.

At 6-11, Seikaly was not the biggest center in the NBA, nor the best, but he was pretty big and pretty good. He was a proven scorer who could play with his back to the basket and run the floor well and rebound if he set his mind to it. Over the course of his ten-year career he had averaged 15 points and nearly 10 rebounds a game. The Jazz had never before had a center who could score, and with Greg Ostertag having come down with a stress fracture in the fibula of his left leg the previous week and struggling besides, it was easy to see why they wanted help.

Ostertag had been playing in pain with what he thought was a bruise for about a week before that, but did not tell the team trainers about it until after the Jazz beat the Clippers, 106–98, at the Delta Center in their first game back after the All-Star break. Ostertag missed practice the next day to undergo tests, and on February 12 he was diagnosed with the injury; he was expected to be out for three to six weeks.

Ostertag refused to talk much about the injury, and claimed he didn't even know how long his leg had been bothering him. Some in the Jazz organization thought Ostertag was keeping his mouth shut to avoid having to make an embarrassing admission about how he really injured his leg, and in concert with that theory, they mentioned Ostertag's trip to Disneyland while the team was in Anaheim to play the Clippers just before the All-Star break, as if he'd been willing to take a foolish risk. Others privately groused that it was simply Ostertag's lack of fitness that made him suscepti-ble to getting hurt.

The team hoped Ostertag would miss closer to three weeks than six, since the stress fracture hadn't actually become a fracture yet. The injury was diagnosed early enough that doctors saw only the kind of inflammation that portends stress fractures, and not a literal crack in the bone. Nevertheless, it was another setback in what already had been a miserable season for Ostertag, who'd been a public target for Karl Malone yet again only a few days earlier. During his All-Star interview session, Malone put a lot of responsi-bility on Ostertag to help the Jazz win a championship.

"One of the key guys for us is Greg Ostertag," Malone said. "I've said, and I've put the pressure on him, he's a key to us and to what we want to do, and we have to get everybody playing well at a particular time. We can't have guys showing up, getting beat by the Clippers one night and beating the Bulls the next night. We're not flowing as a team, and I think Greg has a lot to do with that. And Greg Foster. And we just need everybody playing well every night. That's it."

And now Ostertag was out until March.

The Jazz beat the Boston Celtics, 118–100, without Ostertag before signing 6-10 rookie William Cunningham, who had played for the Jazz during the Rocky Mountain Revue summer league before the season and bore a striking facial resemblance to Michael Jordan. He didn't quite have Jordan's game, though; Cunningham averaged not even 2 points a game in his senior season at Temple

University in Philadelphia in 1996, and had been working out on his own in Phoenix when the call came from the Jazz.

Cunningham made his NBA debut against the SuperSonics in Seattle on February 14, the day before the Seikaly trade, after signing a ten-day contract. He played only ninety seconds in the Jazz's 111–91 victory at KeyArena, but still was as gassed as if he'd run a world-record half-mile. Nevetheless, he scored his first NBA basket, and was able to participate in the Jazz's second win in three tries against the Sonics, who had the best record in the NBA at 39-12.

As pleased as they were with their fourth victory in a row, the Jazz knew they'd had help from the schedule: while they'd had a day off after their home game against Boston to travel to Seattle and prepare for the showdown, the Sonics had gone overtime to beat the Lakers in Los Angeles the night before, and against the Jazz were playing their fourth game in five nights. Players were quick to note, however, that wins are wins and they all count the same when the league draws up playoff brackets at the end of the regular season.

"We've had teams waiting for us at home after a tough road trip," said Malone. "Everybody has to do it."

By beating the Sonics, the Jazz improved to 34-15 and regained their lead in the Midwest Division, and Malone continued his biggest tear of the season.

In the Jazz's victory over the Bulls before the All-Star break and their wins over the Clippers, Celtics, and Sonics after it, Malone averaged 31 points, 10.5 rebounds, and 4.5 assists and won his second NBA Player of the Week award. And with the Lakers suffering a week-long slide to start the second half of the season, the Jazz were in second place among Western Conference teams, behind Seattle.

Then came the trade.

Less than an hour after Foster said he hadn't heard anything about the developing situation in Orlando, with only about twenty minutes until tip-off, coaches and team management told him and Morris to change out of their uniforms because they'd been traded. Few in the Jazz locker room had ever been witness to such a scene, which left the team in something of a daze.

"It was very difficult for the whole team," said Adam Keefe. "Nobody had been in that situation before, where they'd seen guys dressed and ready to play all of a sudden get pulled aside and told to take their uniforms off. I think the whole team was in a bit of a state of shock."

It looked it.

With Cunningham making his first NBA start, the Jazz managed to forge an 11-point lead over the Hornets, but never looked terribly smooth and nearly blew it at the end. The Jazz did not score a basket in the final 2:46 of the game, while Charlotte's Glen Rice scored 15 of his 30 points in the last three minutes to cut the lead to 89–86 with just over a minute left. The only thing that saved the Jazz was their free throw shooting; they made 8 of 10 down the stretch to hang on, 96–90, for their fifth straight victory.

All of that was nearly lost, however, in the chaos of the trade.

After hunting down their wives to deliver the news of the trade, Foster and Morris hunkered down in the Jazz locker room until nearly halftime before emerging to face a throng of reporters who were largely ignoring the game in favor of the more dramatic story behind the scenes.

Foster was much more composed than he had been in the minutes after receiving the news, when he wandered down the Delta Center hallway with his eyes swollen from tears. He said all the right things, about understanding basketball as a business and how these things happen and that the Jazz, after all, had given him the opportunity to make himself marketable. But clearly, he was hurt.

Morris, on the other hand, had to stop himself from handing out party favors. The trade meant for him an early emancipation from his indentured service at the end of Jerry Sloan's bench, and he figured to get much more playing time, and maybe even start, for Orlando coach Chuck Daly, who had coached Morris for a couple of seasons in New Jersey. It was easier for Morris to say the right things, as he did, because he was elated to be leaving.

"It's like a marriage," he explained. "You get a divorce, and move on."

Simple as that.

The Jazz had been working on the deal for weeks, but it was typical that word never leaked out about it. Headed by vice president of basketball operations Scott Layden, the Jazz were perhaps the tightest-lipped organization in the NBA.

But, man, could they swing a deal.

Utah gave up practically nothing to get Seikaly, since all Orlando wanted out of the trade was to make some room under the salary cap so it could be in a good position to lure some of the big-time free agents who would become available during the summer. The Magic took Foster as a replacement in the middle for Seikaly and because he was making only $504,000, and Morris because he made the $3 million necessary to make the trade work under salary cap rules, but would become a free agent on July 1 and thus not count against the Magic's salary limit for the next year.

Acquiring Seikaly was widely praised as the move that would earn Layden the Executive of the Year award and deliver the Jazz their first championship. Newspaper columnists praised the Jazz's decision to damn the torpedos and worry later about the future, and television analysts breathlessly tried to imagine the potency of a Jazz lineup that included not just Malone and John Stockton, but a legitimate center who could take defensive pressure off both of them.

"He's a warrior in there," Layden said of Seikaly. "You look at his numbers and there's a reason that he's had success. He battles. Offensively, he can score, and then look at his rebounding numbers over the years—they're also very impressive. I think he gives us another low-post player and another presence in the middle, and so we look forward to having Greg Ostertag coming back and having Rony Seikaly, and hopefully that will improve the whole situation."

The Jazz had tried to land Seikaly two seasons earlier when he was playing for the Golden State Warriors, but that deal fell through at the last minute. The Jazz were going to re-sign forward David Benoit, package him with center Felton Spencer, and send him to Golden State to rescue Seikaly, who hated playing for the bereft Warriors. At the last moment, though, Benoit's agent, Sal DiFazio, backed out of the deal and allowed his client to test the free agent market after the season. The Jazz wound up dealing Spencer to Orlando several months later, in exchange for Kenny Gattison, Brooks Thompson, and a first-round draft pick. Neither Gattison nor Thompson survived the preseason before 1996–97, but the Jazz held fast to the draft pick, which the Magic had the option of handing over at their discretion until 1999.

That's another thing that made the Seikaly trade a steal: while the Jazz handed over a 1998 first-round draft pick to the Magic, it was their own pick and not the one they'd acquired in the Spencer deal. The difference was more than a dozen spots on the draft ladder.

"It didn't work out last time," said Layden. "But we're happy we were able to make a deal. You look at the depth board for all the teams in the league, and there aren't that many centers around. So we feel fortunate to get a player of his quality."

Malone, however, had a funny feeling about the whole thing. While most of his teammates and employers praised the trade, however cautiously, he remained silent, refusing to speak with the media after the win over the Hornets and walking away again the next morning after practice. He knew something wasn't right, and didn't want to say anything that might come back to haunt him.

He was dead on.

The Jazz had hoped Seikaly would arrive in Salt Lake City sometime the next day, but he didn't, and later that night word began to get around that he did not plan to report unless the Jazz agreed to certain contractual concessions.

At first, it was believed that Seikaly wanted the Jazz to guarantee they'd pick up the option on the final two years of his contract, worth about $8.7 million. He'd given up that guarantee two years earlier, when he was so desperate to escape Golden State that he waived it to facilitate his trade to Orlando, meaning those years would be at the club's option. But now that he was leaving Orlando, Seikaly apparently wanted the guarantee back.

Seikaly's agent, Steve Kauffman, said he wasn't certain whether his client would report to Utah within the forty-eight hours allowed by NBA rules, in time for the Jazz's game against the New York Knicks at the Delta Center on the day of the trading deadline. He refused to be more specific about the dispute.

"We'll wait and see what happens," said Layden. "It's all part of the business and you just have to deal with it and move on. That's why they have deadlines."

Layden appeared calm, but he was the only one. The dispute threatened to derail the entire trade, and that threatened to derail the entire Jazz season. Not only would they not acquire Seikaly, but they probably would wind up with a major morale problem in the locker room if Morris and Foster were forced to return to a team that had tried to get rid of them. Morris would be furious at having his early departure revoked, and Foster was the kind of guy who would feel distraught at having been rejected. Both had already left for Orlando.

Rumors flew on the fast break the next day, in the hours before

Seikaly was due to report and the Jazz were to take on the Knicks. Radio stations had begun to report that Seikaly was in dispute with the Jazz not because he wanted them to guarantee picking up the final two years of his contract, but because he wanted them to promise to *not* guarantee them. Seikaly apparently wanted to play out the rest of the season with the Jazz, then be able to either leave as a free agent or sign a new (and more lucrative) deal to stick around a few more years.

Layden and other members of the Jazz front office spent the entire day in closed-door meetings and on the phone trying to get the deal worked out, but Seikaly was not on any of the four flights booked for him from his home in Miami, and the Jazz arrived at the Delta Center that night preparing for their game against the Knicks without any idea what might happen. The Jazz and Seikaly's agent had until 8:00 P.M. to work something out before the reporting deadline expired; after that, the Jazz would have the option to waive the deadline, try to rework another trade with the Magic before the NBA's trading deadline, or kill the deal entirely.

All the while, Foster and Morris had been holed up in the Marriott Hotel across the street from the arena in Orlando, waiting to find out what would become of them. They had already passed their mandatory physical exams with the Magic, appeared at an introductory press conference wearing Magic baseball caps, and participated in a morning shootaround before the Magic's game against the Minnesota Timberwolves. They were in their rooms dressing for the game, when Magic general manager John Gabriel phoned and told them to stay there; they were not eligible to play against the Wolves because of the complications the Jazz were having with Seikaly. At one point, Foster and Morris phoned Layden to find out what was going on, and they were not happy with what they learned.

The Jazz had killed the deal.

On the floor that night, the Jazz were murdering the Knicks, who shot barely 30 percent in the first half and fell behind, 52–30. Then, at halftime, Jazz owner Larry Miller went first on the Madison Square Garden TV network and then on the local KJZZ feed to tell viewers the deal was off. He did not use those exact words, but only about twenty minutes remained until the deadline, and he wouldn't have gone on TV if the deal still had any life in it.

"What's frustrating is that Rony is saying all the right things," said Miller. "And his agent is just saying he's flat not coming."

The Jazz wound up beating the Knicks, 94–78, for their sixth straight victory, and afterward Miller and Layden addressed the media in a conference room not far from the Knicks' locker room. They confirmed the deal was dead, and expressed frustration that they could not really say why it fell apart.

"The agent never would land on anything concrete that he wanted from us," said Miller. "He made allusions to things, but he would never pin it down. We'd ask him what he really wanted, what the real problem was, and he never would commit to us."

Layden did not want to discuss details of the dispute, but he described as incorrect the media reports that claimed the options or guarantees in Seikaly's contract were at issue.

The son of a wealthy Lebanese shipping magnate, Seikaly grew up in Greece before playing college basketball at Syracuse University in New York. He was widely known to enjoy an upscale, urban lifestyle and warm climates, which fostered the notion that he simply did not want to wind up in Utah. Fans had no problem believing that, either, since Derek Harper of the Dallas Mavericks had refused a trade to the Jazz only a year earlier, fueling the local inferiority complex by derisively telling reporters, "You go live in Utah."

The story grew stranger with every detail that emerged. Seikaly had spoken by phone with Malone and Stockton, and in both conversations said he was eager to play with them and on a team that had a chance to win a championship. But Miller said that when he tried to phone Seikaly, Seikaly never answered. The Jazz administration never spoke with anybody but Kauffman, who they contended was giving them the runaround. There also was talk of an ankle injury, though Seikaly had played just fine in the most recent game for which he'd been eligible.

Either way, Malone didn't care. "If somebody doesn't want to play with me," he said, "I say to hell with him."

It was hard to understand just what was going on, between all the rumors and the Jazz's reluctance to speak about the conflict in detail, but some light was shed on the proceedings the next day, just before the NBA's trading deadline.

Though Seikaly was headed back to the Magic, the team said it would never allow him to wear its uniform again, and fifteen minutes before the deadline, Kauffman and Gabriel phoned a trade in to the NBA office: Seikaly and Brian Evans to the New Jersey Nets for Kevin Edwards, Yinka Dare, David Benoit, and a conditional 1998 draft pick.

The Nets did what the Jazz refused to do and waived the reporting deadline for Seikaly, then announced they thought he might have a stress fracture in his ankle, and added that they had made no contractual concessions to Kauffman.

Seikaly "wanted to be in New Jersey," said Nets coach John Calipari. "That was his number one choice."

That was interesting.

Neither Kauffman nor Seikaly commented immediately on the deal, but it was conceivable that the conflict with the Jazz was nothing but a ruse to force them to kill the trade and make the Magic seek out another offer, ideally from a team Seikaly preferred more than Utah.

Perhaps, as Calipari said, Seikaly really did want to be in New Jersey all along, but was traded to Utah because the Magic liked the offer from the Jazz better than the one from the Nets; Kauffman could not have done anything about that—but perhaps, then,

Kauffman decided it would be worth the risk to try to get the Jazz to kill the deal and force the Magic to find another taker. That he might be able to do. The Magic certainly could not have kept Seikaly once the deal with the Jazz fell apart; their relationship with him had deteriorated beyond repair, and they needed new players to take the places of all the ones they had lost to injury. Perhaps Kauffman guessed that the Nets had offered the Magic the second-best deal for Seikaly, and that the Magic would turn to New Jersey if the Jazz trade didn't come off; then his client could go where he wanted to go in the first place.

Such a plan would have had its risks, of course, but every agent in the league knew the Jazz wouldn't bend the rules and would refuse to waive the reporting deadline. Kauffman may have been comfortable thinking they would sooner kill the deal than be left hanging even longer had Seikaly continued to stay away.

If true, it was pure genius. But the public would never know for sure.

When Seikaly finally spoke about the trades on a national radio show, *The Jungle with Jim Rome,* he claimed to have never given up on the deal with the Jazz. He said he wanted to go to Utah, but two snags held up his departure: the Jazz refused to allow him to become a free agent at the end of the season, then backed out of the deal once they learned about the stress fracture in his foot.

"I definitely did not kill the deal," Seikaly said. "I had my bags packed and ready to go."

Although his former employers in Orlando said they knew nothing about any injury, Seikaly had returned home to Miami after the trade was announced and visited his personal physician, Miami Heat doctor Harlan Selesnick. Selesnick diagnosed the stress fracture, Seikaly said, and estimated Seikaly would be out six to eight weeks. Selesnick sent the Jazz the magnetic resonance imaging exams that revealed the injury, and Seikaly said that information made the Jazz even more insistent on guaranteeing his contract, because they did not want to have to wait two months to acquire his services only to wind up losing him after the season.

The Jazz refused to divulge any particulars of the negotiations, but Layden made it clear that the team's primary wish was for Seikaly to simply report to Utah—as was the condition of that and every trade—and go from there. Layden and Miller conceded they were willing to discuss contractual options with Seikaly, but only if he reported on time.

"It was dead when he didn't show up," said Layden.

Had Seikaly arrived in time, yet failed their physical, the Jazz still could have killed the deal, but they said they wanted to gauge for themselves the severity of his injury before deciding. They might have been inclined to make the trade anyway, had they learned what Seikaly suggested in his radio interview: that despite his doctor's diagnosis, he anticipated missing only three weeks of action.

"It was a chance for me, once in a lifetime, to play for a team like Utah," Seikaly insisted. "Plus with Karl and John, two legends. I mean, all the positives, all the pluses are there, but it wasn't in my hands."

Even the day after the Jazz killed the deal, in the hours before the NBA trade deadline, Seikaly phoned Malone repeatedly and begged him to make something happen.

"I called Karl up to fifteen minutes before the trade deadline," said Seikaly. "I kept on calling him on his cellular. He was shooting a commercial. I was bothering him the whole day. I said, 'Karl, get this thing done. Get this thing done.' He kept on telling me that, 'It's going to get done. Somehow, it's going to get done.' And so, there's no doubt in my mind that I definitely wanted to go to Utah."

Later that night, after he had been traded to the Nets, Seikaly appeared at a press conference in New Jersey. He had his right foot in a cast, validating the injury, yet became the center of an ensuing debate around the NBA about why players were suddenly so able to dictate where they would play, without regard to the clause in their contracts that stipulates they can be traded anywhere in the league. Kenny Anderson did it that same week, proclaiming he would not report to Toronto after being traded there by the Portland Trail Blazers; in so doing, Anderson forced the Raptors to trade him to Boston without Anderson ever having set foot on Canadian soil.

"I'm worried about the direction of the league," said Miller. "When guys are under contract, they should play the contract out. I'm sure players don't always like to be traded, but when they are, it's part of the game. We can't have players dictate where they go and where they don't go."

There were larger issues for the Jazz, though—a little matter of a couple of guys sitting around an Orlando hotel room.

"This is probably the toughest thing in the whole trade," said Layden. "We need to remend relationships and get these guys back in the fold and back in our system, and I think both of them are professional and they are good guys. . . . It's good to have them back, and our focus will be on winning ball games."

As upset as he was about being traded, Foster was not thrilled to have to show his face again around the team that didn't want him, and Morris was furious at having to return to the end of the bench. He had said from Orlando that he did not want to go back.

"You can't go to work and say you're going to try to smile at everybody and pretend like it never happened," said Morris. "It's going to be a difficult situation to accept. . . . I would be surprised if I actually will play."

After the trading deadline passed and there was no threat that they would wind up anywhere but Utah, Foster and Morris gathered their belongings and boarded a plane back to Salt Lake City, uncertain of what awaited them. Could they put the trade behind them? How would their teammates react? Would the rest of the season become a disaster because of the feelings of alienation and betrayal?

"I have no idea," said Foster.

Nobody else did either.

CHAPTER

M oments after Delta Airlines flight 229 from Orlando pulled
up to the gate at the Salt Lake International Airport at 8:45
P.M. on February 18, Greg Foster and Chris Morris stepped from
the jetway and into a cradle of something that they never could
have anticipated.

Adoration.

Scores of fans lined the gate area and the concourse, bearing
banners and balloons and cheering and applauding as if the players
were bringing home a championship instead of returning deject-
edly from a botched trade. Well-wishers offered handshakes and
greeting cards that said "We're glad you're home," while camera
crews from the TV stations turned their glaring lights into the
players' weary eyes. Foster and Morris might have been two of the
most unheralded players in the NBA, but Utah was thrilled to have
them back.

The airport reception was cathartic for Foster, who had been hurt terribly by the Jazz's attempt to deal him. Though he had played for six teams in seven years after his college career at UCLA and Texas–El Paso, he had never felt as comfortable anywhere as he did in Utah. He had grown to like the climate and the land, saw friendliness in the faces of the people who lived there. He'd acquired a steady role with the Jazz, and he felt like he belonged, like he had a home. Then the trade forced upon him a painful reminder that basketball was business, not family, even among the most familial team in the league. As he hugged his wife, Victoria, and his daughters, Victoria and Collette, the applause helped him begin to feel wanted again.

"It was a great feeling," said Foster. "The fans were great. If it wasn't for them, I'd really have a hard time with this."

He had a hard time anyway, just like Morris.

Morris would rather have put his eyes out than have to return to Salt Lake City. Though the hospitality at the airport was aimed as much at him as it was at Foster, it was not nearly enough to soothe the harsh feelings that churned inside him. Only playing time could do that, and, as he said in one of the several interviews Morris gave as he and his family—wife Michelle and sons Michael, Sean, and William—made their way through the airport, he would need about twenty minutes of that per game to make him happy again.

"This is bullshit," he said when the TV cameras clicked off.

By virtue of the phone calls that flooded their offices that day, the Jazz knew ahead of time about the deluge at the airport. They considered sending a public relations representative to meet Morris and Foster and help control the scene, but decided against it because they wanted to avoid the perception of having orchestrated the celebration. That was only the first of several moves the Jazz made in their attempt to smooth relations with their disenchanted players.

The players welcomed back Foster and Morris with relative ease, since they had all been friends and nobody had burned any bridges in the days since the deal tried to go down. Scott Layden and Larry Miller already had praised Foster and Morris for their professionalism in dealing with the situation, and asserted the team's need to put the incident in the past and not allow it to become a distraction.

Then, after Foster started and scored 6 points while Morris did not play in the Jazz's 79–77 victory in San Antonio on February 21, Layden appeared on a Sunday night sports talk show on KSL-TV in Salt Lake City and suggested the Jazz were lucky to have had the trade fall through. Not because Rony Seikaly had yet to play for the New Jersey Nets because of his injury, however: "If a guy doesn't want to be here," Layden said, "maybe we're better off."

Lost amid all the ruckus over the failed trade was the fact that the Jazz had continued to play pretty good basketball. Since beating the Bulls for the season sweep in the last game before the All-Star break on February 4, they'd won seven games in a row and averaged more than 104 points per game before the slowdown in San Antonio. They returned home 37-15 and sitting atop the Midwest Division by one and a half games, and had knocked off some of the best teams in the league—the Sonics, Hornets, and Knicks, most notably—heading into a home game against Miami. They had started to talk quite a bit about their tendency in recent years to play better in the second half of the season; the Jazz had won thirty-one out of thirty-five games after the All-Star Game the previous year, and felt like it might be happening again.

"Everybody is starting to pick their game up," said Antoine Carr. "Hopefully, it will continue into the playoffs."

Usually, in the moments before player introductions at the Delta Center, the Jazz play a short highlight tape on the JumboTron screen, climaxed by John Stockton's three-pointer that sent the Jazz to the Finals for the first time. But with the Heat in town on the night Foster and Morris made their first appearance in Utah since the trade, fans and players found themselves staring up at a different videotape.

In the team's continuing effort to salve the psyches of the players it had tried to give away, the folks in promotions and game operations had put together a highlight reel featuring only Foster and Morris, set to the theme music of the long-dead TV sitcom *Welcome Back, Kotter*.

Eyes rolled.

The players could not believe what they were seeing. As Foster and Morris threw down dunks and pumped celebratory fists on the screen, the real Foster and Morris could not help but feel an overwhelming sense of embarrassment. Certainly, they appreciated the support of the fans and—as much as it might have hurt—understood the position of the team. But this was too much. They still had been traded, nothing could change that, and the reason they were back in Jazz uniforms had nothing to do with being wanted back.

"That was ridiculous," said Foster.

The Jazz similarly failed on the floor that night, getting killed on the glass and allowing four Heat players to score 18 points or more in a 104–102 loss. Foster scored 6 points on 3-of-7 shooting, but Morris sat for the second straight game, and his disgust was as evident as it had been in the myriad times over his Jazz career that coach Jerry Sloan had pulled him off the floor after a wild shot or not called his number at all. Morris was not even leaning into the timeout huddles, preferring instead to stare out into space while Sloan plotted strategy, and took care to always sit at the end of the bench and walk the long way around his teammates and coaches.

Morris was part of a long line of small forwards the Jazz had tried over the years in the hopes of finding the perfect complement to Stockton and Karl Malone. Thurl Bailey was the first, going way back, and he gave way to Tyrone Corbin in a 1991 trade when the

Jazz saw that Bailey's career was pretty much spent. That deal with the Minnesota Timberwolves came only weeks after the Jazz had signed free agent David Benoit, who was still around when the Jazz traded Corbin to the Atlanta Hawks for Adam Keefe in 1994.

Keefe became the backup, and Benoit grew into one of the longest-tenured Jazz players of the early 1990s. As physically talented as he was, though, Benoit acquired a drinking problem that impeded his development and contributed to an inconsistency that became his legacy. He carved out his own ignominious corner of Jazz history by missing all three wide-open three-pointers he tried in the fourth quarter of a Game 5 loss to the Houston Rockets in the first round of the 1995 playoffs, and the next season refused to re-sign with the Jazz to facilitate the trade to Golden State for Rony Seikaly. Instead, Benoit became a free agent, complained later and from a distance that Malone was a failure in pressure situations, and left the small forward spot to Morris, Keefe, and Bryon Russell.

Morris had signed with the Jazz before the 1995–96 season and played sixty-six games behind Benoit while averaging more than 10 points per game. The Jazz won sixty games that year and advanced to the NBA Western Conference finals against the Seattle SuperSonics.

But Morris's relationship with Sloan grew more contentious the next season because Morris never came around to Sloan's idea about how basketball ought to be played. He didn't play defense, first of all. Sloan began to use Morris more and more erratically, and Morris responded more and more rebelliously until he finally erupted during a February game against the New York Knicks. He screamed at Sloan for removing him from the game, and Sloan responded by hollering back and ordering Morris to leave the Jazz bench at the Delta Center. Morris at first refused, but finally relented after the threat of a security detail was raised. He and

Sloan had not been on good terms since, and Russell had developed enough to replace Morris as the starter.

Sloan had always tried to downplay the conflict, and had begun to go out of his way to compliment Morris almost every time Morris did play, in an effort, it seemed, to prove he wasn't holding a grudge. But while Sloan did occasionally give Morris superficial opportunities—unlike a lot of coaches, who might have been more inclined to completely bury a player after a sideline incident like Morris's—he viewed Morris as a hugely talented player whose attitude and command of the game had a ways to go before it caught up with his $3 million salary. Morris had not helped the relationship by missing curfew back in Cleveland, nor by costing himself a chance at a regular starting job in the season's first month when Russell was struggling: the team had planned on inserting Morris in the starting lineup when Russell asked out of it, but Morris missed a workout and Sloan started Keefe instead.

Morris's latest disappointment hardly went unnoticed, either. In the wake of the loss to Miami, Miller visited the Jazz practice facility with a mind to straighten out the hard feelings.

"I just got all the cards on the table," Miller recalled later, "and said, 'You know, Greg, we feel bad that what happened happened, and I know your feelings are hurt, so on and so forth, but you have to decide whether you're going to shut up and play or whether you're going to cry about it. Chris, you just have to shut your mouth, you know. You can either be on the team or be home. Your contract is your contract, you're guaranteed either way, but we're not going to put up with you shooting your mouth off all over the place. And I like you, and everything else, but you just have to decide what you're going to do. What are you going to do?' And I asked them right there, and they were okay. It was kind of just a leveling."

It was then, too, that Sloan showed his players a side of him that they had seldom, if ever, seen. Once Miller finished his speech in the gym that morning, he turned to Sloan at his side and asked if the coach had anything to add. Sloan said yes, as a matter of fact, he did.

By then, Sloan had been more than a month into his new regimen for a healthier lifestyle. He was spending more and more time with his wife, and had begun to quietly consider retirement once the season was over in order to spend even more time with her. He had learned the value of a proper perspective, and his fellow coaches had noticed the positive effect it had on him.

"Last year, every day it was something," said assistant Kenny Natt. "All the way up to the last game of the season, in the Finals, we had confrontations and things out on the floor, whereas now, he's not after every guy. What happened with his wife has made him realize there's more to life. That has settled him down."

And Sloan knew that if Foster and Morris could be introduced to the same appreciation of the things they had instead of the things they didn't have, they could more quickly and easily forget the episode that had so bruised their egos.

"I've learned what's important," Sloan told his players that day. "We'd all like to win basketball games. But winning games isn't as important as your family, and your wife, and stuff like that."

His words were simple, and from someone else they might have seemed bland, but coming from Sloan they left listeners thunderstruck. "It blew my mind; I think it blew everybody's mind because he's never done that before," recalled Miller later. "It was surprising because it was so out of character for him, but it really showed all of us a side of him that he had never been willing to disclose to us, especially as a group. I think it simply boils down to him learning what is really important."

Miller and Sloan were not the only ones who could see the Jazz were teetering on the brink of breaking the season. Team President Frank Layden also knew that if Foster and Morris continued to harbor their grudges and show the same lack of interest that they had since returning from Orlando, the Jazz were sunk. The best they might hope for in such a scenario would be for Foster and Morris to do no damage and just float along for the season's final two months, islands unto themselves. But certainly, the Jazz feared the men would become utterly useless, and that their bad attitudes would multiply among their teammates and perhaps divide the team at the most crucial point of the season.

So Layden met individually with both Foster and Morris, giving them each a $100 gift certificate to former Jazz center Mark Eaton's restaurant south of Salt Lake City as a gesture of goodwill. But he also gave them a lecture designed to guilt them into playing better.

"We are sending men to the Gulf," Layden said, referring to the looming threat of a U.S. military attack on Iraq. "Leaving their jobs, being taken from their homes to go to war, so that you guys can play basketball. You have not made a single contribution to the country, or to the system, or anything else. So why don't you try to have fun, enjoy it, and contribute to this team winning?"

Layden's meeting with Morris came before the shootaround prior to the Jazz's February 26 game against the Phoenix Suns. Both men knew Morris was not going to be back with the Jazz the following season, and Layden asked him, "If you wanted to sell a Mercedes-Benz, would you dent it? Would you go out and hit it with a hammer?"

Morris could see where that was going.

While the team needed calmer waters in which to make its championship drive, Morris needed to make himself more attractive for the free agent market over the summer. Nobody was going to want to hire a player for any amount of money if they were afraid of what negative influence he might have on a team, and Morris carried enough of that kind of history already.

"Why don't you come and help us?" Layden asked.

Morris left the meeting convinced that Layden was right. He went out and, given a chance to play, scored a season-high 20 points that night in the Jazz's 108–97 victory over the Suns in what became the first step in his transformation into just the kind of team player everybody wanted him to be. Not only did he suddenly become more interested in the games, he took to staying late after practice to accommodate any reporter who wanted an interview. He also realized that, by beating his notoriously languorous team-mates out of the shower and into the locker room after games, he could virtually guarantee that all the time-strapped reporters would flock to his locker and give him a good chance of getting his face all over *SportsCenter* and the nightly news. Image wasn't everything, but Morris knew it counted for a lot.

As for Foster, Layden mocked the way he always tried to be cool and tough and mean-looking, when in fact he was simply a tall, skinny journeyman.

"You're a tough guy?" Layden said. "You're a tough guy? If you're tough, what you do is you swallow hard and go out and play. Tough guys recover. Cowards sulk."

Foster needed a bit more time to get over his hurt feelings, but the speeches worked on him, too. He had reclaimed his starting spot even before the trade on account of Greg Ostertag's injury, and within a couple of weeks he started grabbing rebounds like his life depended on it and playing with a ferocity that hadn't been seen all season, if ever.

"I was my own worst enemy since the trade," said Foster. "I was feeling sorry for myself and not playing basketball. . . . I've already been through enough. I don't care what anybody says anymore."

Emotionally, the season had been saved. But the real battle was just beginning.

✿   ✿   ✿

Heading into March, when the Jazz would play twelve of seventeen games on the road, the team was 38-16 and trailed the Sonics by four games for the best record in the West.

The Sonics were showing no signs of slowing down, and had the advantage of playing seventeen of their final twenty-eight games at home in KeyArena. The Jazz, meanwhile, would play seventeen of their final twenty-eight games on the road, where they were only 13-11 so far. Twice in the first three weeks of March, the Jazz would play five-game road trips spanning eight days, with only three home games interrupting the trips. The first was to take them to Houston, Toronto, Boston, New Jersey, and Milwaukee, with the second one hitting Detroit, Minnesota, Charlotte, Philadelphia, and New York.

"This is a big month for us," said Howard Eisley. "It's going to make or break our season."

And considering that they had gained hardly any ground with their recent winning streak, as well as the stack of other disadvantages in front of them, the Jazz seemed to be bracing for the worst.

"It might be better playing without home court advantage," said Sloan.

All season long, the Jazz had been preaching the importance of securing home court advantage so they could have their best possible chance in their championship run, and suddenly it would be better not to have it? Clearly, they did not want to sabotage whatever playoff chance they did wind up with by convincing themselves ahead of time that they couldn't win without the home edge. After all, Sloan pointed out, the Houston Rockets won back-to-back championships in 1993–94 and 1994–95 without having home court advantage either time.

Speaking of the Rockets, they were the first opponent on the big road trip. The Jazz had beaten them twice already, but the Rockets played both games without center Hakeem Olajuwon, who missed thirty-three games of the season recovering from knee surgery. Even after his return a month earlier, the Rockets struggled with other injuries and with personality problems in the locker room, and had won only as many games as they had lost.

Houston led by as many as 14 points in the second quarter, but the Jazz closed the gap with a 20–4 run in the third, and it was tight the rest of the way. Olajuwon made a short jump shot for a 98–97 Houston lead with 2:37 to go, but that was the last the Rockets saw of the lead.

Malone hit a baseline jumper to reclaim the lead for the Jazz at 99–98 with 1:38 to go, and after a Russell miss, Houston's Mario Elie drove to the basket hoping to do the same for the Rockets. Suddenly, though, Carr came out of nowhere to block the shot and send the ball bounding away and into Russell's hands.

"Everybody goes to sleep on you because they think you're old," Carr boasted after the game. "But the old man's still got some ups."

Elie promptly fouled Russell, Russell made one of two free throws and then a short jumper on the Jazz's next possession. Stockton hit two free throws, and Carr hit a pair, and the Jazz had their fifth straight victory over the Rockets, 106–100. Not since 1984 had the Jazz beaten the Rockets that many times in a row.

"They made the plays down the stretch," said Houston's Charles Barkley, "and we didn't."

Sloan again found a way to get Morris into the game, and though Morris did not score 20 points like he had against the Suns, he did help create the first version of a small lineup that the Jazz would use often and well throughout the last two months of the season.

Sloan started using the small lineup mostly because of Ostertag's absence and Cunningham's limitations. The key was Malone, who played center in such situations because, with his strength, he could handle big men like Olajuwon or Kevin Willis on defense. Also, he liked the challenge. That allowed Sloan to mix more of his most athletic players into the lineup at the same time. Against the Rockets, Sloan had Morris on the floor with Eisley, Jeff Hornacek, Malone, and Keefe in the first quarter, and with Eisley, Carr, Russell, and Shandon Anderson at the start of the second.

The small lineup worked even better against the Toronto Raptors two nights later, when it helped Anderson get loose for a career-high 26 points. He scored his baskets mostly by posting up Doug Christie and Chauncey Billups, neither of whom had nearly the strength to keep the muscled Anderson off the block. Anderson's explosion helped the Jazz come back from an early 8-point deficit, something to which they were growing more accustomed in recent days.

"We were just a little sluggish," said Anderson, who had scored his previous career-high of 21 points in the season-opener against the Lakers. "It seems like that first half has always been tough for us."

The Jazz knew how to come around, though. The 108–93 win over the Raptors was their third in a row and ninth in ten games without Ostertag, though they were having a hard time moving up in the standings.

The Sonics had begun their last substantial road trip—a four-gamer that began in Miami and hit Orlando, Charlotte, and Minnesota—the same night the Jazz played in Toronto, and spoiled the Jazz's best chance in that span to gain some ground by ending the Miami Heat's ten-game winning streak. The Bulls won, too, beating the Denver Nuggets to stay two games behind the Sonics for the best record in the league. At 40-16, the Jazz were four games off the pace, and only one ahead of San Antonio in the Midwest Division.

They survived 36 points by rookie Antoine Walker and 23 turnovers to beat the Celtics, 110–94, on March 4, and released Cunningham from his second ten-day contract after the game;

otherwise, the Jazz would have had to sign him for the rest of the season, which they did not want to do since Ostertag was expected back soon.

After three weeks of riding a stationary bicycle and running in a swimming pool to try to stay fit, Ostertag's leg had healed enough that he was cleared to resume on-court workouts, and the team sent strength coach Mark McKown home from Boston the next day to guide Ostertag's workouts until the team returned, when Ostertag was scheduled to be reevaluated.

Whether the Jazz players wanted Ostertag back was another story. Though they refused to say publicly that they were playing better on their own, they were enjoying the trip without him, joking behind closed doors about how well they were playing because Ostertag hadn't been there to goof anything up.

The Jazz caught a break before meeting New Jersey, perhaps the toughest test on their trip. While the Jazz were winning at Toronto, Nets center Jayson Williams pulled an abdominal muscle and had to leave New Jersey's game against the Knicks. By the time the Jazz reached Continental Airlines Arena, the league's second-leading rebounder was on the shelf indefinitely.

That was going to leave Nets coach John Calipari to use Michael Cage and Chris Gatling, two veteran but hardly overpowering players, to try to contain Malone so that rookie Keith Van Horn would be able to roam a bit more freely. A former star at the University of Utah, Van Horn had missed the teams' first meeting in December because of an ankle injury.

The injury to Williams provided an ironic twist, too: having accepted Seikaly in the trade from the Magic after the Jazz killed their attempt to acquire him, the Nets had hoped to have him as a backup for Williams in case of just such an emergency, but Seikaly was still out of the lineup nursing the stress fracture that he said had forced the Jazz to kill their trade for him, so the Nets were without a quality big man who might have helped contain Malone.

In separate interviews before the game—one with Rod Hundley on the Jazz's TV network and one with print reporters outside the Nets' locker room—Seikaly again insisted that it was the Jazz, not him, who killed the deal and that he really did want to wind up in Utah.

"The bottom line," he said again and again, "is that Utah pulled the offer off the table when they found out about my foot."

From the beginning, the Jazz had said that they simply wanted Seikaly to report to them within the forty-eight hours mandated by NBA rules so they could have a look at the injury themselves and go from there. And three times, Seikaly refused to offer a straight answer to questions about why he did not simply do that and allow the Jazz to judge the injury firsthand.

"That had nothing to do with it," he said.

Seikaly kept on about the Jazz's refusal to extend the reporting deadline, whatever that would have meant to Seikaly, but it did not take long for the Jazz to show that they needed Seikaly a lot less than the Nets did.

Though the Nets fought back from a 91–79 deficit in the fourth quarter, they didn't have enough firepower to come through in the clutch. The Nets' Kerry Kittles made two free throws with thirteen and a half seconds left to cut the Jazz lead to 118–115, but Sherman Douglas fouled Hornacek as Douglas stole the inbounds pass, and Hornacek's free throws gave Utah a 120–115 cushion. Kittles then missed a three-pointer, Russell grabbed the rebound and passed to Eisley, who was fouled and put the game on ice, 122–115, with 3.6 seconds left.

"They're a better team," said Calipari. Stockton and Malone "are Hall-of-Famers, not just All-Stars. You can't really close the gap because they don't make mistakes."

Van Horn finished with 23 points, but scored only 4 in the fourth quarter with Malone guarding him, and Sam Cassell led the Nets with 29. But against the mechanical defensive efforts of Cage and Gatling, Malone was able to do whatever he wanted. The Nets tried double-teams and the usual assortment of defensive ploys, but Malone still scored 32 points for the second consecutive game and grabbed 12 rebounds. What he did not know, however, was that he had played the entire game after somebody had telephoned the Nets and threatened to kill him.

The Nets had quietly tightened security for the game, and hustled the Jazz off the court, behind the press table and through a different tunnel than the one they normally used. Guards also refused to allow Malone, Stockton, and Hornacek to return to the court for postgame radio and TV interviews, though even Jazz public relations man Mark Kelly was unaware of the real reason; he thought the Nets' TV people had simply stiffed Malone, and jokingly wondered what would happen the next time they asked Malone for a moment of his time.

"I bet that's the last time Mail gives them an interview," he said.

Meanwhile, Sloan was completing his standard postgame address to the media outside the Jazz locker room when Seikaly walked past on his way out of the building. The player stopped, offered his hand to Sloan, and tried to soothe any hard feelings.

"You know I wanted to be here," Seikaly said, searching the coach's face for some hint of approval.

Sloan did not soften. "I don't know that," he said plainly.

Taken aback by the coach's lack of grace, Seikaly backpedaled and tried to convince Sloan that he was telling the truth.

"I talked to Karl over and over," he said.

Sloan could not have cared less. As far as he was concerned, Seikaly screwed the Jazz by refusing to report, and put Sloan in the embarrassing position of having to repair his team's relationship with Foster and Morris. He shook Seikaly's hand and wished him well because fans and the media crowded the hallway watching, but, judging by the steel in his voice, probably would have taken a swing had he and Seikaly been alone.

Neither the coach nor any of the players were still in the building when the Nets finally made an announcement about having received the threat against Malone. The state police were investigating, they said, without providing any details, and Malone didn't learn of the threat until the Jazz landed in Milwaukee for the last game of the trip. He phoned home the next morning to check in, and like his teammates, found family members worried about what happened. They had learned of the threat from TV or the newspapers.

This was not the first time Malone had faced death threats. In 1991, Malone had smashed Isiah Thomas of the Pistons in the face with an elbow in what the Pistons viewed as retribution for Thomas's scoring 44 points against Stockton a month earlier, in the wake of Thomas's being left off the U.S. Olympic team. There were so many threats made against the Jazz in Detroit that on their next trip through, the team was given a police escort, with extra police placed on the team bus and the bus redirected from its usual route to the Palace of Auburn Hills to avoid trouble. Nothing happened that time, either, but the players and team employees still remember how besieged they felt having to take such precautions.

After Malone scored 40 points against an injury-riddled Milwaukee Bucks team for a 110–92 victory to complete an impressive 5-0 trip, he talked about the threat in New Jersey and bemoaned the lax security at most NBA arenas.

"It stinks," he said. "Terrible. Absolutely the worst. If you wanted to do something to a player, it would be no problem. Until somebody gets shot or something like that—and it's going to happen, I'm telling you—nothing is going to change.... From now on, I'm packing. I'm not going to be one of those 'uh-oh' kind of guys."

Not if he didn't want to be. An avid hunter, Malone said he "could start my own private war" with all the weapons he had at home. Rifles, pistols, *silencers;* he had it all, and the bigger the game, the better. Malone had the stuffed and mounted carcasses of many of his hunting conquests posing around his home—a deer, a bear, a mountain lion—and once joked at practice that the greatest hunting challenge would be for a fellow human being.

"Get some guy, a Vietnam vet, no family, down on his luck," he said. "Offer him $500,000 and give him a half-hour head start. If he gets away, he can keep the money. That would be the ultimate."

For all the stir that Malone created with his vow to carry a gun on the road, he really couldn't follow through; though he did possess a permit to carry a concealed weapon in Utah, the laws in other states varied and were mostly more restrictive than the ones that allowed Malone to stash a pistol with him for safety while out on his long, meditative motorcycle rides. He would need special permission, too, to carry a firearm on the Jazz's plane, even if it was a charter, and so Malone's promise—like many that came straight off the top of his head—veered off into nowhere, never to be fulfilled.

The Jazz had three games at home before their second big road trip of the month, and they won them all to run their winning streak to nine games. They beat Houston, 100–93; earned revenge against Sacramento, 110–95; and stopped Vancouver, 110–101. All the while, Malone was climbing closer to passing Elvin Hayes to become the fifth-leading scorer in NBA history, and Ostertag was growing more and more worried about whether the Jazz would ever want him back.

As they headed back out on the road, the Jazz were 14-1 without Ostertag and had improved to 46-16 while stretching their lead over San Antonio to four games.

"He's chomping at the bit, which is neat," reported Malone. "But it's not a good sign if the team goes 13-1 or whatever without you, whether you're Greg Ostertag or Karl Malone. You know what that means? It's not good."

Sloan said Ostertag was going to have to earn back his playing time, he would not be thrown back into the starting lineup. Though Ostertag had yet to be activated from the injured list, he joined the Jazz for their second road trip and was able to watch the rampage continue after Malone launched yet another round of criticism at him and the organization.

The first game of the trip was against the Pistons on a Sunday, and Malone had the forum of a halftime interview on NBC-TV. He also had taped a "Sunday Conversation" for ESPN's *SportsCenter*, in which he echoed his months-old complaints about Miller, and groused about how Ostertag had acknowledged in a magazine interview his laziness and lack of motivation to overcome it.

"He said that for the whole world to read," said Malone. "I have a problem with that. You know you have a problem and you don't do anything about it? That's a cop-out. If that's not a slap in my face, what is?"

The complaining was getting old, but it was also making clearer the depths of Malone's disgust. Asked once why he kept ripping Ostertag over and over again, Malone explained that reporters kept asking. And no sooner had the words come out of his mouth in the locker room than a writer approached and inquired about Ostertag.

"See?" Malone said.

Yet Malone could easily have refused to keep discussing it, as he did with any other topic of which he grew tired. Instead, he kept on firing away—part of his increasingly professed plan to speak his mind and do what he pleased and stop worrying about what other people thought of him.

And while it seemed from the outside that Malone's tirades were providing one distraction after another for the Jazz, the truth was that the players were hardly distracted at all. Part of the reason was that they mostly agreed with the speeches for which Malone kept getting attention, and part was because they had heard it all before. There was never anything new to be distracted by.

The winning streak hit ten when the Jazz beat the Pistons, 109–98, and eleven when they stopped the Minnesota Timberwolves, 102–98. They hadn't been on a roll like this all season, though it was beginning to resemble the one they put together the previous March and April, when they won fifteen games in a row and twenty out of twenty-one.

Everybody was playing well, too. Malone was still putting up MVP numbers, Russell was shooting 52 percent from the field and 44 percent from three-point range during the streak, Hornacek had improved his scoring average despite missing two games with a sore knee, and Morris had played in ten of eleven games since the team's last loss (he was suspended for the New Jersey game for again breaking curfew). That made it all the more difficult to understand why the Jazz were so willing to activate Ostertag from the injured list before meeting the Charlotte Hornets, the second-hottest team in the NBA, on March 18.

Hadn't they seen *Bull Durham?* You have to respect a streak, because they don't come along very often.

But the Jazz were not the kind of team that believes in superstition. They needed Ostertag back because he was ready to return and because he was running out of time to get back into game shape before the playoffs, when the Jazz would really need him. So in the hours before meeting the Hornets—who had won ten of their last eleven games—the Jazz announced Ostertag's return.

Within hours, they were in ruin.

Carr was hurt. Malone was hurt. Sloan was ejected, and the Jazz were blown out, 111–85.

The winning streak was gone, and Ostertag could not feel like he hadn't been at fault, metaphysically or otherwise, by missing all but one of the 7 shots he took in eleven minutes.

"It has been real hard to sit out," he said. "I've been wanting to play and wanting to play . . . and the night I come back, we get killed."

Coincidence?

Carr strained his right hamstring in the first quarter, and would be out indefinitely. Malone suffered a cut on his nose and a badly swollen eye when Charlotte's David Wesley accidentally raked him across the face while trying to strip the ball in the second quarter. Malone staggered around under the basket after being hit—he actually made the basket on the play, though—and had to return from being fixed up on the Jazz bench to make one of his two free throws to cut the Hornets' lead to 48–31 after Sloan was ejected for protesting referee Joe Borgia's decision that the basket shouldn't count.

The Jazz sliced the lead to 10 points early in the third quarter, but assistant coach Phil Johnson could not cajole any more effort out of the Jazz than Sloan could. Glen Rice made 11 of 15 shots and scored 26 points for the Hornets, who pulled away by shooting 60 percent and taking advantage of the Jazz's shooting only 37 percent and committing 17 turnovers. Malone played only thirty minutes and scored 17 points to fall 9 short of Hayes's mark on the all-time list. The loss was the Jazz's worst since losing to Atlanta, 115–89, two years and six days earlier.

"Great teams come back," Malone insisted after the game, one of his eyes swollen nearly shut from the blow by Wesley. "And I don't expect anything less than that."

Indeed, the Jazz had already made one great comeback in the wake of the failed trade. Why not another?

CHAPTER

10

The Jazz had long ago learned the value of home court advantage in the playoffs. They lost a deciding Game 7 to the defending champion Los Angeles Lakers in 1988, and stopped a three-game losing streak to the Denver Nuggets with a Game 7 victory at home in 1994. But if you had to put a date on their ultimate realization of the power of home cooking, it would be June 1, 1996, when the Jazz played the Super-Sonics in Game 7 of the NBA Western Conference finals in Seattle.

It was the third time in four years the Jazz had advanced to the doorstep of the championship round, and they were getting tired of being turned away. They had fought off a 3–1 deficit with an overtime win in Seattle and a blowout in Salt Lake City, but because of their inferior regular-season record, they had to play the deciding game at KeyArena. They had a chance to win, dramatically fighting back first from an 8-point deficit and then from an 11-point one to trail only 87–86 with thirty-two seconds remaining. But with the home crowd quiet for the sake of his concentration, Shawn Kemp made two free throws for the Sonics, and then Karl Malone missed two amid a hostile wall of noise and put the Jazz's dreams on hold for yet another year.

"Home court is going to be a big advantage," Jeff Hornacek was saying around the end of March. "Obviously, it doesn't guarantee anything, but it's a different story if you get into a playoff series where you don't have the home court advantage. You have to win all your home games and then you have to somehow steal one at the other person's place. There's no chance of a slip-up. If you have home court advantage, you can slip up a game somewhere and go back—say you even lose one at home—you can still go out on the road and win one of them and win the series. It happened to us a couple of years ago with Seattle when it came down to Game 7 and, you know, they had home court advantage and won a close game. Last year we had home court advantage [until the Finals]. I don't know if it helped us any because most of our series were done in six games or less, but maybe it will help us this year."

The Jazz had followed their discouraging loss at Charlotte with an easy 91–79 victory in Philadelphia and a successful 124–119 double-overtime classic against the New York Knicks at the Garden to get where they were—which was 50-17 and dead even with the Sonics atop the Western Conference. Having won nine of ten games on their two big road trips in March, the Jazz trailed the Bulls by only a half-game for the best record in the NBA, with fifteen games left in the regular season.

And now the Jazz would be able to trade the solitude of the road for the comforts of home; only seven of their remaining games would be played away from the Delta Center, and not even half of those were against good teams. However, they knew that they would have to keep playing as well as—if not better than—they had the past few weeks if they were going to surpass the Sonics and Bulls and secure that home court advantage throughout the playoffs.

"We have to start focusing on that," said Hornacek, "taking every one of these games like it's a playoff game and you have to win."

Hornacek was the closest thing the Jazz had to a team spokesman, largely because he was among the most willing to take time out for the media. That might have grown out of his spending the formative years of his career someplace other than Utah, where Malone and John Stockton had developed a disdain for the press and seemed to pass it on to younger players who had no other professional experience to compare it to. But like Adam Keefe, Greg Foster, and Antoine Carr, all of whom had spent time with other teams, Hornacek would talk as long as a reporter needed him, and was smart enough to give wonderfully cogent answers while not betraying any confidences from his teammates. Because of that, he made a great decoy for the players like Malone and Stockton who wanted to slip out of the locker room without stopping to talk.

Widely dismissed as a college prospect coming out of high school in suburban Chicago, Hornacek was a walk-on at Iowa State University. He had always known he was not going to become an athletic superstar—he was skinny, with bad ankles in high school and increasingly bad knees as a pro—so he concentrated enough to get his degree in accounting and develop an identity that was separate from basketball.

But for as much as he looked like somebody who could do your taxes and not much else, Hornacek had the guile and shooting touch—developed shooting over electrical wires in his driveway as a kid—that allowed him to earn a starting spot with the Cyclones after just four games. The Phoenix Suns chose Hornacek with the forty-sixth pick in the 1986 draft, making him one of five current

Jazz players—including Foster, Howard Eisley, Bryon Russell, and Shandon Anderson—who had been discovered in the depths of the draft's second round. He played six seasons in Phoenix before being traded to Philadelphia as part of a trade for Charles Barkley, then went to Utah one and a half seasons later in the trade for Jeff Malone. At the time, everybody hoped Hornacek could be a piece of the championship puzzle, and he wound up fitting in perfectly.

Hornacek's teammates all agreed on the importance of the stretch run. Malone said it was the first time in his career that every game was so important so late in the season, and Stockton said there was no facet of their game that the Jazz could not improve.

"We can execute better," he said. "We can shoot better. We can pass better. It's really wide open, what we have to get better at, and that's good. It's good that we're not at the end of our rope right now, saying we just need to hang on."

After clobbering Phoenix, 92–73, and watching Malone move past Elvin Hayes on the scoring list in their first home game after the big road trips, the Jazz were on their way to Dallas for one of the easier road games when they received a great boost in their fight for the home court edge.

The Sonics lost at Golden State.

Notwithstanding the Denver Nuggets, the Warriors had endured one of the most miserable seasons in recent NBA memory, thanks in part to the Sprewell incident and its fallout, and the team's 14-55 record only fueled the perception that the Warriors would be little more than chum for the bloodthirsty Sonics. But coaches talk all the time about the ability of any team in the NBA to beat any other team on any random night, and the Warriors happened to have their random night of invincibility just when the Sonics needed a victory most.

The previous few days had found the Jazz and Sonics locked in a tie for the best record in the West, and both had lost only seventeen games with about a dozen left. So when the Warriors came alive and stuck the Sonics with that unexpected eighteenth loss, they put the Jazz in the driver's seat for the regular-season championship. All the Jazz had to do was keep pace with the Sonics, and they would finish a game ahead in the standings.

"Golden State really hurt us," acknowledged the Sonics' Detlef Schrempf. "Now we have to make up some ground."

Nobody in Utah seemed to take too much notice of the Sonics' loss, however—or the Jazz's subsequent 99–90 win in Dallas that scootched them ahead of Seattle—because basketball fans there had temporarily turned their attention to the University of Utah, which had advanced to the NCAA Final Four for the first time since 1966.

Having upset defending national champion Arizona the week before, the Utes under Coach Rick Majerus had captured the imagination of just about everyone in Utah by the time they tipped off against North Carolina, at about the same time the Jazz were taking on the Los Angeles Lakers in the Delta Center on March 28 in the first of three big games that could virtually clinch the regular-season championship in the West. After the Lakers, the Jazz traveled to play the Sonics, then returned home to meet Portland; if they swept that trio, the Jazz could pretty much shift into neutral and cruise to the finish line with a solid grip on home court advantage.

Yet for such a big game, the Lakers' visit was practically an afterthought.

Local sports bars, restaurants, and hotels were packed with fans wanting to see the Utes play, and Governor Michael Leavitt even held a game-watching party of his own. Many of the fans who showed up at the Delta Center for the Lakers game wore their red Ute shirts, and some brought portable radios or TVs to keep up with both games at once. One couple sitting behind the Jazz bench waved giant red flags bearing the letter U.

Owing to the enormity of the collegiate event, the Jazz had tried to change the time of their game against the Lakers from 7:00 to 8:30, to allow fans to concentrate on the Ute game from start to finish before turning their attention to the Jazz. But because of obligations in their TV contract, the Lakers were unable to accommodate the change, even though Coach Del Harris would not have minded; he had been an assistant coach at the University of Utah and recommended Majerus for the head coaching job there nine years earlier.

The Jazz considered broadcasting the Ute game on the Jumbo-Tron screen while the Jazz and Lakers played below, but decided that would create too much of a distraction. The team decided to keep the Utes' score posted on the out-of-town scoreboard all night, rather than rotating it with other scores from around the NBA. That turned out to be distraction enough.

Only forty-four seconds into the game, Malone made a free throw that moved him past Moses Malone and into fourth place on the NBA's all-time scoring list with 27,410 points. But the crowd did not offer its standing ovation until two game-time minutes later, between two Shaquille O'Neal free throws, in part because they were listening to the Utes and in part because public address announcer Dan Roberts forgot to announce the milestone. Malone would finish the game with 31 points to bring his career total to 27,440.

Fans became only more engrossed in the news from San Antonio while the Jazz steadily wore down the Lakers.

O'Neal had gone crazy with 22 points in the first half, scoring over Foster, Ostertag, even Malone for a brief stretch, but the Jazz managed to get him in foul trouble and pick up the rebounding effort in the second. Utah led by 10 as the final seconds ticked off the third period, when Eisley swished a running thirty-five-footer for an 83–70 lead. The crowd went crazy in appreciation, as it did again only moments later when the scoreboard screen lit up with the final score of the Utes' game: Utah 65, North Carolina 59.

The Utes were headed to the national championship game, but the Jazz were not finished spanking the Lakers to celebrate the occasion.

As if their rivalry had not become heated enough in the wake of the previous season's playoff series, O'Neal's attack on Ostertag, and Malone's complaint about Kobe Bryant at the All-Star Game, Foster ensured another intense meeting when the teams played the season finale three weeks later. With 4:22 left in what had become a blowout, Foster threw down a fast-break dunk for a 96–81 Jazz lead. He was lost briefly amid the photographers and ballboys along the baseline, but uncoiled himself moments later and bounded back onto the court thumping his fists against his chest as if he'd just won the heavyweight championship. And then, with the beaten Lakers bench as his audience, Foster murderously yanked his thumb across his throat, sending Harris up the sideline in a technical-foul-seeking frenzy.

"Foster clearly had a taunting foul right in front of the referee and he didn't call it," said Harris. "The rules are clear-cut. . . . Besides, Greg Foster hasn't earned the right to taunt anyone. He's been lucky he's been able to stick with a team for a change. He's got no right to taunt anyone. Wait until he does something in this league."

Those were pretty strong words from a normally reserved coach, but that's just how much Foster's cheap theatrics incited the Lakers' fury. Harris did not get the taunting technical on Foster that he wanted, but earned a T himself for complaining to referees Joe DeRosa and Jim Kinsey.

As Stockton was making the free throw for a 97–81 Jazz lead, the Lakers' Rick Fox ambled over to Jerry Sloan and suggested he remove Foster from the game before Foster became a sudden addition to the injured list. Sloan sent in Keefe to finish for Foster.

The Jazz won the game, 106–91, but Sloan was less than thrilled at the motivation his wispy center had provided a team with more than enough talent to run the Jazz out of the gym if it ever harnessed it properly. The Jazz were built on the idea of keeping their composure and not giving opponents any extra motivation, and Sloan had tried to convince Foster to calm himself during the game. Foster, obviously, would not hear of it.

"I'm having fun," he said. "And nobody's going to stop me."

That's where the Lakers came in. Fox said the rivalry had grown "personal," and reminded the Jazz that the teams had one meeting left, while O'Neal suggested he had another Jazz center to put on his hit list for the season finale.

"If he goes up," O'Neal warned, "he'd better go up strong, because somebody might want to take his head off."

The Jazz's victory set up a showdown with the Sonics in Seattle two nights later that could decide the fate of the entire Western Conference playoff race, since the difference between winning and losing meant essentially a four-game swing in the standings for Utah. A victory would improve the Jazz's record to 54-17 and give them a two-game edge over the Sonics in the loss column, as well as clinch a 3–1 victory in the season series that would give the Jazz the tiebreaker edge if the teams finished with identical records. A loss, however, not only would square the Jazz and Sonics at eighteen losses apiece, it would give Seattle a 2–2 tie in the season series and force a season-ending tie to be broken according to the teams' records against the rest of the Western Conference; the Sonics would enjoy a two-game edge in that race.

"It's the biggest game of the year," said the Sonics' Vin Baker. And the Jazz blew it.

They did almost everything right, but they lost for the same reason they had lost one of their previous three meetings with the Sonics—three-point shooting.

While the Jazz made more free throws than the Sonics, shot a better percentage, grabbed more rebounds, and committed fewer turnovers, they could not stop the league's leading long-range attack. The Sonics made 12 three-pointers, including 2 back-to-back by Schrempf and Hersey Hawkins in the final two minutes that nullified an impressive Jazz rally and assured an end to Utah's five-game winning streak. With the loss, the Jazz extended to eleven their streak of games in which they had failed to overcome a deficit at the end of three periods.

Three-point shooting had been the key stat in all four meetings between the teams. In the two Seattle victories—by a combined 10 points—the Sonics made 20 of 41 three-point tries. In the two Jazz wins—by an average of 13 points—they made only 9 of 41. Certainly, that was being thrown into the notebook in case the teams met in the playoffs.

As statistically painful as the loss was, the Jazz refused to pack it in.

"It's too early," said Malone. "Everybody wants to concede something, but we still have eleven games to go. Nothing is over with. If we get to the end of the season and lose the home court advantage by one game, then I'll look back. But we still have basketball to play."

Notwithstanding the loss to the Sonics, the Jazz seemed to be starting to enjoy themselves more. They bounced back by beating the Portland Trail Blazers, 98–89, for the first time all season after three crushing defeats, and they whipped Denver, 97–75, for their twenty-fourth win in twenty-seven games since the All-Star break

188

before heading north to Canada for a game against the Vancouver Grizzlies.

The bus was late picking up the Jazz at the Vancouver airport, and the players and coaches were forced to wait almost twenty minutes at the curb while trainer Mike Shimensky, who handled travel arrangements on the road in addition to being one of the most respected trainers in the NBA, straightened out the problem. Almost anywhere else, the Jazz simply would have stayed on the plane until the bus pulled up on the tarmac to take them away, but because they had arrived in Canada, they'd had to walk through the airport in order to clear customs.

When a group of tourists noticed the players sitting outside on benches, they started to approach with pens and slips of paper. In a flash, Stockton took off.

Hands in his pockets and carrying the small blue duffel bag that he always carried on the road, he walked casually away from the crowd and his teammates and slipped almost unnoticed behind one of the eight large concrete pillars—marked No. 4—that divided the parking bays. But his teammates knew what he was doing.

After one man asked for and received Malone's autograph, he asked about Stockton. Russell jumped in and pointed down the sidewalk.

"He's right down there," Russell said. "Go ask him for his autograph."

The man started walking, hesitantly, and looked back intermittently as if for the players' approval. They did nothing but encourage him.

"Number four!" they shouted. "Number four!"

The words were still echoing off the concrete walls when, on the other side of the pillar, Stockton emerged, walking briskly across several lanes of traffic to the sidewalk on the other side of the street. He turned left and kept going, away from the airport, as the other players roared.

"John! John!" they shouted. "Come back, John!"

Even from across the street, the smile could be seen on Stockton's face.

For a while, then, Russell busied himself by shadow-boxing with his seated teammates, and flirting with a pair of young women who worked at the airport. He encouraged them to ask his teammates for autographs—with a crooked smile on his face, Malone shook his head amusedly and signed—and then spotted Stockton standing with the coaches near the doors to the airport. Stockton had walked a loop around some shrubbery that bordered a parking lot to wind up on the other side of where the players were waiting, and was trying to lose himself in the anonymity of the coaching staff.

Russell was giddy.

"There he is!" he told the women. "That's John Stockton! Go ask him for his autograph!"

Stockton heard Russell, but knew better than to look, and the women were caught between embarrassment and intrigue. They walked toward Stockton and the coaches, then stopped and looked back to see if they were doing right by Russell's instructions.

"Just ask him!" Russell hollered, laughing. "He won't say no."

Hesitantly, the women approached the group, and made their move by addressing first the nearest of the coaches, strength coach Mark McKown, instead of Stockton.

Russell turned to his teammates and rolled his eyes. "She's asking Mark for his autograph," he reported.

It wasn't but a moment, then, before the women returned to Russell and said something too quiet to be overheard.

"Busy?" said Russell, theatrically squinting to find Stockton among the group. "He's not busy! He's standing there with his hands in his pockets! He's not doing anything. Go ask!"

Behind Russell, the Jazz's bus finally pulled into its space, and Stockton saw it coming before anybody else. Without a word, he strode away from the coaches and behind the concrete pillars past Russell and the women and climbed onto the bus almost before it stopped moving.

"There he goes!" Russell yelped. "Get him! Ask him for his autograph!"

It was too late.

Stockton remained as elusive off the plane as he was off the dribble.

❖   ❖   ❖

The fight for the home court advantage was tightening up by the time the Jazz landed in Oakland two days later for what figured to be an easy victory over the Warriors. They had beaten Vancouver, 99–93, to improve to 56-18 and remain a game behind the 58-17 Bulls in the loss column, and then the Sonics lost to Phoenix and fell to 57-19. That opened a window of opportunity for the Jazz to seize a one-game lead in the loss column in the race for best record in the West, and Malone, for one, was not about to let it slip away.

The Bulls had pretty much wrapped up their victory over the Washington Wizards by the time the Jazz and Warriors took the court at the New Arena in Oakland on April 7, so Utah knew it had to win to avoid falling any further behind.

The Warriors were only 16-60, but had begun to play better in the weeks since trading for Jim Jackson, Clarence Weatherspoon, and Jason Caffey. (Remember the helpful victory over the Sonics?) They were more physical than they had been, and early in the game did not have too much trouble whipping the Jazz on the boards and grabbing a 6-point lead.

But Malone felt good from the start. He was comfortable. Everything he did felt smooth, and after a slow first quarter, he began to show it. He made 4 of 5 shots in the second period, and the Warriors were making it clear they weren't going to double-team him all that much. So by the time the Jazz came out of the locker room after halftime, trailing 50–44, Malone was ready to erupt.

Thirty-one seconds into the second half, he scored a layup for his 21st point. The Warriors stretched their lead to 10, but Malone hit again and made a layup after a foul by Weatherspoon. He hit a jump shot, then a layup, then 3 more free throws to cut the Golden State lead to 58–55. None of Malone's teammates had scored yet, and the Warriors were running out of defensive options. They tried the sturdy 6-7 Weatherspoon, they tried 6-8 muscleman Caffey, and they tried 6-11 shot-blocker Erick Dampier. They even tried Malone's former teammate, 7-1 center Felton Spencer, but the results were all the same.

Everything the Warriors tried failed miserably; either Malone scored when he touched the ball or he drew a foul and went to the free throw line. He was hot, and there wasn't anything the Warriors could do about it.

"It's hard to double-team when you can't even let him catch the ball without having a foul called," complained Warriors coach P. J. Carlesimo.

After three more Malone baskets, Hornacek finally interrupted the streak and drove for a layup that cut the Golden State lead to 65–63. Then, naturally, Malone drilled a sixteen-footer to tie it. He was 7 for 8 from the field in the period and 5 of 6 from the line for 19 points. He had 38 points for the game.

"There was a point where everybody was looking for him," said Russell. "He was on fire."

And he stayed that way.

The Jazz fell behind again by as many as 7 points in the wake of Malone's basket-per-minute binge, and trailed by 5 when Malone

The heart and soul of the Utah Jazz: John Stockton, Coach Jerry Sloan, and Karl Malone.

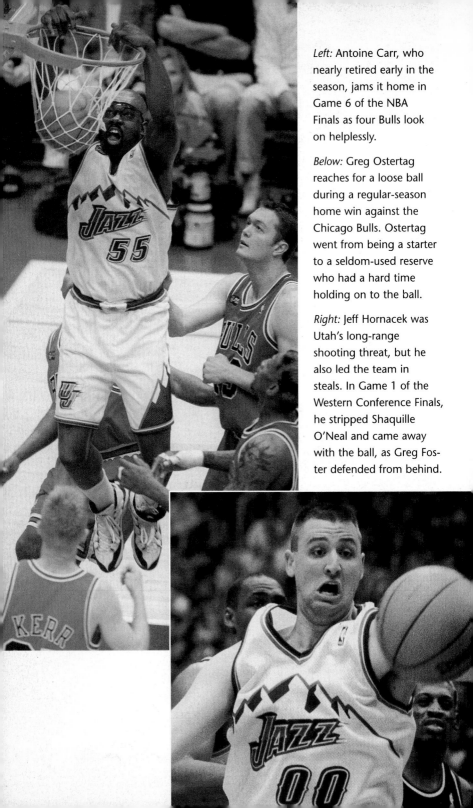

Left: Antoine Carr, who nearly retired early in the season, jams it home in Game 6 of the NBA Finals as four Bulls look on helplessly.

Below: Greg Ostertag reaches for a loose ball during a regular-season home win against the Chicago Bulls. Ostertag went from being a starter to a seldom-used reserve who had a hard time holding on to the ball.

Right: Jeff Hornacek was Utah's long-range shooting threat, but he also led the team in steals. In Game 1 of the Western Conference Finals, he stripped Shaquille O'Neal and came away with the ball, as Greg Foster defended from behind.

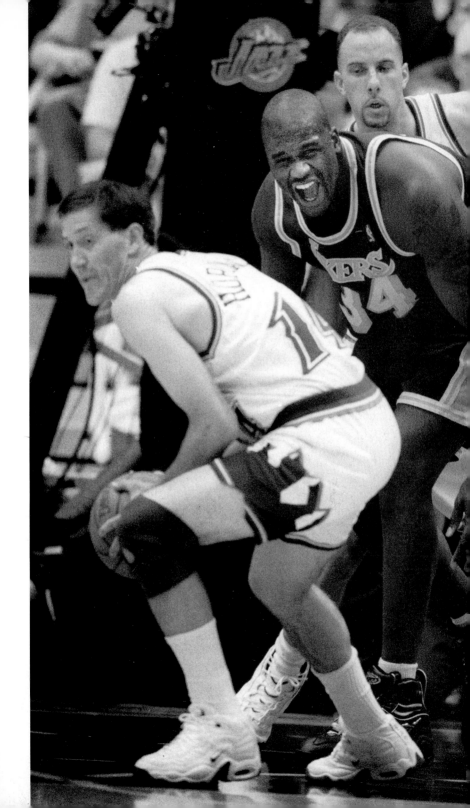

Above: Shandon Anderson reaches in on Scottie Pippen in Game 2 of the NBA Finals.

Below, left: Bryon Russell is embraced by Karl Malone near the end of Game 5 against the Houston Rockets. Russell struggled early in the season, but by the playoffs he was back in Malone's good graces.

Below, right: Howard Eisley garnered NBA experience and developed into one of the league's premier backup point guards after John Stockton went down with an injury.

Above: Poor matchups during the playoffs kept him on the bench, but Adam Keefe had the best season of his career, helping the Jazz win sixty-two games.

Below: Chris Morris spent most of his time at the end of the bench, but he shook off the failed trade for Rony Seikaly to make some solid contributions late in the season.

Left: Greg Foster did what teammate Greg Ostertag wouldn't do—stand up to Shaquille O'Neal of the Lakers.

Below: Stockton-to-Malone: a combination that is sure to land these two men in the Basketball Hall of Fame.

Above: Houston's Matt Maloney elbows John Stockton as the two fight for a rebound during the Utah-Houston first-round playoff matchup.

Right: The Mailman about to deliver: By the season's end, Malone would move into fourth place among the NBA's all-time scoring leaders.

Below: After all his hard work and hustle, Malone lost this ball to Michael Jordan in the last half-minute of Game 6—the play that resulted in Jordan's championship-winning shot.

drove over the Warriors' Donyell Marshall on his way to the hoop with fifty-three seconds left in the third quarter. Marshall had slid himself in Malone's way in hopes of drawing a charge, but instead got no call while Spencer came from behind and blocked Malone's shot.

To add injury to insult, Marshall suffered a fractured rib where Malone kneed him in the side, and lay on the floor as the Jazz grabbed the offensive rebound and reset their offense. Before Spencer fouled Malone to send him to the foul line again, Sloan argued with referee Ron Olesiak that Marshall—curled up nearly in the fetal position down on the right block—should have been called for an illegal defense. (Now *that's* tough.)

Marshall was out of the game by the time Malone made his two free throws, and was not around to watch Malone complete the best quarter in Jazz history by drilling a rushed, fallaway, one-handed twenty-six-footer off an inbounds pass to tie the game as time expired.

"It was just one of those nights," Malone said.

And D-Day was just one of those days. Malone made 8 of 11 shots in the third period and 8 of 10 free throws. He finished the quarter with 25 points, a pair of rebounds, and his second three-pointer of the season, while making all but one of his team's baskets. Only Hornacek infringed on the dominance with that layup, and he missed his other three shots while his teammates combined to take only two others.

The most amazing thing?

Malone was not finished.

He had 44 points, but the game remained tied and was twelve minutes from over. The Jazz still needed to win, too, in order to wedge the Sonics out of the way in the West and keep pace with the Bulls in the East.

So as the fourth quarter began, the Jazz's plan remained largely unchanged: get the ball to Malone. Some of his teammates began to do something other than watch, with Eisley and Russell scoring Utah's first two baskets of the quarter for a 3-point lead before Malone went at it again.

Two free throws after a foul by Spencer.

A driving layup past Dampier, and a free throw for a 3-point play.

Two more free throws on a foul by Todd Fuller.

In a span of two and a half minutes, Malone scored 7 straight points and put the Jazz ahead 83–79. He added another soft jumper after Stockton made a free throw and a three-pointer, and the Jazz led 89–81 with 6:43 remaining.

Weatherspoon, Spencer, and Dampier all had reentered the game in the moments before Malone's jump shot, and they began to pound away at the Jazz on the glass and take the ball strong to the basket. Spencer fouled out trying to guard Malone with 5:08 left, but then Caffey returned and helped Weatherspoon and Jackson complete a 12–4 Warriors run that tied the game at 93–93 with two minutes to go.

The Jazz looked like they might fold when Keefe fouled Caffey and Hornacek picked up a technical foul for arguing about it, which allowed the Warriors to make 3 straight free throws and go ahead 96–95. But Utah regained the lead on Russell's swooping layup with 1:20 left, and after exchanging several possessions, the Warriors had the ball in the final thirty seconds.

Guard Muggsy Bogues dribbled out front, working the shot clock a bit before passing to Jackson on the wing. Jackson threw the ball inside to Dampier, who zipped it back out top to Bogues when Stockton came to double-team. As the Jazz strained to rotate back—and with Malone having fallen after a bump by Dampier— Bogues saw a tiny opening and fired the ball back down toward Dampier. But the pass was too wild, and it flew just past Dampier's outstretched fingertips and out of bounds with only 16.4 seconds remaining.

That looked like it would kill the Warriors.

Bogues immediately fouled Stockton to stop the clock, and Stockton hit both free throws for a 99–96 lead with fourteen seconds left.

But Golden State called timeout, and set up afterward with men at each of the four corners of the key. Jackson bolted from the right block to the top of the circle, losing Russell against a pair of screens along the way. Nobody scrambled out to cover for Russell, and Jackson was left floating all alone on the left side to take the inbounds pass; he caught it, shot it, and buried a three-pointer to tie the game again, at 99–99.

"Where were we?" wondered Sloan.

Sloan did not believe in calling a timeout to allow the defense to set up, so he let the Jazz go with the final seconds of the most important game of the year vanishing from the clock.

With about five seconds left, Stockton passed to Malone at the top of the key. Malone pump-faked Dampier, who bit going left, and drove the right side of the lane. Weatherspoon stepped over to get in Malone's way, but Malone saw him in time and pulled up to float a nice, gentle runner toward the basket.

The guy had 54 points already.

Naturally, his shot hit nothing but net.

With 2.2 seconds left, the Jazz had a 101–99 lead that would turn into a victory as soon as Keefe intercepted the Warriors' attempt at a length-of-the-court inbounds pass. Yet Malone was typically self-effacing.

"It was a big game," he said with a shrug. "You have teammates saying, 'Take this game over,' but it wasn't about taking the game over. It was about staying in the offense and in what we were trying to do."

Malone's 56 points was the most by any player in the NBA all season and the fourth-most in the history of the Jazz, behind Pete Maravich's 68, Malone's 61, and Adrian Dantley's 57. But this was the biggest clutch performance of them all.

The final stat sheet looked like it might have covered a week's worth of games: 18 for 29 on field goals, 19 of 23 from the line, 9 rebounds, 4 blocked shots, and 2 assists. Malone became the oldest player in NBA history to score as many points as he had—the Bulls' Michael Jordan was five months older than Malone, but hadn't topped 50 since hanging 51 on the Knicks back in January —and surpassed 2,000 points for a record eleventh consecutive season.

"He carried us on his shoulders," said Foster. "Like he has done a million other times."

Kissed them on the cheek, too.

That's right: after driving past Dampier and scoring a baseline layup while being fouled for his 48th point and an 80–77 lead early in the fourth quarter, Malone first slapped hands and bumped chests with Eisley, then patted Foster on the head. As he did, he pulled Foster close and pecked him on the cheek. Reporters wondered later what had happened to the high-five.

"There's nothing wrong with that," Malone said. "It's part of the game. People look at our team and sometimes things happen and they don't think we get along and all that, but we have a close team. That's real close, and it's just one of those things that happened. That's just what I thought about doing at the time."

Had he not started quite so slowly—3 for 9 in the first quarter —Malone might have topped his 61-point performance, which is remembered as Malone's response to being snubbed as a starter for the 1990 All-Star Game. Fans had voted A. C. Green of the Los Angeles Lakers to start that year, and the myth has long persisted that an indignant Malone took the floor against the Bucks in the Jazz's next game intent on proving that he belonged in the starting lineup. In fact, though, the Jazz did not play the Bucks until two days after the All-Star voting was announced, and Malone's initial response to being relegated to a reserve role was a 26-point performance in a victory over the New York Knicks. No doubt he was still simmering when the Jazz met the Bucks, and the story fit his reputation for being driven by criticism or disrespect, as cemented earlier that season when Stockton had told him that fable about the Hornets' Armon Gilliam trashing him in a TV interview.

❖ ❖ ❖

Everything seemed to be going the Jazz's way when they played host to the San Antonio Spurs the night after the Golden State victory, with a chance to clinch their fifth Midwest Division championship.

The Spurs had fallen five games back, and their lack of a good small forward in the absence of the injured Sean Elliott was keeping them from becoming a top-quality team. They didn't have much of a backcourt, either, so they wound up throwing it to David Robinson or rookie Tim Duncan most of the time.

Robinson had always had a hard time against Malone, because Malone was so strong that he could keep Robinson from setting up too close to the basket. Malone also had a habit of being able to swat the ball out of Robinson's hands when Robinson tried to make his moves in the post.

It was Malone who had the ball, however, for the most horrifying play of the season.

Not three minutes had gone by at the Delta Center on April 8 when the Jazz grabbed a rebound off a Spurs miss and zipped the ball to Stockton to push it upcourt. As Stockton crossed into Spurs territory and passed the three-point line, he saw Malone setting up for a play the Jazz ran quite often, in which they try to get the ball to Malone quickly for a spin move to the basket before the defense has time to get set. From the top of the circle, Stockton passed it in.

Malone caught it, and turned inside fast as Robinson lunged to knock the ball away. As Malone spun and began to fling his arms skyward to convince the referees that he was shooting as he was fouled, his left elbow crashed hard into the side of Robinson's head. The blow hit the Spurs center so hard and so square that it knocked him unconscious immediately, and Robinson fell to the floor face first, as if he had been shot.

Whistles sounded, and the crowd fell silent.

Malone looked down at Robinson, and began to offer a hand before realizing Robinson was out cold. Malone stepped over him then and headed back to the bench while trainers rushed out to attend to Robinson, who lay motionless on his side.

More than a minute passed before Robinson awoke, and the Spurs by then were furious; not only had their star player been knocked out by what they perceived to be an intentional elbow, but he had been called for the foul on the play. Malone would be going to the free throw line once doctors scraped Robinson off the floor.

"We were pissed about it," said Duncan.

The Spurs finished the game without Robinson, who had to be taken to a hospital, and tried to exact revenge a couple of times. Once, Duncan shoved Malone without the referees seeing it, and Malone retaliated with a vicious elbow to the middle of Duncan's back that earned him a flagrant foul. Later, the Spurs' Will Perdue was called for a flagrant foul for his attempt to clothesline Malone on a breakaway layup, though it was Perdue who wound up on the floor after being unable to knock Malone over.

San Antonio lost, too, 98–88, and coach Gregg Popovich was so disgusted that he appeared after the game at the door to the Spurs' locker room only long enough to tell the media, "I could not be more proud of our basketball team tonight, thank you very much," and turn around and walk back inside. The rest of the Spurs spent most of the time in their postgame interviews demanding that Malone be suspended.

"It's a no-brainer," said guard Avery Johnson, who did not play because of a hip injury. "It's hard to tell what's in a person's heart, but it didn't look good. We don't appreciate that kind of basketball."

Meanwhile, Robinson had been taken to LDS Hospital in Salt Lake City, where he was reported in stable condition with a concussion after undergoing a CAT scan on his brain that revealed no neurological damage.

Malone seemed to be trying to hit Robinson somewhere in order to establish position and send an early-game message, but he swore he did not mean to hit him in the head. He and Robinson were generally regarded as teammates on the NBA's squad of good guys, after all, and had been teammates in the literal sense on two Olympic teams and several All-Star teams. They were friends, Malone said.

"It's just one of those things," he said. "When I turned, I hit him, but I didn't mean to.

"You never like to see that happen in anything," he added. "I was sorry that it happened to anybody. . . . The disappointing thing about it is that a couple of his teammates that weren't even playing out on the floor said I should be suspended and that I tried to do it."

After the game, Malone and Stockton stopped by LDS Hospital to visit Robinson. "My first thing was, 'I'm sorry,' " said Malone. And while Malone said Robinson accepted the apology, Robinson said later that he wasn't certain if Malone was sincere or whether he really had tried to hurt him.

"I don't know," he said.

Duncan vowed revenge. "You know that there is going to be a next time, and next time it comes, we're going to be ready for it."

The NBA suspended Malone one game and fined him $5,000, meaning his streak of 543 consecutive games would be broken against the Los Angeles Clippers. He was furious that the NBA penalized him for an incident that he said was merely accidental, and the Jazz deserved to be a little worried. But the Bulls unexpectedly lost at Cleveland the night after the Jazz beat the Spurs, falling to 59-18 and into a tie with the Jazz in the loss column; that meant that for the first time all season, the Jazz had their fate in their own hands. They could finish in a tie with the Bulls and still claim home court advantage, by virtue of their sweep of the season series. All the Jazz had to do was not fail any more often in the final six games than the Bulls or Sonics. However, they also needed to win with Malone out of the lineup for the first time in six seasons.

"None of us are real happy about it," said Foster. "Every game is so crucial now. We don't want to have any letdown."

Fortunately for the Jazz, it was the Clippers who were in town, and not anybody good. Not only was Los Angeles 16-62, it was playing without center Isaac Austin and Eric Piatkowski, who both were hurt. The result was a starting lineup that included Rodney Rogers, Lamond Murray, Lorenzen Wright, James Robinson, and Pooh Richardson, and might as well have played barefoot for all the effort they gave.

The Jazz built a 13-point lead by halftime on their way to a 126–109 victory, while the Sonics lost to the Spurs (who were playing without Robinson because of the concussion Malone gave him) and fell to 58-20, two games off the Jazz's 59-18 league-leading pace and probably out of the race for home court advantage.

As up and down as the season had been, though, there was no reason to think that things would smooth out now. By committing 20 turnovers and giving up 11 three-pointers in Malone's first game back from the suspension, the Jazz lost their next game, 110–103, at Minnesota, and fell back behind the Bulls. Now they had to win three of their last four—against Minnesota again, the Kings, Suns, and Lakers—and hope the Bulls lost one of their last four. Malone appeared at practice just as sullen and downcast as he had been during much of the early part of the season.

Was it the loss? Was it the pressure?

"What do you know about pressure?" he mumbled. "Try walking in Karl Malone's shoes for a day. For a month, for a year. Then maybe you'll know what pressure is."

Who knew what he was talking about?

Malone acknowledged he was still angry about his suspension, complaining that he learned of it "the same way you guys found out," meaning by fax, just like the media. Malone was mad that he was again shown a lack of respect by Jazz management when nobody from the front office called him to either tell him of the penalty or lend their support in the wake of it. He added that although he had long since sworn off the idea of writing a book, he might do it anyway, just to let people know about all the "bullshit" with which he had to cope.

Malone was steamed, too, that few of his teammates had done much defensive work in the loss at Minnesota, in which he scored 37 points.

"It's a tough time of year," he said. "You work your butt off to get in this spot, you just have to finish it off. . . . We just have to get our defensive attitude back and we'll be fine. A lot of teams are taking a lot of easy shots on us."

Carr, hopeful of returning the next night against Minnesota after missing thirteen games with the bum hamstring he suffered in the big loss to Charlotte, agreed.

"It's playoff time," he said, "and it's time to lay a little wood on people."

Out came the whuppin' stick.

Malone scored 44 points in the rematch with the Timberwolves, giving him a 42-point average over his last four games, and the

Jazz's 126–109 victory squared them again with the Bulls, who had lost to Indiana the night before and wound up losing to Detroit the night after. That set up a tense weekend full of possibility after the Jazz beat the Sacramento Kings, 99–96.

With two games left, the Jazz were 61-19. The Bulls and Sonics were 60-20. As long as the Jazz kept winning, they would have home court edge all the way through the NBA Finals. The Bulls needed to win twice and have the Jazz lose twice to get the best record, and the Sonics had to win twice but needed only a single Jazz loss to sneak past and steal the home court advantage. No wonder Sloan was antsy before the Jazz took on the Phoenix Suns at America West Arena.

The Suns were one of the hottest teams in the NBA, much as the Hornets had been back in March when they snapped the Jazz's eleven-game winning streak. They had won ten games in a row, fifteen straight on Friday nights like this one, and they needed one win in their final two games or one loss by San Antonio to clinch home court advantage in their first-round playoff series against the Spurs. Coach Danny Ainge did not want his players distracted, so he arranged to have the score of the Spurs' game against the Sonics kept off the arena scoreboard. That also kept the Jazz from seeing what Seattle was doing.

Somehow, though, the final score—89–87 for the Spurs—found its way onto the board as the Jazz headed into a timeout huddle, leading 84–82 with 7:36 left in the game.

Russell caught a glimpse of it and told his teammates. If they won now, they could enjoy home court advantage all the way until June.

Word of the victory spread quickly, but it made the task at hand no easier. The Jazz had entered the fourth quarter trailing 78–73, and had not won in a dozen tries all season when trailing after three quarters on the road. They had tied the game 82–82 on

Russell's three-pointer a minute before the revelatory timeout, and again at 90–90 with 4:47 to go.

The Jazz were not going to let this opportunity slip away. They led 96–92 before the Suns' Rex Chapman drilled a three-pointer, but then Stockton hit a basket and Russell scored 2 free throws for a 100–95 Jazz lead with 54.6 seconds left.

Not wanting to allow any more three-pointers, the Jazz allowed Chapman to drive for a layup to cut it to 100–97. But Ainge noticed Chapman straining to get back on defense on his tender left hamstring, which had forced him to miss the Suns' previous game against Denver. Chapman was the Suns' leading scorer with 25 points on 9-of-20 shooting, but once Malone hit a free throw to give Utah a 4-point cushion with 28.4 seconds to go, Ainge pulled Chapman from the game to make sure he would not be hurt so badly that he would have to miss the playoffs.

"As important as this game was to win," said Ainge, "Rex Chapman is a huge part of our success."

Without Chapman to shoot, then, the Suns turned to guard Jason Kidd. He cut the lead to 101–99 with a quick layup with 23.4 seconds left, before Russell finished his best game of the season—21 points on 7 of 9 shots and 6 of 7 free throws—by making a free throw to push it to 102–99.

The Suns had one last chance. They pushed the ball up the floor in the waning seconds, looking inside for a shot, but center Cliff Robinson couldn't handle a pass. Malone grabbed the ball as it bounded off Robinson's hands and passed ahead to Anderson, who dribbled out the final nine seconds near the midcourt stripe.

Finally, the Jazz had their prize.

"This is what we wanted all year," said Keefe. "We did a nice job all year of keeping our focus and not getting distracted. That's what separates us from other teams."

The Jazz had one more game in the regular season, against the

Lakers at The Forum, but even with all the bad blood and nasty words that they'd exchanged during the season, it didn't mean anything to them now. Might as well have been the St. Jude's Boys Choir Junior Varsity, for all the concern the Jazz had for the result. Fox managed a hard foul on Foster as payback for the throat-slashing gesture, and the Jazz lost, 102–98. But a happier bunch of basketball players could not have been found.

"We worked all season to get home court advantage," said Malone. "Now, we have to go out and take advantage of it."

CHAPTER

11

O h, well, this was just perfect.

Here the Jazz had gone and endured perhaps their most challenging season ever—fighting through John Stockton's knee injury and Karl Malone's bitterness and Greg Ostertag's inadequacy, overcoming a failed trade and a five-game deficit in the season's second half to earn home court advantage throughout the playoffs—and this was their reward?

The Houston Rockets?

Maybe just give the Jazz a root canal.

As the eighth seed, the Rockets were supposed to be a sacrificial gift for the Jazz, a foregone conclusion handed to the best team in the league because they had been unable to finish higher than 41-41. But that was just the theory; the reality, as the Jazz saw it, was that Utah had just been handed one of the toughest draws in the first round, on account of the Rockets' recent experience winning back-to-back championships, and their having eliminated the Jazz en route both times.

That happened in 1994 and 1995, the two years Michael Jordan missed while trying out for a baseball team. Several of the players who had been fitted with championship rings remained with the Rockets—most notably Hakeem Olajuwon, Clyde Drexler, and Mario Elie. The Jazz would rather have played the relatively pubescent Minnesota Timberwolves, who won their last two games while the Rockets lost their last two, grabbing the seventh seed in the playoffs and a date with the Pacific Division champion Seattle SuperSonics instead of the Jazz.

"These guys are not an eighth seed," Malone said of the Rockets.

Jerry Sloan agreed: "They're .500 because of injuries. They're not .500 because of talent. There's a big difference. And I've been beaten too many times not to know it."

The Jazz seemed to be bracing for the worst, even though they had owned the Rockets of late, winning their last six meetings. The streak started when the Jazz won Game 5 of the 1997 Western Conference finals in Utah before Stockton drilled the three-pointer in Game 6, and Utah had won all four meetings this season. Stockton had been as lethal in at least two of those games as he had been in the playoffs, scoring 24 points in the Jazz's 107–103 victory on Christmas Day, and posting 17 with 14 assists in their 106–100 win on March 1.

For all the Jazz's expressed fear of the Rockets and their championship experience, though, Houston hardly looked like a team prepared to rear its proud head one last, glorious time. The Rockets had lost nine of their last thirteen games in the regular season, and with victories over only Golden State, Sacramento, and Denver (twice), they hadn't beaten a winning team since March 25.

Charles Barkley had missed nine of the team's last fifteen games, first with a shoulder bruise and then a groin strain and hernia, and was saying he wasn't sure whether he would be able to play much against the Jazz.

Olajuwon had missed the first thirty-three games of the season recovering from surgery on his left knee, and came back looking like a shell of his former self by averaging only 16.4 points per game—under 20 for the first time in his fourteen-year career. Critics said the man once feared as the greatest center in the game was afraid for his surgically repaired knee, and was unwilling to put it too often through the stress of his legendary "Dream Shake" moves. Lately, Olajuwon's right knee had begun to bother him, he said, because he was overcompensating for his left.

And Drexler already had announced that he would retire from the NBA after the season to take a job as the head coach at his alma mater, the University of Houston. Drexler had missed twelve games himself with shoulder and groin problems, and many wondered if he would be willing to cut into his recruiting time by putting in the colossal effort that would be required for an extended playoff run.

The Rockets also had suffered morale problems. Barkley and Olajuwon had bickered over who should take which shots, Drexler was known as a locker room politician with an eye on the stat sheet, and Elie, Kevin Willis, and Matt Maloney all were aware that the team had tried to get rid of them in a trade for Damon Stoudamire that ultimately fell through. Still, the Jazz were not buying any of that as a reason to relax; what they saw was a team with a chip on its shoulder and a lot of legs that had been freshened while their owners sat out nursing injuries.

"This is the kind of team that can come up and bite you in the ass real quick," said Greg Foster. "So we're not ever going to take them lightly. If there's a rivalry in this division, this is it."

Yet it seemed at least a bit odd that the powerful Jazz, the ones supposedly so confident and so driven to win their first championship, would expend so much energy playing trembling victim to their first-round opponent. The Chicago Bulls never did that. Proclaim respect, sure; but the Jazz seemed to be tripping over themselves in their effort to tell everybody just how dangerous the first round was going to be, as if they themselves were not certain they could emerge from it.

And wouldn't you know it? Whether by honest appraisal or self-fulfilling prophecy, the Jazz had just as much trouble with the Rockets as they had anticipated.

Game 1 at the Delta Center was close early, before Houston's three-point touch started coming around. The Rockets had tried more three-pointers than any team in the NBA in the regular season, and they found their groove early in the second quarter. They led 29–25 when Brent Price, in to start the quarter in relief of Maloney, drilled a twenty-four-footer to stretch the lead to 7. Barely a minute later, notorious Jazz-killer Eddie Johnson buried a bomb to make the lead 10, and by the time Price hit his second and third threes over the next two minutes, the Jazz trailed 43–31 and looked lost.

"That came from transition," Sloan said later. "If you can't run the floor, if you can't get back defensively, then, yeah, that's going to happen."

It happened even worse after the Jazz cut the lead to 51–44 at halftime.

The Jazz had not made a basket in the final 3:24 of the first half, and came out in the second still afflicted. Jeff Hornacek committed a turnover. Stockton made a bad pass. Foster committed an offensive foul. And all the while, no shots were falling. The Jazz went another seven and a half minutes without putting the ball through the hoop on anything besides a free throw, and fell behind by 15 before Malone finally coaxed in a sixteen-footer with 4:26 left in the third quarter.

That seemed to be enough for a while.

Malone missed a layup. Hornacek missed a jumper. Howard Eisley blew a cheapie, and Malone was off again. Utah wound up making just 3 of 16 shots in the period and scoring 14 points, while the Rockets put up 28 and took a 79–58 lead that turned into an easy 103–90 victory.

The Jazz did not want to say they told you so.

"We just lost the home court advantage after playing eighty-two games," Sloan marveled in disbelief.

So much for the Rockets being slow and hurt and too caught up in other things to worry about the playoffs. Drexler had scored 22 points to lead their charge, and Olajuwon and Willis combined to destroy the Jazz's interior defense with 34 points and 27 rebounds between them. The Rockets wound up with 10 three-pointers, too, and left the Jazz to listen to the reminders that only once had a top-seeded team lost to the eighth seed. That was back in 1994, when the Sonics fell to the Denver Nuggets.

"They better put the damn brooms in the closet," crowed Elie. "We came to play."

The blame lay everywhere, and ankle-deep.

The Jazz couldn't do anything about Willis and Olajuwon, who seemed rejuvenated by the four days off before the series. They allowed the supposedly infirm Rockets to score 19 points on the fast break. And their attempt to stop Drexler with Hornacek had to be scrapped midway through the first period after the more athletic Drexler drove for three straight layups. Utah also complained about the officiating enough to make Sloan exhort his own players to just shut up and play.

"There's not a lot of excuses you can make," said Malone, who was 10 of 23 for a team-high 25 points and 11 rebounds. "If you want to, you can start looking for some, but . . . We're not going to change the whole scheme of things because they won this game. We've bounced back before and we'll bounce back now. I'm not going to jump off any buildings."

Certainly, part of the Jazz's strength was their ability to put failures behind them and stick with a philosophy that had proven itself over the past dozen years. Since Stockton returned from his knee surgery, in fact, the Jazz had not lost two games in a row; they could not afford to start bucking the trend now. Only four of seventy-one teams since 1984 had rebounded from a 2–0 deficit to win a first-round playoff series, and the Jazz were 2-10 all-time in series in which they lost the first game.

"The pressure really is on Utah," said Price.

And it was a lot of pressure. The Game 1 loss deflated the entire community in Salt Lake City, which seemed to have picked up its playoff enthusiasm right where it left off after the Finals the year before.

Women painted their fingernails in Jazz colors. Men wore Jazz baseball caps. T-shirts were everywhere. People were mowing "Go Jazz" into their lawns and painting Jazz logos on the pavement in the middle of their subdivisions. Everywhere you looked, cars flew miniature Jazz flags or posted placards bearing the "Feed the Fever" catchphrase in their windows. Three television stations were broadcasting live thirty-minute programs about the Jazz every night, and one of them drew hundreds of fans who wanted to be part of the "studio" audience out in front of the Delta Center.

Not surprisingly, the excitement was suddenly muted once the Rockets finished with the Jazz in Game 1, almost as if a pall had fallen over the city. Given their team's history of playoff failure, fans seemed to collectively wince at the thought that tragedy might strike down the Jazz during what was supposed to be their finest hour.

"I'm going from Genesis to Revelation," said Rev. Jerry Lewis, the Jazz's team chaplain, in the hours before Game 2. "And I'm not leaving anything out."

It must have worked, because Utah's prayers were answered.

The Jazz came out with a whole new attitude in Game 2, taking the ball strong to the hoop, playing aggressive defense, and not worrying about what the referees were doing. That turned out to be the Rockets' job.

Houston grew frustrated early as it tried to match Utah push for push and hard foul for hard foul, because the officials—from the Rockets' perspective, at least—seemed to be whistling everything the Rockets did wrong and none of the Jazz infractions. By the end of the first quarter, Maloney, Price, Drexler, and Elie all had two fouls, and the Jazz, who had five fouls altogether, led 29–19.

The Rockets' irritation boiled over early. Coach Rudy Tomjanovich picked up a technical foul for complaining about Maloney's second foul against Stockton not even five minutes into the game. Two minutes later, Drexler earned his second personal and a technical for griping about it, and had to be practically dragged off the floor by Willis so he didn't add another T and get thrown out.

"They weren't saying anything in the first game," said Bryon Russell. "I don't know why they're complaining, acting like sissies."

The Rockets cut the Jazz lead to 40–39 in the second quarter, but Stockton took over early in the third. He scored on a fast break layup that developed after Malone—all but absent to that point, with 9 points on 3-of-11 shooting—made a steal, then drove to the basket twice more in the next four minutes. After Hornacek and Drexler nearly got into a fight over a Hornacek foul, Stockton drained a jumper for a 59–47 lead that did nothing but grow. It reached 22 points, and all the Rockets fighting in the world couldn't do anything about it.

Not that Houston didn't try, however.

The game was out of the Rockets' control with 4:50 left, and they still were seething over the flurry of calls that had buried them early in the game. Olajuwon had been ejected for back-to-back technicals not a minute before, and Barkley, with five personals, apparently decided he was ready to call it a day, too.

So when Stockton ran to the middle of the key to set a screen on Barkley, Barkley simply rammed out his right arm and slammed Stockton square in the chest. Then, showing a callous arrogance that turned Sloan's stomach, Barkley immediately raised his hand in a mocking admission that the foul was on him, and headed toward the Rockets' bench while Stockton pushed him from behind.

"That was a good one, don't you think?" Barkley said after the Jazz put away their 105–90 victory.

Barkley already was a target of scorn around the Delta Center for his attempt during Game 1 to fight with a fan behind the Rockets' bench, a move that, combined with his swearing and obscene gestures, cost him a $10,000 fine from the NBA. The Jazz were even more angry because it was Barkley who, in the Western Conference finals the previous season, plowed over Stockton as he set a screen, then claimed he was trying to injure the Jazz star in retaliation for setting illegal screens.

"Stockton was working hard out there, and when Barkley tried to take him out like he did . . . I don't know," said Sloan, straining to contain his rage. "So help me, I think it's ridiculous. It's still a game of basketball. Unfortunately, the sideshows get more important than the game itself. I respect this game. I don't respect the sideshows. It just makes me want to throw up."

Most importantly, though, the Jazz had evened the series as it headed to Houston by keeping the Rockets from doing well all the things they did in Game 1, while getting more characteristic performances from their own players.

Malone wound up with 29 points and 10 rebounds, while Stockton had 17 points, 10 assists, and 4 steals and went back to making Maloney look like a sixth-grader trying out for the varsity. Hornacek, Russell, and Shandon Anderson all had good games, and even Ostertag played big, grabbing 11 rebounds in 26 minutes. Congratulations, however, remained far in the future.

"All we really accomplished tonight was stopping the bleeding," said Stockton. "Now, the work starts. We more than have our hands full. It's an uphill battle for us."

Because the Jazz had lost Game 1 at home, they would be forced to win at least one of the two games on the road in order to win the series. And with three days before Game 3 at the Compaq Center in Houston, the aging Rockets would have ample time to rest up for the effort at winning twice and avoiding a return trip to Utah for Game 5. That time off figured to be a big deal, since the Rockets had seven players who were thirty-four or older (compared to four for the Jazz), and it became a bigger deal when Stockton injured his back in practice two days before Game 3.

Nobody said anything about it at the time, especially not Stockton, who had played much of the 1996 playoffs with a hyperextended elbow that he refused to acknowledge even after team doctors had. The Jazz almost never mentioned injuries; they believed that if you dressed for the game, you played. Period. It took the notations of journalists and TV analysts to inform fans that Malone, for instance, had played all year with a damaged tendon in the middle finger of his shooting hand that would require surgery after the season. Or that Hornacek was constantly battling sore knees and back spasms. Or that Adam Keefe's arches had bothered him so badly during the second half of the season that he put special magnets in his shoes, hoping they would speed the healing process the way Japanese baseball pitchers claimed they did.

But Stockton's discomfort turned out to be every bit as detrimental to the Jazz in Game 3 as was Olajuwon's rejuvenation. While Stockton did score 15 points, he made only 6 of 14 shots and committed 5 turnovers while handing out just 6 assists, and allowed Maloney to score 11 points—more than he had in the first two games combined. The difference might not have been so noticeable, though, had it not been for the renewed futility of the Jazz's men in the middle.

While they had not been able to stop Olajuwon in the first two games, Ostertag, Foster, and Antoine Carr had done a respectable job of giving the Jazz some production when each was in the game. Foster had 15 points and 6 rebounds in the two games, Carr hit 4 of 8 shots in the first one, and Ostertag grabbed those 11 rebounds in Game 2.

But Foster picked up 2 fouls in the first eighty-one seconds of Game 3 and wound up contributing nothing in only three minutes. Carr had 2 points and 4 boards in twelve minutes, and Ostertag—despite playing thirty-seven minutes—could score only 4 points and get 4 boards.

Meantime, Olajuwon killed the Jazz with 28 points and 12 rebounds in Game 3, and the Rockets took a 2–1 series lead with an 89–85 victory.

"I don't know if we were intimidated, I don't know what happened," said Sloan. "We played like we've never played on the same team with each other."

The Jazz had actually led 86–85, but Ostertag fouled Olajuwon with 37.6 seconds left and Olajuwon made 2 free throws to take the lead before Drexler hit 2 more free throws for a 3-point lead. Malone tried to tie the game with a three-pointer with ten seconds left but missed, and Barkley stole the Jazz inbounds pass after one more free throw to allow panic a seat at the Utah table.

One more loss, and the resilient Jazz would be finished yet again.

"When this series started," said Barkley, "they were the hunter and we were the rabbit. Now, the rabbit's got the gun. Let's see what happens. Let's see how the hunter reacts."

The hunter reacted with predictable bewilderment.

Sounding like he was back in the preseason, Sloan bemoaned the Jazz's willingness to take the Rockets one-on-one rather than play team basketball. Foster said the Rockets' outside shooting was hurting the Jazz. Hornacek, while noting the bad timing, said the team simply wasn't clicking like it had been at the end of the regular season. And while the Jazz largely tried to maintain their stoic demeanor and profess their usual businesslike approach to Game 4—in many cases reminding the media about how the Rockets were not a true eighth seed—Russell broke ranks and said what many fans had begun thinking. After scoring 19 points off the bench in a futile Game 3 effort, Russell threw down a gauntlet for his teammates.

"It's all about heart, if you've got heart," he said. "We're playing the eight seed and the eight seed is kicking our butt. We have to play with a lot more heart. . . . It was an easy chance. We could have swept. But we didn't, and now we're down 2–1. We're making it tough for ourselves."

Russell might well have been talking about Malone, who had not enjoyed a particularly good series. He made only 24 of 58 shots in the first three games, and was nowhere to be found in the formative stages of Game 2, scoring 18 of his 29 points once the Jazz had stormed to a double-digit lead. Some critics suggested he was not using his strength enough to go inside, and settling instead for too many outside shots. In the Game 3 loss, Malone was only 6 of 16 with 5 turnovers—not the sort of performance the Jazz needed out of their superstar.

"The shots were there," he said. "You just keep trying. I'm looking to get it done. We realize there is no tomorrow if we don't win. It's a matter of convincing ourselves. It's a matter of now."

Oddly, he added later, "If we lose, it's not the end of the world."

It would be close, though, and the Jazz could sense it. They had yet to play at the level that helped them win fourteen of their last seventeen games of the regular season, Stockton was aching, and the Rockets had all the confidence in the world.

"If you come out and play like we did in Game 1, and you come out and put that kind of effort into the game, you don't deserve to win, whether you're the first seed or whatever," said Sloan. "I would like to say that we did, but when you don't play the game the way you're supposed to—as a team—and the way you've played all year long, and you change your whole philosophy around, I don't think we can beat anybody.

"We have to stick to what made us a pretty decent team, and that's play basketball together. Set screens for each other and help each other defensively. I don't really think we've done that, except for maybe four or five quarters in the whole series."

Things grew worse before they improved.

The Jazz started horribly in Game 4, and right away it was apparent that Sloan probably should have shaken up his starting lineup as he had considered doing. Instead, the Jazz scored but 2 baskets in the first two minutes, and watched as Olajuwon put Houston ahead 6–4 with his second basket over Foster.

After two more minutes of scoreless basketball, Sloan sent in Ostertag as a replacement for Foster, and Olajuwon scored over him within seconds. Then Matt Bullard hit a three. Drexler took a full-court pass from Olajuwon and beat Eisley, who had just come in, with a spin move to the basket that gave the Rockets a 13–4 lead and what looked like enough momentum to start shoveling dirt on the Jazz coffin.

"They were blowing us away," said Sloan. "I don't know what we were doing."

Playing like they all had tee times in the morning (although Malone thinks golf is a waste of good pastureland), the Jazz had never been so ripe to be picked. Barkley entered the game for Olajuwon, and scored over Malone to answer the Jazz's first basket in seven minutes, a Russell dunk over Bullard. Then Barkley stole the ball from a slipping Eisley and ran the length of the court for a layup, and Drexler made 4 straight free throws.

By the time the first quarter was over, the Jazz had made just 4 of 16 shots and tied the record for the fewest points scored against the Rockets in a playoff quarter with 10. They trailed by 11 and, judging by the looks on their faces on their way back to the bench at the quarter break, had conceded the game and the season and all their hopes of finally winning a championship. Their sagging shoulders all said the same thing: "We quit."

But there was a savior. Two, actually.

Russell had already made a couple of good plays when Anderson entered the game at the start of the second quarter like he always did, in place of Hornacek. And Anderson must not have been paying attention enough to know that the Jazz had given up and already were preparing their we-gave-it-our-best-shot speeches. Promptly, he scored a layup to cut the lead to 21–12. Then Barkley scored, and Anderson answered. Johnson hit a three for Houston. Then Anderson stole the ball from Barkley and was fouled, and he hit 2 free throws. Then Barkley scored again. The Jazz were not making up much ground—the Houston lead was 28–16 at that point—but they were finally starting to make some baskets and find a rhythm and feel the tide turn. Barkley was killing them, but with their entire backup unit in, the Jazz were gaining some long-lost momentum.

"We needed it," said Anderson.

For all the inspiration Anderson provided, however, the Jazz might not have been able to get back into the game had what happened next not happened at all.

Within seconds of an Eisley layup that cut the Jazz lead to 10, Barkley leapt to grab a rebound but came down grabbing his arm instead, and grimacing in pain. At first, it looked as if Barkley might have aggravated his hernia, because he was gripping his right arm against his body in a way that put his hand near his groin. But it turned out that Carr had somehow elbowed Barkley in the triceps in a freak way that actually tore the muscle. Barkley had to leave the game and have his injury treated, and right away Russell drilled a three-pointer. Suddenly, the Jazz were on the move.

"Once we lost Charles," said Elie, "we lost a big part of the team."

Barkley tried twice to return to the game with a bandage protecting the torn muscle, once later in the second period and once late in the third; he didn't last very long either time, though, and behind the inspiration of Anderson and Russell, the Jazz just kept catching up.

By halftime, they had cut the Houston lead to 42–36, and fought back to take a 57–56 lead on a pair of Malone free throws just as Barkley was starting his second comeback attempt. But Barkley couldn't even catch the ball; he had to stop passes with his left hand and balance the ball against his body just to hang on to it, and he lasted only twenty-one seconds before Tomjanovich took him out, never to return.

From there it was all Jazz, even though they had to finish without Hornacek and Russell, who crashed into one another in the final minute of the third quarter and exchanged stitch-requiring cuts around the eyes.

After a 59–59 tie, Utah embarked on a 34–10 scoring run that turned the game into a blowout and turned the Jazz back from the edge of oblivion. Malone and Anderson erupted, combining for 19 points in the fourth quarter, by which time Olajuwon was exhausted after carrying the Rockets with 27 points in the first three quarters. He missed all 4 shots he tried in the final period, and his teammates made only 3 of their 13. The Jazz held the Rockets to a Houston-record-low 29 points in the second half, and with 15 points apiece, Anderson and Russell could claim all the credit they wanted for the 93–71 victory.

"Those guys were terrific," said Sloan.

As unwilling as he was to use injuries as an excuse for losing, Malone was disgusted to see the Jazz's victory portrayed as a product of Barkley's injury, the veracity of the description notwithstanding. He hated hearing that the Rockets would have won if only

Barkley had not been hurt. Yet Malone could take plenty of solace in the feeling that the Rockets, now, were pretty much spent.

Barkley was out for the rest of the series, Willis and Drexler had been nowhere in Game 4, and Olajuwon was not going to get much rest with only one day off before Game 5. What's more, the Jazz had administered the kind of whipping that tended to inspire surrender rather than resolve, coming as it did in front of the whippee's home crowd and before a long trip back to Utah for the deciding game.

Now, said Eisley, "it swings back in our favor."

Indeed, the hunter had his gun back.

Just to be sure, Sloan made the move he had considered for Game 4, replacing Keefe in the starting lineup with Russell, which forced the Rockets to start Elie instead of Bullard and further deplete the help they could expect from their bench. Russell responded to the promotion by scoring 10 points and grabbing 8 rebounds in a team-high forty-five minutes of Game 5, and he provided the final knell to the Rockets' hopes of an upset.

The game had gone back and forth through the first three quarters, with the Jazz going ahead by 12 and then allowing 11 straight Rockets points, and then building the bulge back up to 61–54 at the beginning of the fourth period. The Rockets closed the gap again, cutting the Jazz lead to 3 on Johnson's jumper with 8:17 to go, but that was as close as they would come.

On the next possession, Ostertag rebounded Russell's missed dunk for a dunk of his own. Seconds later, Russell buried a three-pointer, and that was that.

Ostertag redeemed himself to a small degree by blocking a playoff-record 5 shots in the final period to keep the Rockets from mounting another challenge, and the Jazz won, 84–70, to hand the Rockets their first defeat in eighteen playoff series in which they had won the first game.

Finally, the Jazz had shaken loose of the Rockets and now, free of the emotional burden of potential playoff infamy, appeared poised to get their heads right and play the rest of the playoffs the way they had played the second half of the regular season—like a bulldozer.

"We did what we needed to do in this series," said Malone. "And that's the important thing."

No question about that. The championship dream was still alive.

CHAPTER

12

Fresh off scoring 31 points in the series-clinching victory over the Houston Rockets, Karl Malone sat at a podium, dripping sweat and drinking a bottle of water and waiting for the first question from the assembled media.

"You've got San Antonio next—" a reporter began.

Malone interrupted.

"Let me clear that right now," he said. "I don't want to talk— the only thing I want to talk about San Antonio—and I know where you're going with that question—I'm not even going to get caught up in what you guys are going to say. That's all I'm going to say about it. I'm going to play my game. I'm not going to stop playing physical, and I'm not going to listen to all the bullshit that's going to be said. I'm going to play basketball, and that's my job. And I will not talk about it anymore, so you guys put that on the AT. The A . . . A . . . whatever the hell it is. What is that?"

Malone looked to the side of the podium, at Kim Turner, the Jazz's director of media relations, for help.

"The AP wire?" Turner asked.

"The wire," Malone confirmed. "You put that on the wire. I don't want to talk about it no more. I almost said AT&T. Shit."

Malone smiled and laughed, and the reporters crowding the interview room in the Delta Center laughed with him. But for a guy who didn't want to talk about "it," Malone certainly did a lot of talking.

"That was my question," the reporter said. "I wanted to know how you—"

"Well," said Malone, interrupting again, "I'm done talking. I'm done talking about it. I'm going to play my game. I'm not going to stop playing physical. I'm not going to get caught up in all the stuff that's said, or done. Karl Malone has a job to do. I have one goal. I have one goal in mind. I'm not going to take anything. I'm going to protect myself. I'm going into this series to play basketball, and that's the most important thing to me and I'm not going to talk about that answer anymore."

Nobody had actually specified what it was that Malone was not talking about, but everybody knew: his elbow, and its relation to David Robinson's head. The Spurs still believed Malone slammed Robinson on purpose, and many observers were anticipating trouble after the way the Spurs had talked back in April.

"It's time for payback," Tim Duncan said then. "That's the only thing we can say about that. If it gets to the playoffs and we're up against them, it's going to be a whole different ball game."

And here it was, the playoffs.

Different ball game time.

But the notion that the Spurs would wind up with anything other than a second—if less literal—headache seemed almost ludicrous as the series approached. Certainly, that was the general feeling around Utah, where fans were reviving their playoff passions in the wake of the Jazz's first-round victory over Houston. Some might have viewed the onerous victory over the Rockets as a harbinger of more trouble, but most observers seemed to think the Jazz had played their one bad series, and were ready to relax and return to their role as the NBA's steady assassin.

What's more, the Spurs simply did not seem all that fearsome.

Yes, Robinson had his All-Star wits about him again, and fellow 7-footer Duncan had been voted the nearly unanimous Rookie of the Year for displaying an amazing grace and maturity for a man only twenty-two years old. But after that, who was there?

Sean Elliott? He was hurt.

Avery Johnson? The point guard had had a great series in the Spurs' first-round triumph over the Phoenix Suns, but was more typically a 10-point scorer who shot from outside like he was trying to stick tennis balls in a chain-link fence.

Vinny Del Negro? Jaren Jackson? Will Perdue?

Fans already were looking forward to the Western Conference finals, and paying attention to the series between the Los Angeles Lakers and Seattle SuperSonics to see which team would meet the Jazz for the right to go to the NBA Finals.

Even San Antonio coach Gregg Popovich suffered from light regard around the league, having used his position as the general manager to fire coach Bob Hill early in the team's disastrous 1996–97 season and seize the job for himself. Popovich then presided over the rest of the team's injury-ravaged 20-62 season, before having the good fortune to land the number one draft pick and use it on Duncan, who helped the Spurs finish 56-26 and make the biggest season-to-season turnaround in NBA history.

Part of the Spurs' image problem was the same one that had afflicted the Jazz for so many years: the Spurs had never won an NBA championship, or even made it to the Finals, and bowed quietly out of the playoffs more often than they raised a ruckus in the later rounds.

Their reputation as a "soft" team was not helped, either, by their response to Malone's elbow back in April. Though Perdue had tried to clothesline Malone in retaliation later in that game, none of the Spurs had sprung into Malone's face the moment Robinson went down, and an awful lot of the postgame revenge talk came from Elliott and Johnson, both of whom were out hurt at the time.

The Jazz did have two serious problems on their hands in Robinson and Duncan. For all the faults of their teammates, the two big men were among the best in the league, and were especially dangerous against a team as weak in the middle as the Jazz. Neither Greg Ostertag nor Antoine Carr was quick enough to guard either of the Spurs' stars effectively, leaving Foster as the man the Jazz would use primarily against Duncan. The task of guarding Robinson fell naturally to Malone, who historically handled him just fine, and who might have been (ahem) in Robinson's head to some degree anyway.

Figuring his team could endure the routinely impressive performances of the Spurs' twin towers—who combined to average more than 40 points and 25 rebounds against the Suns—as long as none of their teammates erupted, Sloan plotted a strategy in which the Jazz's smaller players would seldom leave their men on defense to go help double-team.

That's what had doomed the Suns in the first round: because they had no true big men, the Suns were forced to double-down a lot in an effort to reasonably defend Robinson and Duncan in the post. But that left open guys like Johnson, who made a killing by using his devastating quickness to take. passes on the perimeter and dash to the basket past Suns defenders still straining to recover from the double-team. Johnson had averaged a team-high 20.5 points in the series.

Since the Spurs were trying to create even more mismatches by putting a third 7-footer, Perdue, on the floor, coach Jerry Sloan put Adam Keefe back into the Jazz's starting lineup instead of forcing

Bryon Russell to try to guard a man so much bigger than him. All of the Utah strategies worked just fine, as a matter of fact, for the first quarter of Game 1 of the best-of-seven series at the Delta Center.

Then the second quarter began.

The Jazz had opened a 26–16 lead, but Foster needed a break and Sloan sent in Carr to guard Duncan. Within 34 seconds, Duncan had induced two fouls on Carr, and Sloan had to send in Ostertag to see what he could do about the rookie. Another ninety seconds later, Ostertag had his second foul, and Duncan proceeded to score over him at one end of the court and block 2 of his shots on the same possession at the other.

"That guy's unbelievable," said Jeff Hornacek.

Utah forged a 52–46 lead at halftime, but most of that had been built when the Spurs managed only 7 baskets and 16 points in the first period. By the time the third quarter began, Robinson and Duncan had begun to find their grooves, and Johnson had not missed in 5 tries at the basket. The three of them had 35 of the Spurs' points.

Malone and John Stockton were similarly dominant for the Jazz, with 27 points between them, and Malone asserted himself enough in the third quarter to make Robinson miss all seven shots he tried. The Spurs fell behind by 8 points, and figured to be finished in the face of the Jazz's hostile crowd.

But they weren't. Not with Duncan around.

He already had supplanted Robinson as the team's go-to guy on offense, but he might have given new meaning to the term in the final twelve minutes of Game 1. He scored the Spurs' first 3 baskets of the quarter to trim that 8-point lead to 70–66, then threw down a dunk and made 4 straight free throws to cut it to 4 again with about five and a half minutes left. By then, the Spurs could see he was on fire—3 for 4 in the quarter with 27 points overall— and that none of the Jazz could stop him. They threw Duncan the ball at every opportunity.

He made a thirteen-foot jump shot to cut the Jazz lead to 79–76.

He drilled a sixteen-footer to make it 79–78.

Then, after Malone's running jumper put Utah in front 81–80, Duncan scored a sweet little ten-foot jump-hook that gave the Spurs an 82–81 lead with 1:23 remaining. It was their first edge since the opening minutes of the game.

"He's better than everybody told us he was," said Sloan.

Malone put the Jazz back in front with another running jumper with 1:12 to go, before the teams settled into a sort of late-game anxiety attack that manifested itself into one missed scoring opportunity after another.

Robinson was called for an offensive foul, but Foster could not make a short jumper at the other end. Chuck Person grabbed the rebound with thirty-seven seconds left, but threw up a wild three-point try five seconds later that missed.

Person was trying to set up a two-for-one opportunity for the Spurs, firing quickly in hopes of giving San Antonio the lead and at the same time preventing the Jazz from exhausting the clock on one final possession. But failing to wait just a couple more seconds to get the ball to Duncan was criminal; the Spurs were so eager to steal the first game of the series on the road that they momentarily lost their heads, just as the Jazz were terrifying themselves with the thought that they might blow their home court advantage for the second series in a row.

The Jazz had the ball, then, with twenty-eight seconds left. Wanting not only to score but to give the Spurs as little time as possible with which to work, the Jazz worked the ball around and worked it around and worked it around, until only single digits showed on the game clock. Then Malone squared up from nearly twenty feet and let one fly just as the shot clock buzzer sounded.

He missed.

The air seemed to get sucked right out of the arena as Person rebounded and called timeout for the Spurs. The clock showed 4.6 seconds. That was plenty of time to get off a shot, and everybody in the building knew who the Spurs wanted to take it. Hell, the guy had hardly missed all night.

Duncan was 13 of 21, a remarkable 6 of 8 in the fourth quarter, and had 33 points to go with 10 rebounds. As the teams emerged from their timeout huddles, thousands of eyes stayed focused on the rookie from Wake Forest, to see where he would set up and how the Spurs would try to get him the ball against a Jazz defense certainly aware of the intention.

"I knew the ball was coming to him," said Foster.

Yet there was little Foster could do, since the last thing he needed to do was commit a foul and put Duncan on the line with the chance to win the game. So as the pass came in to Duncan near the top of the key and Duncan began to pivot, Foster simply thrust his arms straight up above his head, wordlessly telling the refs, "No foul, see?" and hoping somehow to impede the vision or comfort of a man already an inch taller, and leaping for further advantage.

Time was nearly gone.

Duncan finished his leaping turnaround, and with Foster still standing there, reaching for the sky, he flicked the ball gently toward the rim as the clock raced toward zero. Eyes tracked the ball's path. Players held each other in a nervous push for rebounding position. And fans held their breath as the ball came down toward its target.

For the first time the whole game, it seemed, Duncan's aim was off.

His shot bounced harmlessly off the rim, and Russell corraled the rebound as time expired. It took a moment to register, the Jazz's 83–82 victory, as if nobody could quite believe they'd escaped. But they had, and, in spite of a performance that portended trouble in the future, avoided the doubts that would have accompanied another series-opening loss at home.

"We had moments of everything," said Stockton, who finished with 15 points and 8 assists and whose back had improved a good deal since the Rockets series. "We had moments when we executed very well, moments when we defended very well. The effort was good, for the most part. But until I can say all those things for forty-eight minutes, we're in trouble."

That already was clear, compliments of Mr. Duncan.

Obviously, the Jazz had nobody who could guard him, except perhaps Malone, and pulling him off Robinson to guard Duncan might be like choosing the firing squad over the guillotine. (Robinson had 16 points and 16 rebounds in Game 1 as it was.) Considering the Spurs had received precious little help from anybody outside Duncan, Robinson, and Johnson, and Popovich made it clear he needed more than three points' worth of contribution from his bench players, they could not have been more pleased to have had the ball and a chance to win in the playoffs on the Jazz's home floor. Opportunities like that are typically hard to come by.

"If we can do this in four trips into this place," said Robinson, "we'll win one of them."

Especially if the Jazz kept up their end of the deal. By scoring only 31 points in the second half of Game 1 and shooting barely 40 percent for the game, they showed they hadn't quite shaken the malaise that had plagued them against the Rockets. They had struggled to get off good shots against the taller Spurs, been killed in the rebounding battle, and shot only 16 free throws to the Spurs' 31.

They wore their disappointment plainly, too, with Sloan talking about how the victory felt more like a defeat because the Jazz had blown a 9-point lead in the final seven minutes to, essentially, one guy.

"I thought we were getting beat, the game I was looking at," agreed Foster. "But we made a lot of hustle plays that allowed us to stay in it. Other than that, we got our butts kicked in every aspect but the scoreboard. Another ugly win."

The dramatic finish had erased practically all memory of Malone's elbow and its supposed sinister intentions, but Robinson did not need long to start pointing another finger at his adversary. The next day at practice, Robinson complained that the referees let Malone get away with kicking.

"That's one of the most dangerous things a guy can do," he said, "and I have a problem with that. I've been kicked before, and I don't like it."

Robinson's complaint stemmed from one play in particular in Game 1, when Malone hit his running jumper with 1:12 left that turned out to be the game-winner. The Jazz found the entire discourse laughable, but the Spurs clearly were trying to plant a thought in the minds of the officials so they might incite a favorable call when they needed one most. Whether such tactics really ever worked was hard to gauge, but the Spurs certainly seemed to try as the final minute was ticking off a tight, tense Game 2 at the Delta Center.

The game was tied 96–96 before Duncan scored his 8th point of the fourth quarter and 24th of the game over Carr with thirty seconds left for a two-point Spurs lead.

On the next Jazz possession, Malone was jockeying against Robinson and drove the lane to take another running jumper. Robinson fouled him, and as Malone shot, he flared out his legs as he often did and as the Spurs had charged was illegal. Robinson and Popovich were furious; they argued that a foul should have been called on Malone, which would have negated the tying basket and given the Spurs the ball with sixteen seconds left.

But the referees—Bill Oakes, Hue Hollins, and Terry Durham —wouldn't hear it. They stuck with their call of a foul on Robinson, and Malone went to the line for a free throw to put the Jazz ahead. But just as he had late in Game 1, with the chance to complete a 3-point play and give the Jazz a 2-point lead, Malone missed. Fortunately for the Jazz, Carr somehow fought through the tangle of Spurs defenders and grabbed the rebound, giving the Jazz the chance to take the final shot and put the Spurs away.

Fortune turned fast, however, and more than once.

Stockton drove past Del Negro with less than five seconds left, hoping to either draw a crowd on his way to the basket or get through for a tie-breaking layup. As Stockton cleared Del Negro, Robinson and Duncan stepped in his way to prevent the easy layup, and he tried to whip a pass out to Russell on the wing.

But Johnson saw it coming. He stepped in the way of Stockton's pass and intercepted it, and quickly called timeout with 2.1 seconds left. Suddenly, the Spurs had hope again.

After the timeout, they set up much like they did in the waning stages of Game 1, and Del Negro inbounded the ball to Duncan near the top of the key. This time, the Jazz collapsed on Duncan, intent on not letting him get off another good shot and adding to his 26 points. As the Jazz defenders arrived, Duncan spied Jackson wide open in the corner. He kicked it out, and Jackson hoisted. But he missed, too, and the buzzer sounded.

For all the chances they were getting, the Spurs could not get anything to fall when they needed it in this series, and they headed to overtime wondering when a shot would finally fall their way.

It would be a while.

Not even thirty seconds had run off the clock in the extra period before Duncan rose to swat Hornacek's attempt to beat the shot clock and came down funny on his left ankle. He had to leave the game to have the injury examined, and though he returned within a minute after his trip to the locker room, he was nowhere near the player who had leapt to block Hornacek's shot.

The Spurs had actually claimed a 100–98 lead on Robinson's

baseline jumper while Duncan was gone, and moved ahead by another point on Robinson's free throw before Stockton cut it to 101–100 on a jumper with 2:35 left.

But Duncan missed a short jump shot, and found himself at Malone's mercy at the other end of the court. Malone knew he could take advantage of the rookie's injury, and Duncan had no chance to do anything about Malone's hard drive to the basket. With his ankle throbbing, Duncan could not move fast enough to impede Malone even a little bit, and Malone threw down a ferocious dunk with 1:17 remaining that put the Jazz ahead for good, 102–101.

"You have to try to make the plays when you need to make the plays," said Malone.

Duncan had another chance, but missed 2 free throws with fifty-five seconds left before Russell scored from the right angle twenty seconds later. The Spurs managed a couple more baskets, but the Jazz made 5 of 6 free throws in the final fifteen seconds to hang on and win, 109–106. Again, it wasn't pretty, but it was a victory, and only a handful of teams had ever come back from a 2–0 deficit to win a seven-game series.

"We saw it from everybody tonight," said Foster.

And how. Malone had 22 points and 12 rebounds. Stockton had 18 points and 12 assists. Hornacek had 21 points, 7 assists, and 4 rebounds. And Russell and Carr combined to shoot 10 of 17 off the bench and add 31 points.

Perhaps more glaring on the stat sheet was the fifty minutes logged by Duncan. He would have played fifty-one but for his ankle, which was diagnosed as a mild sprain, and the Jazz were wondering if that might wind up having an impact later in the series. Because Popovich was using Perdue in the starting lineup, he had precious little resource with which to give either of his big guns a rest and keep any height on the floor. Carl Herrera was the closest thing to a power forward the Spurs had in reserve, and

Popovich used him only seven minutes in Game 2. Meanwhile, Duncan had played forty-five minutes in Game 1, while Robinson worked forty-two in each of the first two games, mostly against the challenge of Malone.

"Hopefully, in the end, it will pay off," said Foster. "They'll get tired. We just need to be physical and keep beating on them."

The series certainly wasn't turning out to be the whole different ball game that the Spurs had hoped it would be. In fact, it was all but lost after just two games, and the fact that the Spurs managed a record-breaking blowout in Game 3 back at the Alamodome in San Antonio served only to prolong the punishment.

The final score of Game 3 was 86–64, and not since before the NBA added the shot clock for the 1954–55 season had a team scored fewer points in a playoff game than the Jazz did at the Alamodome.

The carnage was magnificent. While the Spurs shot under 40 percent themselves, they held the Jazz to 28.6 percent. Malone was 6 for 21. None of his teammates scored more than 9 points, which was precisely how many the whole team scored—to set a record for both the Jazz offense and the Spurs defense—in the entire third quarter. The Jazz made only 2 of 17 shots in that period, and finished it with a grand total of 44 points before their comparative explosion in the fourth quarter.

"They killed us about every way you can," said Sloan. "We just closed up shop."

Malone was not around to see the finish; he sprained his right ankle late in the third quarter and did not return before describing himself as the "goat" after the game. The 26,000 fans at the Alamodome had booed lustily when Malone left the floor, and wildly cheered every one of Robinson's 21 points and 9 rebounds. Robinson had even summoned the courage to shove Malone and incite double technical fouls late in the second quarter, after Malone had

232

given Robinson a bit of a push in the back after fouling him on a drive to the hoop.

"It was just the same stuff," said Robinson.

That was true for the Jazz, too, in a way. Though only three other teams had scored as few as 64 points in a playoff game, the Jazz had some experience bouncing back from blowouts in the playoffs. They'd lost 104–84 to the Los Angeles Lakers in Game 3 of their Western Conference semifinal series the year before, and rebounded with a 110–95 victory that helped them win the series in five games.

"We might as well have not even shown up," said Russell. "We didn't want it. I don't think we wanted it enough. . . . But knowing this team, I know we're going to bounce back. It won't be like this, I guarantee you that."

Russell found that it was easy to make guarantees when he had Malone on his team.

The Jazz had but a few hours between Games 3 and 4 in San Antonio, since Game 3 was played on a Saturday afternoon and Game 4 on Sunday night, and that probably kept them from dwelling too much about how badly they had been beaten. Malone had considered going out after Game 3 to a favorite restaurant near the team hotel downtown, but decided against it because he couldn't be sure there wouldn't be some rabble-rousing Spurs fans —"boneheads," as he called them—inebriated enough to give him a hard time or make trouble. That, too, probably helped the Jazz and hurt the Spurs, since Malone opted instead to meander around his room and the rest of the hotel, and pretty much just think about the things that had not gone his way in Game 3 and consider ways to correct them. He knew he'd been shooting "flat," for instance, and reminded himself to get a little more arc on his jump shots.

Man, the Spurs should have taken him to dinner.

* * *

When the fourth quarter rolled around the next night at the Alamodome, the Jazz and Spurs were locked in a battle reminiscent of the first two games rather than the third one. The Spurs had started slowly, but kept up enough to stay within striking distance as the fourth quarter dawned. Already, though, they had been victimized by Malone and his jump shot, which he had corrected just enough to make 12 of his first 21 shots for 24 points through the first three quarters. But the Spurs hadn't seen anything yet.

By the start of the fourth quarter, Malone had pretty much given up going to the basket, since he hadn't gotten a call all night (the man who annually led the league in trips to the free throw line would finish the game without a single free throw attempt for only the third time in his career), and was content to sit out on the perimeter and gently stroke the Spurs to death. Starting at the 7:16 mark of the fourth quarter, Malone scored 8 straight Jazz points on 4 soft, floating jump shots from well beyond fifteen feet, while working around a pair of awfully blown calls that earned referee Ronnie Nunn one of the longest glares in NBA history.

"It's hard to defend jump shots like that—nineteen, twenty feet away," marveled Robinson, whom Malone had defended into a 5-of-13 shooting performance. "Those are not shots that I want to take when games are on the line, but that's why he's the player he is."

Ten-time All-NBA first team, thank you very much.

The Spurs cut the Jazz lead to 75–72 when Duncan scored a tip-in with 2:54 remaining, but Ostertag miraculously made 2 free throws twenty seconds later to give the Jazz a 5-point lead before holding the Spurs to only one free throw the rest of the way. Ostertag had shot 48 percent from the line in the regular season and was but 6 of 18 before Game 4, and both of his foul shots surely touched every last inch of the rim before doing him the courtesy of falling through the net.

"They went in," he said later. "It doesn't matter how they go in."

He was right. The Jazz had an 82–73 victory and a 3–1 lead in the series, which was enough to almost certify that the Spurs would not be advancing to the Western Conference finals. San Antonio was not among the six teams that had ever come back from a 3–1 deficit, and the Spurs had never won a playoff game in Salt Lake City, site of the upcoming Game 5.

Furthermore, the Spurs' big stars had begun to fade, without getting any compensatory help from the rest of the roster. Duncan and Robinson combined for 37 points and 17 rebounds in Game 4, but they made only 13 of 31 shots between them (Jaren Jackson added a 3-for-15) and again played more than forty minutes apiece. That would really hamper Duncan; his injured right ankle was not getting the rest it needed to keep responding when asked, and would swell up, Popovich said, on the Spurs' flight from San Antonio to Salt Lake City. Had the Spurs known that ahead of time, they might not have even bothered making the trip.

Coincidentally, Sloan had reinstalled Russell among the starters for Game 4, just about two years after Russell had established himself as one of the Jazz's better postseason performers against— who else?—the Spurs.

Russell had nearly been cut during the 1995–96 season, but managed to stay on the squad by virtue of injuries to other players. He was coming off the worst season in his brief NBA career, having played just fifty-nine games behind David Benoit and Chris Morris, when the Jazz found themselves facing an unexpected Game 5 against Portland in the first round of the playoffs. When Benoit came up with a sore knee, Morris earned the start, and that cleared the way for Russell to get some minutes off the bench. He responded with 10 points, 8 rebounds, and 4 steals in the Jazz's 102–64 series-clinching victory, and he never left the rotation in the Western Conference semifinals against the Spurs. The Jazz won that series, and went on to lose to the Sonics in Game 7 of the Western Conference finals.

"I got the chance to do something," said Russell, "and I did it."

Since then, Russell had averaged nearly three points more in the playoffs than in the regular season. He was doing the same thing now; he'd averaged just 9 points per game after suffering his miserable start, but was scoring 11.8 in the playoffs while shooting nearly 50 percent from the field. Though his indifference to the regular season had landed him in some trouble with Malone early in the year, Russell acknowledged that the playoffs inspired him to make more of an effort on the floor, to dive for loose balls and "do all the little things that make a difference."

"One thing he does is give us more space," said Sloan. "He's a deeper shooter, and they have to guard him farther out on the floor. It's pretty tough for them to run from one corner of the floor and help off of Karl. If Bryon can make a couple of shots out there, he can keep people pretty honest."

It worked in Game 4, when Russell's presence helped give Malone a lot of one-on-one opportunities against Robinson while the other Spurs were too far away to lend much help, and it worked again in Game 5. Russell made another start, scored 15 points, and was one of four starters who reached double figures in Utah's 87–77 victory, which earned the Jazz their fifth trip to the Western Conference finals in seven years. It was also the third time since 1994 that the Jazz had eliminated the Spurs.

"It's like they're the parents and we're the children," said Johnson.

In the wake of their loss, the Spurs conceded they had simply ridden their horses too hard and too far. Duncan was clearly exhausted and hurting, and he had managed just 14 points on his sore ankle against the defense of Malone and Foster in Game 5.

And while Robinson led the team with 21 points and 13 rebounds, he again shot poorly to finish the series shy of the 40 percent mark.

"It looks to me like the best team is going on," said Popovich.

The Jazz could not have agreed more, and they did not even need sharp elbows to convince anybody.

"I'm in this thing for one reason," said Malone, "to do something that's never happened here. Now, we're one step closer to getting that goal."

CHAPTER

13

The Western Conference finals were nothing new to the Jazz; they had been there four times in the previous six years. But for all the varying results they encountered in the NBA's penultimate playoff round—losses to Portland in 1992, Houston in 1994, and Seattle in 1996 before the breakthrough victory in 1997—the one constant for the Jazz was their reliance on a single strategic cornerstone: the pick-and-roll.

It was one of the oldest and most basic plays in basketball, yet it was nearly unstoppable when executed properly—which is to say, when the Jazz executed it. Having spent the better part of a decade with the play as the primary staple in the team's offensive diet, the Jazz had long since raised its execution to an art form. The play was one of the main reasons the Jazz had advanced to the Western Conference finals so many times—and at the same time was perhaps the reason they had failed so many times to advance any further than that. In any event, no other team in basketball history has been as inextricably linked to a single play as the Jazz are to the pick-and-roll.

"It made this team," said Bryon Russell.

And in return, John Stockton and Karl Malone made the pick-and-roll a thing of beauty. The premise of the play was simple enough; Malone would run up to the top of the key and set a screen for Stockton (the "pick") before spinning and cutting to the basket (the "roll"). What made the play dangerous, however, was all of its options. Stockton could either drive past the Malone screen for a layup; drive a little bit, but then pass to Malone either cutting to the basket or flaring out for a jump shot; pass right away; or step back and take a jump shot. His decisions were based on what the defense did; if opponents tried to crowd Malone and prevent him from driving or taking a pass, Stockton could simply shoot or drive himself. If defenders tried to pressure Stockton, they usually left Malone a bit too unprotected to be stopped if he got the ball near the hoop.

"You can't defend the pick-and-roll if you have two guys willing to run it and use their options," said Malone. "The pick-and-roll starts with the screener, and if you're willing to do your job and are willing to slip [cut to the basket] and are willing to come at different angles and all that, then you get the defense turning their head. Then, you've got 'em."

That the Jazz happened upon the pick-and-roll was as much of an accident as having happened upon a pair of Hall-of-Famers with middle-round picks in back-to-back drafts. The Jazz ran the play originally because it was a basic one that worked. They ran it more and more often as they became more successful with it, and now, the vast majority of the team's offense is built around the play.

But the play probably would never have been as successful for the Jazz had Stockton not had the amazing ability to make all manner of passes to Malone at all the right times, a talent that

Stockton had seemed to develop even more as the years went by. Similarly, as Malone improved as an outside shooter over the years, he made the pick-and-roll all the more threatening because opponents could no longer concentrate on him as solely an inside threat; since they had to worry about him rolling outside as well as to the basket, that left more space in the middle for Stockton's drives. A vicious circle was born.

The Jazz have been criticized for being too reliant on the pick-and-roll and therefore too predictable; opponents knew that if they could stop the play, they could pretty much stop the Jazz. That was still very much true when the Jazz qualified for their fifth Western Conference Finals in seven years, but stopping the Jazz's pick-and-roll was probably harder than ever. Stockton and Malone were as precise as surgeons when operating the play, and their teammates showed the greatest understanding of the play and their roles in it as any group the two had ever encountered. Russell and Jeff Hornacek, in particular, were such good outside shooters that opponents could not focus on Stockton and Malone as fully as they once had. Only in the previous couple of seasons had the Jazz developed these consistent alternative threats, and combined with Stockton's and Malone's ever-improving synchronicity, they made the play tougher than ever to defend.

Still, the Jazz had yet to give anybody a reason to take out a second mortgage and put it all on them to win the NBA title.

They'd come perilously close to suffering an embarrassing exit from the first round, having been saved, perhaps, only by that timely injury to Houston's Charles Barkley. And then there were those last-second victories against San Antonio, when the Jazz did less to stop the Spurs than the Spurs did to stop themselves, and the humiliating Game 3 defeat that hardly stamped the Jazz as championship material. The Jazz did win when they had to win, there was no disputing that, but they had yet to run roughshod over anyone the way title contenders could fairly be expected to do.

And now they had a real challenge. Now, they had the Lakers.

After losing Game 1 of their Western Conference semifinal series against the higher-seeded Seattle SuperSonics, the Lakers erupted in a fit of running and gunning and won four straight games, two in Seattle, by an average of nearly 18 points—and remember, the Sonics had won sixty games. Shaquille O'Neal was playing like the best center in the league, his teammates were hitting three-pointers like they were softballs at the company picnic, and the Lakers were making their fans believe they might be watching a prelude to their first NBA championship in a decade.

"We're the underdog," acknowledged Malone. "That's how it's been my whole career. We just have to play good basketball. They're playing the best basketball, probably, out of everybody still playing."

"We can go a long way if we show up," said the Lakers' Nick Van Exel. "And lately, we've been showing up."

The series had all the hallmarks of a classic clash between teams with contrasting styles. The glamorous Lakers were the highest-scoring team in the league, with nobody born before the Summer of Love and a center recognized the world over as a star of movies and music as well as basketball. The Jazz, on the other hand, were a team comprised largely of onetime nobodies who placed a greater value on teamwork and defense and who possessed a center—hell, three of them—who could just barely be identified as such.

It was at the center position that most observers felt the series was going to be decided. O'Neal had been simply unstoppable in the playoffs, averaging nearly 30 points per game, and the Jazz looked unlikely to be able to derail Shaq with Greg Ostertag, Greg Foster, and Antoine Carr.

But Jerry Sloan had a plan.

Instead of rushing to double-team O'Neal as soon as he caught a pass, the way most teams did, the Jazz were going to be selective with the way they used defensive help on the big man. They would not double-team O'Neal on every possession, allowing Foster or Ostertag or Malone to occasionally guard him one-on-one and hope they could do just enough to keep O'Neal from making too many shots. That hope was fueled by the second part of the plan, which called for the Jazz to double-team O'Neal using a variety of defenders from a variety of spots on the floor, and at varying stages of O'Neal's possession. The Jazz might use Howard Eisley to double just as easily as they would Russell or Malone, and they might wait until O'Neal dipped his shoulder on his way into the lane before they came with the double-team, or until he began to dribble. Other times, they might indeed swarm him right away.

The idea was to confuse O'Neal and keep him off-balance by not letting him get used to the rhythm of a pattern of double-teaming. And if O'Neal could be kept uncomfortable, the Jazz had a better chance of making him miss shots or fail to find teammates with passes out of the post. The Jazz hoped to keep the Lakers' outside shooters from getting comfortable, too, since their defenders would not be leaving them unattended quite as often as they had in series past. The whole plan could be ruined quickly if the Jazz didn't come out aggressively in Game 1 and prevent the Lakers from getting a good start that would dictate a change in the defense, but the Jazz's only alternative was to make themselves more susceptible by exposing more of their weak spots—strength at the center position and speed in rotating to the open man on the perimeter—from the very start.

Sloan also scrapped the idea of playing Adam Keefe even the cursory minutes as a starter that he had throughout the San Antonio series, opting instead to use Russell almost full-time to negate some of the advantage the Lakers enjoyed with their superior athleticism. Plus, Russell had been such a big spark in several of the playoff games so far that he could have argued that he'd won back the position he'd held early in the year.

And the Jazz, finally, seemed to have won back their desire.

They came roaring onto the court for Game 1 of the series with the exuberance and energy of the Runnin' Utes. Right away, Foster blocked O'Neal's layup, rebounded a missed layup, and threw down a dunk. Then he hit a baseline jumper. Stockton stole the ball from O'Neal on one of the quick double-teams, threw long to Russell for an easy layup, and in a frenzied flash, the Jazz had a 6-point lead before the Lakers could say "Showtime."

The Jazz hadn't started like that the entire playoffs, and now, nearly three minutes into the game, the Lakers were crouched in a timeout huddle trying to figure out a way to get on the scoreboard and take the deafening crowd out of the game.

The timeout did nothing to help the Lakers' shooting touch; they were only one of 8 when Foster stuck his nose right up in O'Neal's face and did what Ostertag never dared: he talked back.

"I got pushed in the back," Foster explained. "I have to let him know I'm not going to take it. I'm not no punk. . . . It's always important to stand up for yourself. Not even for your team, you have to stand up for yourself. If you let someone take your heart away from you, he's going to smash you, step on you. He can do that to a lot of people. I don't lack no heart, and I'm not going to be pushed around by nobody, and that's just the way it is."

Moments later, Ostertag checked in. Still, the Jazz never missed a beat. They stole the ball from O'Neal again and held him without a basket until nearly two minutes into the second quarter. They kept O'Neal's teammates from giving much help, staying in the Lakers' faces as they missed three-pointer after three-pointer and strained to slow the Jazz charge.

"We didn't do anything extra special," Foster insisted. "They just missed shots they normally make and we just got off to a good start."

Then, behind the pick-and-roll, they piled on. By the time O'Neal hit his first basket, the Jazz bench was beginning a contribution that would earn it praise as the deepest and the best in the league. Eisley came off a screen to hit a jumper in the key on the Jazz's first possession of the second quarter, then drilled a baseline jumper the next time down, and wound up hitting 6 straight shots while the Jazz built a 42–18 lead and made the Lakers look like they'd never even heard of the pick-and-roll. Meantime, O'Neal was called for traveling on back-to-back possessions, Lakers coach Del Harris earned a technical complaining about it, and the Jazz lead grew to 61–35 at halftime.

The Lakers had no idea what hit them. The best they could do in the second half was push and shove while watching the Jazz methodically drill them into the ground. Eddie Jones elbowed Stockton to the floor midway through the third period for one flagrant foul, and Van Exel tackled Keefe on a breakaway minutes later for another. In between, they had to watch Foster throw down another vicious dunk on the fast break, then spring back past the Lakers' bench much as he had in that regular-season blowout, only this time he held a finger in front of his pursed lips: "Shhhh!"

The final score was 112–77, the worst loss in Lakers' playoff history, surpassing even the notorious "Boston Massacre," the Lakers' 148–114 loss to the Boston Celtics in Game 1 of the 1985 Finals. O'Neal shot just 6 of 16, and his teammates combined to go 16 for 62, missed nearly half their free throws, and got pounded in the rebounding battle. The Jazz plan had worked, and the Lakers clearly were befuddled by it.

"We couldn't get anything going for ourselves," Jones complained. "Shaq is our number one option, and if he can't get going, then it's really hard for everybody else to really get going."

The Lakers also expressed shock at the eruption of the Jazz

bench. Besides Eisley's 14 points, Carr scored on four straight possessions at the start of the fourth quarter and finished with 10 points, as did Chris Morris and Shandon Anderson. Meanwhile, Van Exel and Kobe Bryant were horrible for the Lakers.

"It wasn't pretty, folks," said Harris. "A bad combination—with one team playing great and one team playing lousy. We'll look at the films, lick our wounds, see if we can't defend the pick-and-roll better and come back for Game 2. That's why they call this a series. If this was high school, we'd be out."

O'Neal was loath to give much credit to the Jazz, complaining instead that he was getting fouled "all the time" while the referees refused to whistle the infractions. He promised to start swinging his elbows for protection, now that he had seen that the officials were going to let the teams play rather loosely.

"To become a Hall-of-Famer, I'm just going to start flaring my elbows," said O'Neal, in an obvious reference to Malone. "I kind of see how they're going to let us play, and that's fine with me. I just hope that a couple of people don't get their noses broken. I'll be throwing elbows. They're coming up now. That's it."

The Jazz were accustomed to hearing such innuendo, and the verbal shots from O'Neal were not the only ones flung Malone's way early in the series against the Lakers. In the hours before the teams played Game 2 at the Delta Center, the NBA announced that Michael Jordan had beaten out Malone for his sixth Most Valuable Player award, which afforded Chicago coach Phil Jackson the chance to take another swipe at Malone's controversial victory the year before.

"It was a joke," said Jackson.

Jordan received ninety-two first-place votes compared to twenty for Malone, which came as no surprise to anyone considering the events of the previous year. Voters gave the award to Malone in 1997 in part because he had enjoyed a remarkable season, but also because they felt he deserved it as something of a lifetime achievement award. When Malone missed those two free throws at the end of Game 1 of the 1997 Finals and Jordan hit the game-winner, newspapers all over the country proclaimed Jordan "the real MVP," while many voters acknowledged making a mistake by choosing Malone. If that backlash hadn't been enough to swing the MVP momentum back toward Jordan for 1998, there was the season-long threat that Jordan was playing his last season in the NBA. Nobody, it seemed, wanted to be the one to vote against Jordan for MVP in the final year of his unprecedented career.

Certainly, Malone had enjoyed another outstanding season, one that some observers felt was superior to the one for which he won his MVP award. He averaged 27 points, 10.3 rebounds, and 3.9 assists while shooting 53 percent and carrying the team for the eighteen games when Stockton was out hurt. The trouble for Malone was that many of the things he had done, Jordan had done better: he'd led the league in scoring for a record tenth time with 28.7 points per game, shot nearly 47 percent from the field, and ran his streak of double-figure scoring to a record 840 games. For good measure, he carried the Bulls for the first thirty-five games of the season while Scottie Pippen was out hurt—nearly twice as long as Stockton was out—and led Chicago to the same sixty-two victories as the Jazz.

But comparisons could wait; with any luck, Malone could make his case on the same court as Jordan in the NBA Finals. And it was looking more and more like he would get the chance.

❂   ❂   ❂

With O'Neal asserting himself, and his teammates similarly intent on proving they were not the collection of crash-test dummies they had appeared to be in Game 1, the Lakers predictably played better in Game 2. (They could not have played any worse.) They led throughout the first three quarters by keeping the Utah bench from erupting and by getting better looks at the basket for them-

selves, yet led only 75–72 when Russell went to the free throw line
for the Jazz early in the fourth quarter. When Russell made both
shots to cut the lead to 75–74, that seemed to suddenly remind
the Lakers that they could not afford to make any mistakes down
the stretch if they were going to make their thin little lead hold up
in the final ten minutes against one of the most precise teams in
the NBA.

With that thought, the young Lakers panicked.

Sloan had gone to the small lineup with Carr at center against
O'Neal, along with Morris, Anderson, Russell, and Eisley, and right
away Morris turned a missed three-pointer by Van Exel into a
jumper that gave the Jazz their first lead since the game's fourth
minute. Bryant missed a layup, Carr grabbed the rebound, and
Russell fed Anderson for a fast break layup, and the run was on,
just as Malone returned to the lineup.

Bryant committed an offensive foul; Morris scored a layup.

Robert Horry threw the ball away; Malone made a three-point
play.

The Lakers wasted two more possessions with turnovers, and
scored just a single free throw before Malone threw down a dunk
with 6:24 left that gave the Jazz an 85–76 lead that shrank but
never disappeared. All the while, O'Neal was on the floor but was
nowhere to be found because his teammates couldn't avoid mistakes long enough to get him the ball. He hadn't scored since the
10:25 mark, seconds before he floored Carr with an elbow to the
nose that validated O'Neal's pregame warning but did little for
the Lakers' bottom line.

"I'm cool," said Carr. "He said he wanted to play that way, so we
played that way."

Stockton, meanwhile, was killing the Lakers with his deadly
efficiency on the pick-and-roll. He had 22 points on 9-of-12 shooting, including 14 in the second quarter when the Lakers failed to
follow him around or through screens and he kept working his way

into the key for short jumpers. Then, in the fourth quarter, after the Lakers cut the lead to 90–88 with 3:08 to go on Shaq's last basket of the game, Stockton drew an offensive foul that was the sixth on Corie Blount, who was in the game at least partly to disrupt the pick-and-roll. With Blount thus dispatched, Stockton was able to drive the lane and find nobody bothering him, so he pulled up for a runner for a 4-point lead with 1:55 left.

Carr was making it worse for his counterpart, too. The Lakers had trimmed the Jazz lead to 94–93 with about a minute to go when the Jazz ran the pick-and-roll again. The Lakers collapsed around Stockton, who fired a perfect pass to Carr, wide open on the perimeter. With nobody even close, Carr squared up and drained an eighteen-footer that pushed the Jazz to a 99–95 victory and dumped the Lakers into a huge hole.

Since they had moved to Los Angeles from Minneapolis in 1960, the Lakers had only once in twelve tries recovered from a 2–0 deficit to win a playoff series—and no team, since the NBA swapped divisions for conferences in 1970–71, had ever come back from such a hole to win the Western Conference championship.

What's more, the Lakers already seemed out of ideas on how to beat the Jazz. They had tried throwing it to O'Neal, not throwing it to O'Neal, throwing it away (they had 18 turnovers in Game 2), and crying like babies. O'Neal had refused to retire to the locker room after Game 2 until he accosted referee Steve Javie at midcourt and screamed at him for screwing the Lakers with his calls and no-calls.

"We didn't really get any breaks," O'Neal said later.

Perhaps it only seemed that way. The Lakers shot 34 free throws to the Jazz's 38 in Game 2, yet made only 23 of them for not even 68 percent. That was horrible, and it was actually better than they'd shot in Game 1, when they made just 27 of 46. They were not going to advance to the Finals performing like that, especially when the Jazz had suddenly started to look so good.

In the postgame press conference, coach Del Harris said he thought the Lakers had done a better job against the pick-and-roll; by some formula, he figured they had allowed less than a point per possession on which the Jazz ran it, and that was a good result, he said. Reporters who'd watched the Jazz expose the fundamental weaknesses of the callow Lakers, especially at the crucial moments down the stretch, were left wondering if they'd seen the same game.

The Lakers had so many problems that only the play of O'Neal and their pending return home stood out as positives. On the other end of the floor, the Jazz's defensive scheme was allowing O'Neal to score while keeping the rest of the Lakers under wraps. Van Exel and Bryant had combined to shoot just 12 of 45 in the first two games, while Horry had only 8 points total after averaging more than 10 in the first two rounds of the playoffs. Forward Elden Campbell was playing as if he'd stepped on the floor for the first time in Game 1.

A repeat of the year before?

"I don't think so," said guard Derek Fisher. "We feel confident that we can win two games at home. We feel that the comfort level of being at home will provide us with a little energy and spark in those situations where the momentum maybe has changed. Your home crowd gets behind you and you feel good. So we feel like we can win those two games and put the pressure back on Utah to come back and win Game 5. The series is far from over. Two games is not insurmountable. We'll be okay."

The rumblings had already started, though, that Harris was not long for his job if the Lakers didn't improve—and some believed that the Lakers were playing so poorly in an effort to get him fired. But as poorly as the Lakers had played, they hadn't really blown anything yet; yes, they would have to win in Utah eventually, but in the playoffs it seems that no team is in real trouble until it loses a game at home. And coming up at The Forum was Game 3, the game that the Jazz had lost four times in their past five playoff series, including by 20 points to the Lakers the previous season.

But this time the Jazz just kept right on rolling.

Just as they had the previous two games, they plowed right over the Lakers in Game 3, with no consideration for history or sympathy or job security. In fact, the whippings were getting worse, considering that the Lakers had now had two chances to adjust to the same plan they saw in Game 1, yet couldn't.

Malone suffered through what was for him an off night by shooting just 9 of 22, but he made all 8 free throws he tried while Russell did not miss any of his 6 shots and Anderson and Morris combined for 28 points off the bench. Sloan seemed to make more adjustments in the fourth quarter than Harris had made the whole series; with the Jazz on the verge of pulling away, Sloan left Anderson on the floor instead of replacing him as he usually did with Hornacek, who had shot just 3 of 13 in the series. Anderson scored 11 of his 13 points in the final 7:26 to help the Jazz pull away for a 109–98 victory that left the Lakers all but eliminated.

"They've kicked our butts three times now," said Van Exel. "They're definitely the better team right now. Maybe we're not ready yet."

O'Neal again had done his part, with 39 points and 15 rebounds (although he did miss 8 free throws, including 4 in the final 4:22), but his teammates couldn't have backed the car out of the garage without running over the mailbox. They shot 18 for 55, and contributed almost nothing as O'Neal was left to keep them in the game by himself, scoring 16 of the 18 Lakers points spanning the third and fourth quarters. But the Jazz were too strong, getting, as they were, so much out of so many people.

"It was nice to be able to come in here and win," said Sloan. "We haven't won in this building in a long time."

It had been since the previous season's playoffs that the Jazz had won in The Forum, and victory was especially sweet considering the indignities they had suffered there early in the season. But now the suffering was in the other locker room, where the most impressive team of the postseason had been reduced to a collection of sniveling young fools, uncertain what had gone wrong and entirely lacking the means to fix it.

"We've pretty much tried everything," said Van Exel.

And though the Jazz professed no level of comfort, even in the most insurmountable of leads—the Lakers did win four straight against Seattle, remember—the truth was that the series was over.

The Lakers were dead.

No team had ever come back from a 3–0 deficit to win a playoff series, and Los Angeles had just failed by 11 points in a game on their own home court, during which they took more shots, grabbed more rebounds, and tried more free throws than the Jazz on a night when Malone wasn't on his game. Opportunities don't come much more gift-wrapped than that, and still the Lakers had been unable to pilfer a victory. Forward Rick Fox suggested that in Game 4 the Lakers should do exactly the opposite of everything they had been doing, since nothing they had tried had worked so far.

As surprisingly satisfying as the series had been for the Jazz, it was a stark contrast to their last trip to the Western Conference finals. Of course, that series was capped by Stockton's shot and the Jazz's championship-style celebration, but the Jazz and Rockets had until then entertained fans with a passionate and exhilarating series that featured three great finishes.

This one? Not so much.

The Jazz had shut down the Lakers in almost every respect, and in little more than a week had transformed themselves from a team with too many inconsistencies into the greatest threat to the Bulls' championship reign. The Jazz had stopped the Lakers' transition game, stopped them from hitting a lot of three-pointers, and made them so frustrated that they had begun to criticize each other.

The biggest challenge the Jazz faced now was not betraying their growing confidence to the press—"it's not closed out until we win our fourth game," said Anderson—and perhaps not openly mocking the Lakers for the way they had fallen apart after all the talking they'd done over the course of the season.

The Jazz were set on making it back to the Finals and winning their first championship, and they promised that their post-series celebration would not resemble the one from the year before, when the Jazz had joyously swarmed Stockton for a massive group hug at midcourt of the Compaq Center. It would be nice to win, certainly, they said; a fine accomplishment, they all agreed. But winning the Western Conference without topping it with something greater was not quite what they had in mind, so another big party was out of the question.

"Our focus is to win it all," said Foster. "Not just this."

So it was that Game 4 came and went at The Forum with almost no semblance of real drama. Sure, the Lakers cut a 13-point Jazz lead down to 90–87 with a minute to go, but nothing that happened in those final sixty seconds was anything the crowd had not already seen or could not have anticipated.

O'Neal missed 2 free throws after referee Jack Nies waved off a basket that would have turned the sequence into an opportunity for a 3-point play, and the spry Lakers could not catch the supposedly creaky Jazz to foul them and stop the clock after cutting the lead to 92–90 with twenty-two seconds left.

From there, Stockton made 2 free throws, then hit Foster for a long, press-breaking pass that matched Van Exel's layup and gave the Jazz the final cushion for a 96–92 victory.

Experience had beaten youth, hard and into the ground.

"I want to congratulate Utah for a great basketball game to finish the series," said Harris. "They were able to stop us from doing what we did all year."

As they promised, the Jazz did not jump up and down when the final buzzer sounded, or leap into one another's arms. Instead, they walked off the court as if they had been playing in the driveway when mom called for dinner. Though the Jazz knew that later that night thousands of fans would greet them cheering at the airport, that the next morning would bring huge headlines and congratulatory advertisements in all the papers, and that within hours finding someone in Salt Lake City without a Jazz hat or a Jazz T-shirt would be like finding a winning lottery ticket, they also knew that their biggest celebration would be reserved for an even bigger victory. They all said the same thing:

"We haven't done anything yet," said Russell.

Indeed, the Jazz were just getting started.

Just as they had the year before, thousands of fans crowded the private airport where the Jazz landed in their chartered plane just a few hours after winning the Western Conference finals.

The crowd was a little smaller, not quite the 20,000 who flocked after Stockton made The Shot against the Rockets, but it was no less enthusiastic. Many of the throng held aloft brooms, symbolizing the Jazz's unexpected sweep of the Lakers, and others brought posters and flags and signs, and alternated between chants of "Let's Go Jazz" and "Bring on the Bulls." Coach Jerry Sloan encouraged the crowd with his waves, and Bobbye Sloan stood at his side, happily videotaping the arrival rather than shuddering with fear alone in her bedroom.

But this was far from a repeat celebration in the evening sun.

The smiles on the players' faces were not quite as wide as they had been the year before. Karl Malone doffed his cap in appreciation of the welcome, but that was about all. Stockton rolled up the windows of his car when a TV news camera crew approached. Chris Morris was not riding on his hood, and Antoine Carr was not out high-fiving the faithful with tears in his eyes. No, the Jazz were all business this year, jaws set and bracing for the fight.

"No one else probably did, but we expected to be back," Malone said as he maneuvered his sport utility vehicle through the throng. "We didn't break out the champagne or anything like that, because we haven't done anything yet."

That wasn't quite true.

The four-game sweep of the Lakers was the first of its kind in Jazz history, and it proved that all the team's hard work had paid off by burying the petty doubts and insecurities that had so marked the season.

Fat-asses? Failed trades? Disrespect?

They were nowhere to be found now; after 104 games, the Jazz had grown confident and united. And they could not help but think that this destination had been their destiny all along. Teams don't go surviving a knee injury to one superstar and the incessant complaining of another, fighting through a botched trade and a nearly disastrous first-round playoff series, and then sweep Shaquille O'Neal and the Los Angeles Lakers—sweep them, for crying out loud—and not emerge with the faith that somehow all the forces of justice and fair play had finally pitched a tent on their side of the fence and decided they had suffered long enough without a championship trophy.

This simply had to be the Jazz's year.

Hadn't it?

Technically, the Jazz were not yet sure whom they'd be playing in the Finals. The Bulls and Indiana Pacers were but three games into their best-of-seven series in the Eastern Conference finals when the Jazz polished off the Lakers, but really, in their hearts, they knew, just as everybody knew. The Bulls would beat the

Pacers. It was simply meant to be. The Pacers were a fine team, and the Bulls would need more effort and a little more time to beat them than the Jazz had needed against the Lakers, but certainly Michael Jordan would go back to the NBA Finals one more time, with a chance to win his sixth championship in what could be his final season in the NBA. Certainly, fate would have her rematch.

That was exactly what the Jazz wanted.

Most of the players publicly proclaimed a respectful indifference to the proceedings in the East. But aside from Howard Eisley, who came right out and said he was cheering for the Pacers because he wanted to play in the Finals against his childhood friend and high school teammate Jalen Rose, the Jazz desperately wanted the Bulls again. They wanted to beat the team that had beaten them, to prove themselves against one of the greatest teams in basketball history.

Once Reggie Miller drilled a game-winning and series-tying three-pointer for the Pacers in Game 4 against the Bulls the day after the Jazz arrived home, the Jazz were assured of having ten days off by the time the ball went up in Game 1 of the Finals. Only the 1981–82 Lakers had more time off before a Finals series, with twelve days between sweeping the San Antonio Spurs and beating the Philadelphia 76ers, 4–2, for their second of five championships in the 1980s. The Jazz were hoping the Pacers would soften up the Bulls a bit to ease their own run at the champs.

In the meantime, the Jazz had to find something to do with themselves. Some fished, some golfed, some spent time at home with their kids. Malone rode his Harley and lay by the pool. But they all were a little worried about the effects of the layoff, and had a hard time enjoying themselves. Sloan especially; he knew his team's rhythm could easily be ruined by the sudden change in routine, and was trying to inspire his players to re-create in practice the intensity they brought to games. The Jazz were far from appeasing him early in the week, when they were so gassed and inattentive during one workout that they could not finish a four-quarter scrimmage to Sloan's liking. Sloan complained that the players had lost all their fitness in a mere three days of rest.

"If you can't work," he said, "then I guess we don't get much done."

The Bulls beat the Pacers in Game 5 of their series in Chicago, then lost Game 6 in Indianapolis. The deciding Game 7 was May 31 in Chicago, and the Jazz claimed they were not planning on watching it. Sloan, for one, had planned a trip to Idaho to see about buying a tractor for his farm.

What they missed was Jordan scoring 28 points to become the NBA's all-time leading scorer in the playoffs, and the Bulls coming back from a 12-point deficit to win, 88–83, and earn their third straight trip to the NBA Finals. The rematch with the Bulls was set, for all the Jazz wanted to talk about it.

"We're here. They're here," said Malone. "We'll see what happens."

The Jazz could only hope it wasn't the same thing that happened the year before, when they blew a close Game 1 and rolled over in Game 2 and eventually watched Steve Kerr drive a season-ending three-pointer into their heart in Game 6. The vision of Jordan dancing on the press table was still fresh.

It was hard to imagine the same outcome, considering the ease with which the Jazz had dispatched the Lakers and the difficulty the Bulls had had with Indiana. Historically, the Bulls had been so good that simply being forced to play a Game 7 was cause for alarm, so their having to come from behind at home to beat the Pacers in that Game 7 inspired all kinds of commotion. Suspicions arose that the Bulls were too old and too tired, too worn out from their ordeal against the Pacers to stand much of a chance against the Jazz, all rested and ready after their ten days of vacation. Even Scottie Pippen joined in the day before Game 1 at the Delta Center, when he and the rest of the Bulls landed at the airport, drove straight to the arena for practice and declared that the five-time champions were the underdogs in the series.

"The pressure is not on us," Pippen explained. "No one is expecting us to win. Everyone is expecting the Jazz to walk away in this series. We came here last season and we were expected to win. This season, we're not. So the pressure is on them. It's a different feeling. We've never been in this situation, where we've sort of been written off. It's a great feeling being underdogs because you want to go out and prove everybody wrong."

At first, it sounded absurd: the five-time champions—with *Michael freakin' Jordan*—as underdogs?

Yeah, right.

Odd as it seemed, though, he was right. Everybody was talking about the Jazz, about their efficiency and their work ethic and their masterful game plan against the Lakers. And an awful lot of people seemed willing to tell the Bulls: Hey, great run, but step aside please, there's a new champion coming through.

The Finals were radically different from anything else a basketball team experienced. The attention was almost unfathomable. Fans flocked outside the team hotels in hopes of seeing a player or two on their way in or out, and the media throng was so thick that come game time, there wasn't enough room for every reporter to watch the game live. Scores of journalists simply watched the games on TV, in the press room under the stands.

The NBA issued more than 1,300 press credentials to reporters from more than 100 countries for the Jazz's rematch with the Bulls, turning every interview session into a virtual mosh pit. Each team was required to be available for thirty minutes on nongame days, and to accommodate the press, the league usually ushered the coaches and one or two top players into an interview room, where every word was amplified on a speaker system and every word transcribed by a court reporter. Meanwhile, the rest of the players were allowed to mill around on the floor and answer questions, and because of the sheer volume of reporters, even the most marginally significant players could find themselves besieged by a circle of cameras and microphones four people deep.

It was this kind of attention that distracted the Jazz just enough in their first visit to the Finals, when they were awed by the whole experience and did not snap out of it until the series was lost. Not this year. Knowing what to expect gave them just one more reason to believe that this would finally be That Championship Season.

"It's obviously our best shot," said Jeff Hornacek.

To take advantage of it, the Jazz felt they had to survive the early stages of Game 1, which they figured would be the most difficult on account of their long layoff. Since their legs hadn't known the burn of a game in so long, they might need a little while to get loosened up and feeling right. But as long as they could stay close through their readjustment, the Jazz felt they could win the opener and start off on a good note. In more than fifty years of NBA playoffs, nearly 80 percent of the teams that had won Game 1 of a seven-game set had gone on to win the series.

"We've got to go lay it out on the line," said Greg Foster. "That's all there is to it. Game 1 is going to be huge. The way we come out in Game 1 is going to tell the tale of this whole series."

It was a nightmare disguised as a dream, complete with a cold sweat.

Both teams started slowly, owing to their respective disadvantages. The Jazz shot just 35 percent in the first quarter, and threw the ball away more than once. Yet they kept the Bulls from taking advantage, and spent most of the game with a four to eight point lead. Regulation ended in a 79–79 tie.

The overtime was tense, but the enduring image would be of Stockton, driving the lane late in the extra period, with the Jazz up by two, and leaving his feet halfway toward the basket, only to find the myriad Bulls defenders fanning out to guard against the pass instead of collapsing on Stockton to stop the shot. Chicago coach

Phil Jackson had left little Steve Kerr in the game to defend Stockton, so Stockton did not have to worry about the gangly arms or six-inch height advantage of Ron Harper on the crucial play. And with the Bulls' other defenders scrambling to check their men and not be the ones to be beaten by one of Stockton's famously brilliant passes, you could almost see Stockton shrug right there in midair and make his decision.

"Oh, all right already!"

He flipped the ball toward the basket somewhat off-balance, it appeared, and there it went. Bingo. Just like always. Stockton was 9 of 12 for the game, and had given the Jazz an 86–82 lead with 9.3 seconds left. He would be declared the hero after making 2 more free throws to bring his scoring total to 24 points, rendering Toni Kukoc's three-pointer with 3.5 seconds left merely frightening and not fatal. Pippen had one last chance for a three-pointer at the end, but it missed, and the Jazz survived, 88–85.

Suddenly, the Finals looked easy.

The Jazz didn't even need Malone to emerge from his notorious NBA Finals shooting slump to beat the Bulls—Malone made just 9 of 25 shots—and they had received another awe-inspiring performance by their reserves on a night when both teams showed some weariness.

Utah also demonstrated some stiff defense. Hornacek stripped Pippen early in the overtime, for instance, and Jordan lost track of the shot clock and could not get his jumper over Bryon Russell and Greg Ostertag in time to avoid a violation. Then Luc Longley, who had sent the game into overtime with his jumper in regulation, tried to drive past Ostertag and to the basket, but lost the ball off the dribble; Russell recovered, and on the next possession, Stockton made his shot.

"It's a relief to win," said Stockton. "The ten days off was a very long time. I'm not claiming I was rusty or anybody else was . . . it's just a long time to sit there and wonder and think about the next series. Last year, we were just thrust into it, and in a way I think that helped us go out and play."

Rough drafts of the Bulls' eulogy were being written all over the country, with all their aforementioned disadvantages as causes of death. The Bulls were too old. Too tired. Too distracted. Too much Jordan and not enough Kukoc. One newspaper columnist, in fact, declared the series over. Finished. Done. Jazz were the champs, so give 'em the rings.

But it was just one game. The Jazz needed three more, and they just might have given themselves a false sense of security with their success in the opener.

The aftermath of Game 1 was typically eccentric for the Bulls, who, after losing by just three points in overtime and on the road, had to answer charges of everything from insurgency to intransigence. Wasn't Harper pissed that Jackson left him on the bench for the final moments of the game? Wasn't that Jordan screaming at Pippen during a timeout late in the game? What about the bench; shouldn't it be expected to contribute more than 8 points?

And then there was Rodman.

Having arrived for Game 1 with another new hairdo (lime green, with black spots) and a mysterious injury to his thumb (apparently suffered in Game 7 against the Pacers), he had grabbed 10 rebounds and helped hound Malone into his forgettable shooting performance. But then Rodman hopped a private plane for Las Vegas in a move that, in the wake of a loss, appeared more distracting than appropriate. What about him?

"He's free to go," said Jackson. "It's better than his hanging around this town and upsetting some Mormons."

During the Finals the year before, Rodman had so insulted the Utah-based Mormon Church that the NBA hit him with a $50,000 fine and forced him to apologize. That did not help his image in Utah, of course, where Rodman was widely viewed as the anti-Malone—a depraved, ranting lunatic so bent on self-promotion that he had let slip away all semblance of pride and honor and good taste, who was not fit to hold his counterpart's jockstrap on the court, or off it for that matter. Little did anybody know that even as the Finals were taking place, Rodman and Malone had signed a deal to grapple with each other in a pro wrestling event in San Diego a month after the Finals. Maybe they weren't so different after all.

The Bulls skillfully countered all the charges that came flying at them in the wake of their series-opening loss. Harper said he wasn't mad. Jordan was simply shouting to be heard over the din of the crowd. And quite simply, yes, the Bulls needed more production out of their reserves. Just that easy. The Bulls had, after all, been through this wringer after every game all season, on account of the smothering media interest that attended the possibility that this was their last season together. "The Last Dance," Jackson was calling it.

Perhaps owing to their experience on the spot, the Bulls showed no lagging confidence after Game 1, in spite of the fact that they had lost three straight games to the Jazz and five of six at the Delta Center. They talked about taking fuller advantage of Hornacek if he guarded Jordan, and about getting more of their teammates involved in the offense. They displayed a confidence that probably crossed well into arrogance, but they had the credentials to back it up.

"We're not worried," said Kukoc.

It was easy to believe him.

If the Jazz could win Game 2 at the Delta Center, they would be in great shape. Only two teams in NBA history had rebounded from a 2-0 deficit to win the Finals—the Boston Celtics in 1969 and the Portland Trail Blazers in 1977. But like its predecessor, Game 2 was tight the whole way, and came down to a crucial sequence in the final minute.

Malone had been awful all night, proving that he had yet to

overcome whatever it was that kept him from being in the Finals the kind of player he was during the regular season. Hornacek was left to keep the Jazz close by scoring 20 points in his best game of the playoffs; his three-pointer with 1:46 remaining gave the Jazz an 86–85 lead, after the Jazz had spent most of the fourth quarter watching their shots glance harmlessly off the rim. They had not made a basket in the first seven minutes of the quarter, yet found themselves within 4 after Russell hit a three a few minutes before Hornacek's.

The Jazz were trying to build on their lead in the final minute when Stockton drove the lane, much as he had in the defining moments of Game 1. But this time Rodman stepped in his path, and Stockton collided with him as he tried to flip a last-second pass out to Russell on the wing. Kukoc leapt to make an interception, then passed to Kerr as the Bulls rushed upcourt.

With Stockton struggling to regain his feet, only Malone stood between the streaking Kerr and the hoop, and Kerr knew Malone did not want to be drawn too far away from the basket. So, with 48.9 seconds left on the clock, Kerr pulled up at the three-point line in front of the Jazz bench and fired.

The shot was sure to fall. The entire arena sensed it; the fans had had too much experience in this situation to expect anything less. How many times in the previous season's Finals had the Jazz been right there, ready to take the game over, when the Bulls pulled some spectacular play out of nowhere and whisked away the victory? Almost all of them, not the least of which was Game 6, when the same guy who was shooting now had drilled a jumper from top of the key to put the dream to rest for another year. Yeah, that shot was going down.

The most peculiar thing happened, though: it didn't.

Kerr missed.

The ball bounced high and long off the rim, and the Jazz appeared as genuinely surprised as the crowd to see it happen. The entire arena seemed to gasp at once, eager for the Jazz's chance to escape such a near-death experience and extend their tenuous lead and—oh, the opportunity!—take a 2–0 lead in the series.

But with surprise sometimes comes inaction, and the Jazz players who were in the neighborhood of Kerr's missed shot seemed unwilling to go grab it, as if they wanted to see it land and hear the noise before actually believing that it had missed. And in the split second that they stood and watched, Kerr scrambled up the right side of the key and snared the ball as it came back down. Right between Malone and Russell, the smallest man on the court grabbed the biggest rebound of the game. The crowd groaned.

"That's true desire," said Jordan.

In a flash, then, Hornacek lunged at Kerr, and Kerr spotted Jordan wide open under the basket. Kerr fired the ball to his teammate, and Jordan scored the layup just as Stockton arrived to foul him. One free throw later, the Bulls enjoyed the same 88–86 lead they would have had if Kerr's shot had fallen, but now they enjoyed it with less time on the clock and considerably more certainty of the outcome. The Bulls never gave up the lead.

Malone missed a jumper on the Jazz's next possession, and Kerr made two free throws to seal the eventual 93–88 victory.

"It's ironic, isn't it?" he said. "I think that was maybe my first rebound of the series."

Now, the Jazz were on the defensive.

They had committed 20 turnovers, allowed twice as many offensive rebounds than they grabbed, and were headed back to Chicago for three games in a row. Worse, Malone was showing no signs of breaking out of his Finals funk; he made only 5 of 16 shots in Game 2 for a mere 16 points, and did not score a single basket in only 4 shots during the second half.

Counting his abysmal performance in the 1997 Finals, Malone was shooting less than 42 percent in the championship round and scoring only 22.5 points per game—nearly 5 below his season average. The pressure clearly was wearing on him, yet he kept up his stoic demeanor and refused to make excuses for his failures.

"My main thing right now—even though it's the second game—is I don't want to start rushing," he said. "I don't want to start saying, 'Hey, you have to do it.' I want to try to do it within our offense. . . . I don't know. Maybe last year, maybe the second game, the third game, I started saying, 'Oh, I got to pick it up,' instead of just playing relaxed. I don't think that in these two days I've played relaxed yet."

Somebody asked why not.

"I don't know," he said, rolling his eyes. "It's only the NBA Finals."

So, he was rattled. He was nervous. All that glowering and macho posturing was just a cover. As much as he yearned for it, and as much as he strove to attain it, Malone simply did not have the appetite for intense pressure that Jordan did. Jordan *snacked* on big games, and licked his fingers when he was through. Malone, however, tensed up. And though he held his head high and valiantly absorbed the critical blows that he knew were coming his way, Malone was left to simply wonder further about whether he would ever win a championship ring. He was left to grow more uncertain. He was left with that fear.

"It's just that I know what's at stake here probably more and I want it, you know?" he said. "I want to win it so bad, instead of just playing and playing relaxed."

Imagine Jordan saying that.

Malone knew the Jazz were not going to be visiting the jeweler anytime soon if he didn't start playing better, and he acknowledged as much, even though his teammates and coaches tried to take the heat off him by complaining about their flat defensive start and inconsistent rebounding. Sloan pointed to the fact that the Jazz had the lead with less than a minute to go in Game 2, despite Malone playing poorly.

"I never said I didn't want Karl Malone to take shots," said Sloan. "But the important thing is, how hard do you work to get open to get shots? They were doing a great job. They stood us up and took us out of some of the things we wanted to do. That's when you have to be tough mentally and stay with it. I don't think we were sometimes. I thought we lost our ability to compete against them."

He hadn't seen anything yet.

Because they had barely escaped Game 1 with a victory after blowing their lead, the Jazz were feeling almost as if they had lost both of the first two games, and nothing was going right for them.

The day after the Game 2 loss, they planned a workout at Westminster College before traveling to Chicago. Sloan was so disgusted with the effort in the game that he had his players watch nearly an hour's worth of film in the coaches' room on the lower level of the gymnasium, which kept them there long after members of the media began to arrive and wait on the nearby stairs that led up to the court.

The Jazz's practices had been closed since early in the season, meaning the media simply had to wait for the workout to end and for a PR rep to open the doors so they could go in to conduct their interviews. That's what was happening the day after Game 2, when suddenly the door to the downstairs coaches office opened and the Jazz began to spill out in front of the surprised reporters, who had no idea the team had been in there. Sloan, however, thought the media knew and had been eavesdropping.

"Why don't you just come into the locker room?" he grumbled, as his players marched silently up the stairs.

Several reporters expressed surprise and said they hadn't heard a thing, jokingly promising not to print any of the Jazz's game plan. Sloan, however, was not in a joking mood.

"You better not," he said. "If I see anything in the paper, I'll find you."

Gulp.

What film session?

Then, when the Jazz reached the top of the stairs, they found the doors to the court locked. What next, goldfish in the Gatorade? Disgusted, they were ready to turn around and head back downstairs and walk around to the entrance on the other end of the court when a pair of newspapermen, who had been wandering through the gym wondering where everybody was, pushed open the doors and let them in. Oh, the indignity.

The Jazz tried to maintain their composure throughout the buildup to Game 3, but had already made up their minds that they were not going to sit back and let their problems from the first two games doom them again. Malone set his mind toward coming out strong and having a good game for once, and Sloan decided that he could no longer afford to start Foster at center because the Jazz were getting killed on the offensive glass. Sloan chose to start Ostertag in Game 3 at the United Center, which seemed a reasonable enough alternative, given Ostertag's size and presumed ability to guard the equally immobile Longley. As it turned out, though, it was the most disastrous decision of the Finals.

Ostertag had played all of twenty-four minutes in the first two games, scoring 9 points and grabbing 6 rebounds in the wake of his reasonably successful effort against Shaquille O'Neal in the Western Conference finals. He had shown slivers of improvement as the year wore on, but had never returned to the level he had reached the previous season. He still had trouble catching the ball, and he still couldn't make free throws, yet the Jazz were hoping he could at least pull down a few boards and relieve some of the rebounding pressure on Malone so Malone might concentrate a bit more on his offense.

What the Bulls saw was an opportunity.

So little did they respect Ostertag and the offensive threat he posed—which was all but negligible—that Jackson decided to let the 6-7 Pippen guard him. That way, the Bulls could keep Longley on Malone and not be forced to use someone more slight who would be much more vulnerable to Malone's strength inside.

The plan did not work at first.

The first few moments of Game 3 belonged to Malone, who came out determined to prove he could play big in the Finals. He hit a jump shot thirty-five seconds into the game for the Jazz's first points, grabbed a rebound, then hit another jumper for a 4-0 lead. He sandwiched another jump shot between two hard drives to the basket past Longley, and stuck a twelve-footer that gave the Jazz a 14–9 lead with 3:32 left in the period.

It looked like trouble in the making for the Bulls.

Malone was 6 for 6 for 12 points, and had in his eye that same gleam he had when he went for 56 against the Golden State Warriors late in the regular season. But while Malone was off to his hot start, his teammates were not; Stockton, Hornacek, Russell, and Ostertag combined to make just 1 of 16 shots in the first quarter, and the Jazz trailed 17–14 when it was over. That's when the Bulls' plan really went into effect.

Since Ostertag had missed four layups or tip-ins in the first period, the Bulls saw he could be left entirely alone with virtually no fear of getting burned by him. Even when Ostertag was playing well, he was the last of the Jazz's offensive options, and he rarely scored except off rebounds or loose balls. So Jackson told Pippen to guard Ostertag only in the most cursory way, and to use most of his energy roaming the floor and helping his teammates double-team the more potent Jazz players. Most notably, Jackson wanted Pippen to help Harper harass Stockton before he could set up the Jazz's offense.

The result was devastating.

Though the Jazz hung on while Malone took his customary breather early in the second quarter, and trailed only 24–19 when he returned with about eight minutes to go, they absolutely folded the rest of the way. The turning point came halfway through the second period, after the Jazz had weathered a nearly six-minute scoreless stretch and Malone drove to the basket hoping to cut into a 29–23 Bulls lead. Malone knocked over Pippen on his way to a layup, and referee Hue Hollins waved off the basket and called Malone for an offensive foul.

Malone was aghast. The Bulls were enthused. And the game, for all practical purposes, was over.

"That was the key," said Pippen of the controversial call. "We've been trying to continue to force him to make jump shots, and Karl is the guy who's going to try to get to the basket. . . . You have to be man enough to take the charge, because he comes to the basket pretty hard."

From there, it was all Bulls, all the time. They forced 9 turnovers in the second quarter and turned Stockton into an irrelevancy by using Harper and Pippen to converge on him at midcourt before he had a chance to orchestrate the offense. Stockton could hardly even see over the taller Bulls, let alone get off crisp passes through the tangle of long limbs. The Jazz complained and complained that Pippen was playing illegal defense by roaming in no-man's-land in his effort to slow Stockton and Malone, but never once got the call from Hollins, Ronnie Nunn, or Dick Bavetta (remember that name).

Worse, Malone not only quit hitting, he quit shooting, in large part because the Jazz could not get him the ball amid the Bulls' oppressive defense. Malone tried only one shot the entire second quarter, and missed it, while his teammates could do little to stop the Bulls' surge. Chicago led by only 37–29 with 2:39 to go in the half, but made 2 steals and 4 layups during a 12–2 run that put them ahead 49–31 at the break.

"They turned it up a couple of notches," said Stockton. "And we did not respond by gritting our teeth and executing, despite the pressure. . . . I don't know what's a good word for it, we tried to do it our own way, and that doesn't work. And that just snowballed on us."

The Jazz only played worse after halftime. They made just 4 of 15 shots in the third quarter, and fell behind by 28 points while Jordan worked his way toward 24 points and Harper closed in on a triple-double. Utah careened into the fourth quarter trailing 72–45, and once the Bulls built their lead to 30 in the next few minutes, the Jazz simply quit. Just utterly and totally gave up. They scored only 9 points the entire fourth quarter, lost, 96–54, and set enough ignominious records to make people wonder how in the hell they had made it so far in the first place.

Worst loss in Finals history.

Fewest points ever in a Finals game.

Fewest points in any NBA game since the shot clock debuted in 1954.

The Jazz also scored a Finals record-low 23 points in the second half, committed 26 turnovers, shot 30 percent, and made only one of 9 three-point tries. Malone finished with 22 points on 8-of-11 shooting, but was only 2 of 5 after the first quarter and committed 7 of the Jazz turnovers. Ostertag did grab 9 rebounds—4 of them offensive, even—but the retributive cost was unconscionably high. He would play a total of seven minutes the rest of the series, and the fans would wonder what might've happened had the trade for Rony Seikaly gone through. The Game 3 problem had returned, at the worst possible time and in the worst possible way.

Sloan was discussing that very point after the game when an NBA staffer handed him a final stat sheet. He put on his glasses and looked down.

"This is actually the score?" he said, looking up again and pretending to search the room for the person who gave him the sheet. "Is this the final? I thought it was 196. Seemed like they scored 196. . . . They ate us alive."

Now, everybody wondered: were the Jazz dead?

The team that four days earlier had been heralded as the one about to end the Bulls' reign of terror was now in worse shape than it had been during their maiden trip to the Finals. The Jazz trailed 2–1 in 1997, too, but they at least were coming off a victory as they headed into Games 4 and 5 at the Delta Center. Combined with the frustration of blowing their lead in the opener, the Jazz felt as though they had lost three in a row, and still had to play two games in Chicago in the wake of the worst blowout in Finals history before even getting back to their home court. So much for any advantage.

The Bulls began adding insult to injury, too.

Rodman missed practice the day after Game 3, and wound up participating in a pro wrestling event in Michigan that night. Jackson fined Rodman for missing the team's workout, but the Bulls almost unanimously said they didn't care what Rodman did on his own time, as long as he came to play. He had been doing that, too, uncharacteristically handling Malone because, Rodman said, the referees were letting him play.

"Karl Malone is used to getting his way down low," said Rodman. "He gets ticky-tack fouls. Now, he's not getting those calls. You let me play, and Karl Malone will never beat me."

Meanwhile, the city of Chicago was beginning to make plans for the Bulls' victory parade and celebration in Grant Park. Chicago smelled blood.

If there was anything the Jazz could do now to save themselves, they seemed wholly unaware of what it was. They talked about trying to expose Pippen's illegal defense by holding the ball longer and allowing the referees to see how he was improperly playing zone, and they discussed the need to be more physical with the Bulls and not let them go to the basket with such impunity. But they had none of the confidence and swagger that they had brought into the Finals; the Lakers series might have been six months ago for all the good it was doing them.

Sloan sensed enough desperation in the wake of the blowout to insert Adam Keefe into the starting lineup at center for Game 4, in hopes of keeping Pippen from causing as much havoc as he had in Game 3. It almost worked, since Keefe played reasonably well in twenty minutes and the Jazz committed only 11 turnovers —by far their fewest of the series. But Pippen erupted offensively for 28 points and 5 three-pointers, and Rodman embarrassed Malone by making 5 of 6 free throws late in the game and holding Malone to one basket in the fourth quarter of the Bulls' 86–82 victory. Malone had started strong as he did in Game 3, but was 4 of 12 over the final three quarters. The critics were not letting up.

"Everybody is experts now," he growled on the postgame interview stand. "I have opportunities to score on Dennis as well as Luc, and I just haven't. It's no excuses. But in a situation like this, all you guys have all the answers, so I don't know why I answered that myself."

Certainly he knew that, ultimately, the Jazz were finished. No team in the history of the NBA Finals had ever recovered from a 3–1 deficit.

"They have to beat us three games in a row to win this series," said Jackson. "And we know that's a pretty difficult task for any team."

How difficult? The Bulls had not lost three games in a row since the middle of January in 1995—before Jordan returned to the team from his baseball experiment—and now they had a five-game winning streak against the Jazz at home in the Finals. Neither trend figured to be coming to an end anytime soon, not with Jordan and the rest of the world sensing the most glorious moment of his career.

The stage was set for him to go out in style, to play the last game of his basketball career at home, in front of an adoring crowd, while winning the sixth championship of his storied NBA career.

Everybody presumed he would try to put on an epic show to certify his greatness one last time, perhaps like he did in Game 5 of the 1997 Finals, when he overcame illness and fatigue to score 38 points in a Bulls victory at the Delta Center. Tickets were selling for thousands of dollars, and the police were closing streets and clearing jail space in anticipation of a riotous championship celebration.

Faced with such anticipation, the Jazz had nothing to fear. Perhaps that, as much as anything, was the reason they won Game 5: the pressure was off. Nobody but the most faithful of Jazz fans believed the Jazz could win the series now, and the absence of expectation seemed to allow them to finally relax and play their game. Yet if they were to make history and become the first team ever to recover from a 3–1 Finals deficit, the Jazz had to start somewhere, and denying Jordan and the Bulls the party they had so anticipated was as good a place as any.

By game time, some of the Jazz players were disgusted enough with Chicago and its fans that they were ready to do whatever they could to make their lives just a little less enjoyable. As had been the case the year before, fans and the occasional radio station had taken to phoning the players in their hotel rooms in an effort to harass and disturb them.

"How does it feel to have Michael Jordan in your head?" somebody asked Chris Morris.

One caller told Carr that his young son had been in an accident with the boy's mother, and that Carr should get to the hospital right away. Other players also reported receiving phone calls, though most of them had learned from the previous year's experience to either refuse calls or not pick up. Malone, in fact, was not even in his room to answer the phone; he was out riding in a squad car with an Illinois state trooper (whom Malone later identified only as "Ty") in an effort to get his mind off the Finals.

"I went riding and went out to the weigh station and weighed some trucks," Malone reported. "That's what I did, because I like that kind of stuff."

And boy, did it work.

Combined with the Jazz's return to the role of hopeless underdog, Malone played his finest game of the Finals, scoring 39 points, including 25 in the second half, to help the Jazz win, 83–81, and send the series back to Salt Lake City. Carr was huge, too, scoring 12 points on 5-of-6 shooting and making 2 free throws with 10.4 seconds left that helped the Jazz hang on in spite of Kukoc's three-pointer five seconds later and a Jordan shot at the buzzer that missed.

"We knew it was do or die," said Malone.

It would be do or die again, too. And a third time, if necessary. But the sense of relief among the Jazz was overwhelming. At least now they had made the Finals respectable. And with Malone having finally snapped out of his bad spell, they began to think that maybe—just maybe—they could make an unprecedented recovery in the comfortable confines of their own home arena. If they could just win Game 6 and tie the series at 3–3, they would force the Bulls to Game 7 of a Finals for the first time, and then, hey, anything could happen.

"Momentum is an interesting beast," said Keefe. "It changes in a hurry. Obviously, we had it going into the series with how well we played against the Lakers and winning Game 1 in overtime. It was just a tough Game 2 loss, and all of a sudden the momentum changes. Now they're in a little bit of the same boat, you know? They had a tough loss. They didn't want to go to Salt Lake and come back here. It's going to be tough. There's no easy way for either team."

He had no idea.

*   *   *

Game 6 arrived on a Sunday afternoon in Salt Lake City, two days after the Jazz had ensured their survival for at least one more game, and the predictably hopeful local sentiment had the Jazz winning at least once more to set up what would be the biggest basketball game the state had ever seen. (That wasn't as obvious as it might have sounded; Magic Johnson and Larry Bird had squared off in the 1979 NCAA tournament championship game at the Huntsman Center, just up the hill from the Delta Center.)

Before the game, thousands of fans milled around the plaza in front of the Delta Center, where the Jazz had set up concession stands and basketball courts and souvenir booths, but their mood seemed more anxious than it had when the series was last in Utah. Everybody had been festive and carefree then. But now, even though the kids were still getting their faces painted with Jazz logos, and those without tickets were still staking spots on a lawn from which to watch the game on a giant TV screen, fans seemed to be searching for a validation of their faith, as if sharing their fears would help banish them.

Inside the arena, the ticket holders were bracing for history. Either the Jazz would stave off elimination yet again and force the Bulls into the first Finals Game 7 in their history, or they would fall short for the second straight time, in what would be widely presumed to be Jordan's last game in the NBA. At 5:42 P.M. the ball went up, carrying all the hopes and dreams of two decades' worth of Jazz players and fans.

The Bulls won the tip, and took the game's first lead on a dunk by Pippen. Malone hit a jumper to tie it, and the seesaw battle was on. The game would be tied six times in the first quarter alone; when Malone and Jordan began an epic duel for supremacy that could go a long way in erasing all of Malone's and the Jazz's mistakes through the first four games.

Malone made all 4 of his shots in the first period, and went to the line five times to finish with 12 points. Jordan, on the other hand, was not having the same success with his jump shot, but was not about to stop shooting. He had 8 points on 3-of-8 shooting, and the Jazz led 25–22 after the first quarter.

The Jazz were getting good help from their other players, too, unlike Game 5, when Malone did everything on his own. Hornacek jumped out to a fast start, as did Carr when he entered the game for Keefe late in the first quarter. But the second quarter was not even three minutes old when the roaring crowd witnessed the first of several plays that they would always remember as the ones that screwed the Jazz out of their championship.

Kukoc had just cut the Jazz lead to 28–24 with a layup when the Jazz reserves found themselves running a rotten possession and in sudden need of a shot before the shot clock expired. So Eisley hastily pulled up and fired a jumper from the top of the circle.

The ball snapped through the net—a three-pointer—for a 31–24 lead and some badly needed Jazz momentum. But before the points could even be posted on the scoreboard, referee Dick Bavetta began to wave his arms furiously and blow his whistle hard enough to be heard over the frenetic crowd.

"No basket!" he shouted. "No basket!"

The crowd turned on him.

What? No basket!

Bavetta patted his palm on the top of his bald head, signaling that the shot clock had expired before Eisley had released the ball. Sloan went nuts on the sideline, screaming to Bavetta what nearly 20,000 people already knew: the shot was good. It should have counted. So badly had Bavetta blown the call, in fact, that TV replays showed that the ball was nearly halfway to the basket before the shot clock hit zero. But there is no rule in the NBA by which referees may view replays, and, oddly, neither Hollins nor Danny Crawford made any attempt to correct Bavetta's blunder. Three referees had just missed the most obvious call of the series.

"Those are very difficult things to swallow," Sloan said later, obviously trying to hide his true feelings. "But that's part of this business."

With Eisley's basket nullified, the Jazz's lead was only 4 instead of 7. And it was cut to 2 almost immediately, when the Bulls' Jud Buechler drilled a long jumper with 9:23 left in the period.

The Jazz survived the blown call well enough that they didn't get buried, but a combination of turnovers and missed shots kept them from pulling away. They went ahead by four on a layup by Malone, but trailed 36–35 within two minutes after Jordan scored a layup, a three-pointer, and a free throw.

That's when the fun started.

Hornacek missed a short jumper for the Jazz after Jordan's layup, but Anderson grabbed the rebound and tried to tip it back in. Anderson missed, but Malone was right there. He grabbed the rebound, and finally scored to put the Jazz back in the lead.

Jordan traveled on the Bulls' next possession, and Malone responded with a layup for a 39–36 edge.

Then Jordan drilled a three-pointer to tie.

Then Malone buried a seventeen-foot jump shot.

It was a full-scale scoring war, and Malone was winning. He had 20 points, and Jordan had 19. But while Malone cooled off and let his teammates get back in on the action—Russell, Hornacek, and Stockton all scored again before the half was over—Jordan just kept casting. And casting. And casting. He made his first 2 shots after Malone's last one to tie the game at 45–45, but missed 4 more in the final 1:16 of the second period. The Jazz went to the locker room at the half ahead 49–45.

The third quarter was much less spectacular, as the teams settled into a tension that seemed to arrive with the realization that they were on the threshold of history. After Malone's jumper twenty seconds in, the Jazz embarked on a stretch of nearly eight minutes without a basket. Fortunately for them, the Bulls were not hitting with much more frequency, and were not going to the line as often.

At one point, it was left to Rodman to score a pair of tip-ins and represent the Bulls' offense in the middle part of the period. His second bucket tied it again at 59–59, before the Jazz managed a little streak at the end for a 65–61 advantage.

Through all this, Pippen hardly was contributing to the Bulls' effort because of a sore back he had suffered, he said, taking those charges from Malone in Game 3. He played only seven minutes in the first half before leaving to the Chicago locker room to have his injury treated, and managed but a single basket in nine minutes of the third period. That was part of the reason Jordan was doing all the work.

Jordan was 11 of 25 through three periods for 29 points, while only Kukoc was giving him much support with 13. The Jazz had been much more balanced, but still teetered on a slim lead as they huddled before the start of the fourth quarter. With twelve minutes between them and infamy, the Jazz had a moment to revisit all the trials and tribulations they had endured to reach this point, and to consider all the historic fortuities that had allowed them the opportunity.

Then they dove back into battle.

Eisley scored over Kerr.

Jordan hit a jumper.

Back and forth it went, and the tension mounted.

The Bulls took a 74–73 lead with 6:50 left on two Jordan free throws and a jump shot, but Malone scored twice in the next three minutes and put the Jazz back in front, 79–77, before the second of the horrible calls that went against them.

This time, it was a jump shot that clearly did not beat the shot clock out of Harper's hands, yet the Bulls guard was not signaled for a violation. The basket counted, the crowd went triple-ballistic, and the game was tied yet again, 79–79.

"You can't argue about it," said Hornacek, meaning it would do no good.

But the argument could easily have been made that the Jazz should have been 9 points ahead, rather than 4, after Malone buried another jumper with 2:32 left for an 83–79 lead. And who knows what might have happened had Eisley's basket counted and Harper's not? Bavetta's name would forever elicit venom from Jazz fans who believed he cost them the series.

Still, the Jazz had the game in their hands.

Jordan drew fouls on consecutive drives to the basket and made 4 straight free throws to tie it, but Stockton pulled up and drained a three-pointer with 41.9 seconds left that gave the Jazz an 86–83 lead and gave fans a flashback to Game 6 against the Rockets. Sitting in the stands as the crowd went wild, former coach Dick Motta—the man who trained both Sloan and assistant Phil Johnson—turned to his grandson. "That ought to do it," he said.

The words had barely left his mouth, though, before all the pain of the previous year came rushing back to the Jazz.

Jordan needed only four seconds to drive past Russell for a layup that cut the Jazz's lead to 86–85 and reminded everybody that the game was not over yet. The Jazz did, however, still have the lead and the ball on their own floor, and Stockton dribbled upcourt hoping to extend the advantage at least enough to force the Bulls into needing a three-pointer just to tie the game.

As Stockton crossed into the halfcourt, Malone stood near the low post to the left of the basket with Rodman leaning on him. Hornacek was coming past along the baseline to use a Malone screen to shake Jordan and perhaps get free on the other side of the hoop. Malone set the pick, and Jordan absorbed it as Hornacek cleared out.

Then Malone opened up, and Stockton threw him the ball.

What Malone did not know was that Jordan had not followed Hornacek all the way through the key. He had seen the Jazz run that play before, and he knew what was coming, so he took a chance. He waited just a split second beneath the basket, just long enough for Malone to catch the ball, lean into Rodman, and glance over his left shoulder as he plotted which move he was going to use to give the Jazz a lead that would ensure them at least five more minutes of basketball life.

Drive through the lane?

Jump hook?

Step-back baseline jumper?

Before he could decide, tragedy struck the Jazz. It wore No. 23.

With Malone holding the ball about waist-high and not paying attention to the weak side, whence Hornacek had passed and Jordan still lurked, Jordan took one good hard swipe down between Malone's hands. His swing found its mark, and he punched the ball loose from Malone's usually unassailable grasp.

"Karl never saw me coming," said Jordan.

The scramble was on, and Malone and Rodman both dove after the ball. Jordan recovered it, though, after it had bounced around a bit, and all the world knew what was coming next. He brought the ball upcourt, saw the clock read about eighteen seconds, and rejected the idea of calling timeout because he did not want to give the Jazz a chance to set up their defense.

Russell was guarding Jordan, trying to remember all the lessons he had learned the year before, when Jordan burned him for the game-winner in Game 1: Stay in front. Don't reach. Don't foul.

The crowd held its breath. It checked the clock. It prayed.

With less than ten seconds left, Jordan drove right.

Russell shadowed him, but somehow forgot what he himself had outlined at the start of the series as a key to defending Jordan: he reached in, hoping to tap the ball away, and just as he did, Jordan moved to dribble past and brushed Russell with his left arm. That sent Russell falling backward, on his behind, and gave Jordan the clearest, most crystalline view of the basket that he had ever seen.

"I saw that moment," he said. "I took advantage of that moment. And I never doubted myself."

The shot was wide open from seventeen feet, and this was Jordan stopping hard and pulling up to take it, with time winding down and the chance to win the game. No way was the greatest basketball player on the planet going to miss. No way was he going to be denied the opportunity to complete his brilliant career with such an astonishing sequence. No way were the Jazz—in spite of their heroic perseverance and hard work and tenacity—going to win their coveted championship.

No way. No way. No way.

Splash.

EPILOGUE

The next day dawned in Salt Lake City with nothing but bright sunshine and the usual morning traffic. That was not how it was supposed to end. The day after the final game of the Jazz's magnificent campaign was supposed to find the streets littered with the debris from a long-overdue victory celebration, not silent with the gnawing ache of another lost season.

There were no champagne headaches in Utah that day.

No parade.

No trophy.

The Delta Center, a roaring cauldron of passion only hours before, stood virtually silent, entombing only the shuffling noise of network technicians coiling their miles of TV cable into giant loops to be loaded back onto huge trucks and driven off to the next destination: Wimbledon, maybe, or the U.S. Open.

One by one, the Jazz players filtered into the building to clean out their lockers and meet with their coaches one last time before departing for another summer of wincing at the memory of what might have been. The players hadn't been hit by the finality of it all, perhaps, until now. Until they had wheeled all the boxes of basketball shoes out to the car, and autographed all the hats and basketballs for each other as mementos of a glorious season stopped one game too soon.

"It's an eerie feeling," said Greg Foster.

In another city, thousands of miles away, the Bulls were puffing cigars and holding aloft that gleaming golden trophy, while in the bowels of their own home arena the Jazz waited for their rookie, Jacque Vaughn, to fulfill his traditional postseason obligation to buy the rest of the team lunch. Crown Burger this year. Everybody said it was delicious.

Karl Malone arrived on his Harley-Davidson, driving it down the cement concourse and parking it outside the locker room before growling his way past a group of waiting reporters. He was still furious at having lost, and at the criticism that had been leveled at him from members of the Jazz's own radio broadcast team. While Malone struggled to score in the pivotal games of the NBA Finals, the broadcasters had wondered aloud whether fans wouldn't start to lobby for the Jazz to trade him for somebody who could produce more under the pressure of the biggest series of the season.

True to his nature, Malone could not ignore the scrutiny.

"Either they shake that situation up," he said, "or they've got to do something else with me. So it's me or them."

It was hardly the most stately of farewells, Malone lowering himself to threaten the jobs of talk-radio hosts on the heels of the official word that he would participate in that pro wrestling match over the summer—especially after he had been so graceful in boarding the Bulls' bus to offer congratulations the night before. But Malone's final outburst surely owed to the pain of failure as much as anything else.

One layup, one steal, one jump shot.

Michael Jordan did all of those things when it mattered the most; Malone and John Stockton did not. The Jazz had had one last chance to win Game 6 after Jordan hit his jump shot with 5.2 seconds left, but Stockton missed a three-pointer at the buzzer, and the Jazz were left with an 87–86 loss that not only cost them the Finals for the second season in a row, but threatened them with a legacy that emphasized failure rather than the pride, sacrifice, and determination upon which the team had been built.

That pride kept the rest of the Jazz organization from reacting as bitterly as Malone had; owner Larry Miller knew he had one more chance with this group, and team president Frank Layden claimed to have gotten over the loss in about five minutes, because it was just a game. Even Jerry Sloan, who privately fumed over the blown calls that cost the Jazz five points in Game 6, said all the right things and gave all the proper credit to the Bulls.

"Altogether, I guess you can look back and say it was a pretty good year," said Jeff Hornacek. "Most people had written us off—last year was the one year and that was our chance—but we came back and gave it another shot. Hopefully, they write us off again and next year we can try again."

Like Hornacek, the rest of the players came and went with dignity that day, expressing bitter disappointment in the past but a seemingly unspoiled hope for the future. Antoine Carr said he would like to return to the Jazz if the team would have him, and Foster said the team had everything it needed to contend for a championship again. (How soon that chance would come remained a mystery, with a lengthy labor lockout on the horizon.) Even Stockton handled his disappointment with grace and good humor, in spite of the possibility that he had just missed the last chance he would ever have at winning a championship. Though everyone knew he was crushed on the inside, he joked with reporters when asked how much of the team's playoff bonus the players had voted to give the media.

"About what you'd expect," he said.

Whenever the next season did start, the Jazz could probably

expect to be counted out again, just as they had been counted out practically every year since losing to the Portland Trail Blazers in the 1992 Western Conference finals. But for each of the previous seasons in which they had been left for dead, the Jazz had emerged with ever more drive and motivation in their attempt to finally claim what had eluded them for so long.

Might that happen again?

Might they fight back one more time, and finally win?

Or had the Jazz finally succumbed to the fate that had been so often prescribed for them?

"You look at the style of our players and the style of our game, and we're not going to change," said Hornacek. "As you get older, the teams that are very athletic are going to struggle a little bit, I think, when they lose that athleticism. You know, John and myself, we don't play with that. And Karl uses his strength, which he's not going to lose. So age, I don't think, is that big a factor for us. And our young guys have come along and proved they can play, so I don't see why we can't be in this position next year."

Next year.

Always next year.

With the lockers empty and the sun gone down on another season, that's all that was left to talk about.

—June 16, 1998
Salt Lake City, Utah